PRAISE FOR *PARK LIFE*

"Recurring lockdowns have reminded us all of the importance of parks in our lives – as places of refuge, respite, relaxation and reconnection. In Park Life, *Tom Chesshyre guides his readers around the world in 50 parks, opening up all sorts of intriguing historical, cultural and environmental vistas along the way."*

Jonathon Porritt, founder director of Forum for the Future

"Ever enterprising, Tom Chesshyre has made a virtue of necessity in this celebration of 50 worldwide parks he has explored over the years. As all our physical horizons shrank, his mental horizons expanded, prompted by memories, old notebooks and photographs and background reading. With an engagingly light touch, his recollections and descriptions are by turns wry and reflective. A truly imaginative 'Look Back in Lockdown'."

Stephen McClarence, travel writer

"Everyone has their favourite park. Whatever influences your own preference, Chesshyre's inspired selection from around the world amplifies how parks are so much more than green spaces. It is also a timely reminder that green is the colour of the outdoors; we ignore it at our peril."

Richard Hammond, *Green Traveller*

*"*Park Life *is a journey into memory, and the pleasures of those places that we once took for granted. Parks are the increasingly contested common ground where people – meant to stay apart – come together to share more than just space. However, because they are public they are often under threat, and Chesshyre shows how these urban refuges are essential parts of our cities. This is a book to dream in."*

Leo Hollis, author of *Cities Are Good for You: The Genius of the Metropolis*

"It's one thing to write a travel book when you can go almost anywhere you want; quite another to do so during a pandemic when largely confined to barracks. This is some achievement and is due largely to Tom Chesshyre's unbridled curiosity, sharp journalistic eye and boundless enthusiasm. Apart from anything, I feel the urge to reacquaint myself with Tom's local, Richmond Park, which he brings to life admirably."

Mark Palmer, *Daily Mail*

PRAISE FOR *SLOW TRAINS AROUND SPAIN*

"A lovely book."

Michael Portillo

"Chesshyre takes us on a wondrously hypnotic meander across Spain. His attention to detail and unwillingness to be rushed, either as passenger or author, make this a highly relaxing and subtly addictive read. What's more, if train travel is to play a bigger part in our travelling future, as many feel it might, Slow Trains Around Spain *makes it feel like a future well worth embracing."*

Glen Mutel, *National Geographic Traveller*

"If you ever need convincing that it's better to take the train than to fly, this is the book that makes a persuasive case."

Nicky Gardner, *Hidden Europe*

"You'll be entertained and inspired."

Richard Hammond, *Green Traveller*

"By turns humorous and sharply insightful, [Chesshyre] affectionately paints a vivid portrait of a deeply divided and contrasting country, bringing to life its characters and landscapes like few other travel writers can. Always curious, witty and intelligent, his writing style and subject matter are deeply rewarding… this is armchair travel at its satisfying best."

Francisca Kellett, travel writer

PRAISE FOR *SLOW TRAINS TO VENICE*

"He casually, and beautifully, bats away the earnestness of travel literature."

Caroline Eden, *The Times Literary Supplement*

"There is something nostalgic about the clatter of wheels and sleeper trains… by the end, the reader will struggle to resist the urge to follow his lead."

The Economist

"Bristling with vitality, Chesshyre's new tome is a joyfully rudderless romp through Europe's railway system… It's a work of brilliant geekery, but for the

most part it's a love letter to the continent, a Eurocentric work for our Brexit-beleaguered times."

National Geographic, Top Ten Travel Books for Summer 2019

"Like the trains he travels on, Tom Chesshyre meanders through Europe and the result is entertaining and enjoyable."

Christian Wolmar, author of Blood, Iron and Gold:
How the Railways Transformed the World

"A diverting and thought-provoking read."

Simon Bradley, author of The Railways

"An engaging picaresque series of encounters and reflections on Europe as many of its countries struggle to find common ground amid the populist reaction to its dilemmas."

Anthony Lambert, author of
Lost Railway Journeys from Around the World

"Beethoven with attitude, masochism in Lviv, the smell of cigarettes in the corridor, adventurous great aunts who travelled on the roofs of crowded trains, Carniolan pork-garlic sausage, Jimi Hendrix in the Slovene Ethnographic Museum and, of course, the 13:49 from Wrocław. Tom Chesshyre pays homage to a Europe that we are leaving behind and perhaps never understood. Che bella corsa! He is the master of slow locomotion."

Roger Boyes, The Times

PRAISE FOR *FROM SOURCE TO SEA*

"An enjoyable refuge from everyday life."

Clive Aslet, The Times

"Chesshyre's book stands out from other accounts of walking the Thames Path in its contemporary (post-Brexit, pre-Trump) immediacy. A portrait of England and the English in our time, it is peppered with fascinating historical and literary markers. It's also a usefully opinionated guide to watering-holes and B&Bs from the sleepy Cotswold villages to the dystopian edgelands of the estuary."

Christina Hardyment, author of Writing the Thames

"*A highly readable and entertaining saunter along England's iconic river.*"
Christopher Somerville, author of *Britain's Best Walks*

"*Readers should perhaps prepare themselves for a whole new wave of Whither England? type books in the months and years ahead, and Chesshyre's is a not unwelcome early attempt to answer that seemingly urgent question.*"
Ian Sansom, *The Times Literary Supplement*

PRAISE FOR *TICKET TO RIDE*

"*Like mini-odysseys, Chesshyre's railway journeys are by turns gentle and awesome, and full of surprises.*"
John Gimlette, author of *Elephant Complex: Travels in Sri Lanka*

"*Funny and illuminating from Crewe to Korea,* Ticket to Ride *is a hugely entertaining account of the author's travels on the rails the world over – chance encounters fly like sparks.*"
Sara Wheeler, author of *The Magnetic North*

PRAISE FOR *TALES FROM THE FAST TRAINS*

"*Compulsory reading…*"
Mark Smith, *The Man in Seat 61*

"*Transforms seemingly unsurprising familiar territory – whether the Eurostar terminal at St Pancras or the cities of Frankfurt and Antwerp – into the stage for insights and adventures.*"
Dea Birkett, author of *Serpent in Paradise*

"*If you've 'done' Paris and Bruges and are wondering, 'Where next?', then this may be a quiet revolution.*"
Andrew Marr

"*Splendid twenty-first-century railway adventure. At last this IS the age of the train.*"
Simon Calder, *The Independent*

PRAISE FOR *TO HULL AND BACK*

"Tom Chesshyre celebrates the UK... discovering pleasure in the unregarded wonders of the 'unfashionable underbelly' of Britain. The moral, of course, is that heaven is where you find it."

Frank Barrett, *The Mail on Sunday*

"You warm to Chesshyre, whose cultural references intelligently inform his postcards from locations less travelled."

Iain Finlayson, *The Times*

PRAISE FOR *HOW LOW CAN YOU GO?*

"Highly readable Bill Bryson-esque travel writing."

Clover Stroud, *The Sunday Telegraph*

"A hilarious record of a low-cost odyssey around the least salubrious corners of Europe."

Celia Brayfield, *The Times*

PRAISE FOR *A TOURIST IN THE ARAB SPRING*

"This witty, perceptive book provides a fascinating read for lovers of thoughtful, imaginative and well-written travel literature."

Frank Barrett, *The Mail on Sunday*

"A charming travel companion, entertaining and engaging."

The Times Literary Supplement

PRAISE FOR *GATECRASHING PARADISE*

"Chesshyre, one of the most dependably interesting modern travel writers, explores the offbeat atolls of this sinking archipelago."

Wanderlust

"It should be mandatory reading for all visitors [to the Maldives]."

Francisca Kellett, *Tatler*

An Hachette UK Company
www.hachette.co.uk

Summersdale Publishers Ltd
Part of Octopus Publishing Group Limited
Carmelite House
50 Victoria Embankment
LONDON
EC4Y 0DZ
UK

www.summersdale.com

Printed and bound in the Czech Republic

ISBN: 978-1-80007-009-7

Substantial discounts on bulk quantities of Summersdale books are available to corporations, professional associations and other organizations. For details contact general enquiries: telephone: +44 (0) 1243 771107 or email: enquiries@summersdale.com.

PARK LIFE

AROUND THE WORLD IN 50 PARKS

TOM CHESSHYRE

summersdale

For Kasia

ABOUT THE AUTHOR

Tom Chesshyre is the author of ten travel books and spent 21 years on the travel desk of *The Times*. He now contributes mainly to the *Daily Mail* and the *Mail on Sunday*. He has also written for *Condé Nast Traveller*, *National Geographic Traveller*, *Monocle*, *The Critic* and *Geographical*, the magazine of the Royal Geographical Society. His books are *How Low Can You Go?: Round Europe for 1p Each Way (Plus Tax)*, *To Hull and Back: On Holiday in Unsung Britain*, *Tales from the Fast Trains: Europe at 186 MPH*, *A Tourist in the Arab Spring*, *Gatecrashing Paradise: Misadventures in the Real Maldives*, *Ticket to Ride: Around the World on 49 Unusual Train Journeys*, *From Source to Sea: Notes from a 215-Mile Walk Along the River Thames*, *Slow Trains to Venice: A 4,000-Mile Adventure Across Europe* and *Slow Trains Around Spain: A 3,000-Mile Adventure on 52 Rides*. He lives in Mortlake in London, close to Richmond Park.

Stockholm,
Sweden

Helsinki,
Finland

Berlin, Germany

Warsaw, Poland

Minsk, Belarus

Vienna, Austria

Venice, Italy

Odessa, Ukraine

Dubrovnik, Croatia

Athens, Greece

Pyongyang,
North Korea

Beijing, China

Tokyo, Japan

Shimla,
India

Kathmandu,
Nepal

Eilat,
Israel

Hong
Kong

Suez,
Egypt

Vientiane,
Laos

Ho Chi Minh City,
Vietnam

Tripoli,
Libya

Manila, Philippines

Khartoum,
Sudan

Malé,
The Maldives

Stone Town,
Zanzibar

Mahé,
The Seychelles

Anuradhapura,
Sri Lanka

Cape Town, South Africa

Sydney,
Australia

CONTENTS

NOTE: Exactly what constitutes a "park" is open to interpretation and the 50 "parks" to come range in size from many hectares to tucked-away half acres or sometimes less. My *Collins English Dictionary* includes 19 definitions, the first being: "A large area of land preserved in a natural state for recreational use by the public." This is fine for most parks in the countryside although the specification of "large" does not work for most urban parks. The second definition in the Collins list of 19 is: "A piece of open land in a town with public amenities." This is closer in relevance for this book on urban parks. At times I have included places officially referred to as "squares" or "gardens", but whatever the terminology, a "piece of open land" with greenery and a "natural state" of some description is to be found.

Martha Gray [gatekeeper]: Where is your ticket?

John Lewis [a local]: What occasion for a ticket? Anyone may pass through here.

MG: No – not without a ticket.

JL: Yes, they may; and I will.

MG: You shan't.

JL: I will.

Events at Sheen Gate, Richmond Park, London, 1755

PREFACE

During the recent global lockdowns something strange happened. With travel out of the question as the coronavirus spread – and "movement" of any sort tricky – horizons shrank and a question soon formed: what on earth were we going to do with ourselves?

So began a quick succession of events. We watched *Tiger King* on Netflix (or read about others doing so). We ordered delivery meals. We attempted to bake bread (dwindling flour supplies permitting). We followed online fitness gurus (or read about others doing so). We drank wine at lunch while "working" from home. We learned how to use Zoom. We had weird dreams. We finally fixed the blind in the front room and sorted out that pesky broken shower curtain.

Then we all went to the park.

Before we knew it, regular perambulations were established. Dog walkers raised eyebrows as paths filled with pallid newcomers seeking fresh air after hours staring at screens (surveys revealed that the average person was spending a quarter of their waking hours online, many much more). Places that during weekdays might have been deserted were soon swarming with escapees from living-room sofas, slightly swivel-eyed from the brightness, greenery and birdsong – like prisoners set free from windowless cells.

Parks suddenly became important in a way they never quite had been before. Restrictions, as the seasons turned to spring and summer, relaxed. Rendezvous on benches began. Backpacks bulged with chilled Sauvignon Blanc, tubs of hummus and six-packs of San Miguel. Mini pork pies! Tubes of Pringles! Packets of Mini Cheddars! Philadelphia cream cheese! Let's live life to the full! Sales of tartan picnic rugs soared. Cooler-pack shelves at supermarkets emptied as al fresco congregations gathered pace, much to the disquiet of local authorities perturbed by bins overflowing with the detritus of the jamboree. Crushed cans spilling sticky liquids and wrappers with half-eaten food were bumper pickings for foxes (and other creatures).

All of this, of course, concerns city dwellers. Country folk had plenty of open space in which to pace about and speculate on the future, happily removed from politicians flanked by scientists making solemn pronouncements about "R" figures. Yet for so many of us, it was urban parks that took on an unexpected new centrality in our day-to-day lives.

For we are becoming a planet of city people. More than half of the world's population (55 per cent) lives in cities. By 2050 the United Nations predicts this figure will rise to 68 per cent, meaning parks will become even more important than ever. Given that the world's population has risen from 1.6 billion in 1900 to 7.8 billion now, this represents *a lot* of people in cities all of a sudden, when you take a historic perspective. After all, the number of human beings on the planet had previously crept up to the 1 billion mark only in 1800, taking a period of 2 million years to do so. Pushing this forward, more than 9 billion people are expected to live on Earth by 2050, assuming Covid-19 or other diseases do not run out of control. If not quite already so, we are poised to become one great city world – societies squashed together cheek by jowl, many of us in small apartments without balconies, let alone gardens. It is estimated that one in eight British households has no access to a garden (one in five in London). For our sanity and health, we will need green spaces close by. Plenty of them.

There is another consideration here (recent lockdowns aside).

It is impossible to deny the connection between climate change and travel, be it flying, driving, taking trains or hopping on cruise ships. Greta Thunberg and global warming scientists have won that argument and there is little point in repeating it here. The simple fact is, as the teenaged Swede has so many times said in one form or another: *sending fumes into the heavens is no good for us.* During the lockdowns, air quality improved dramatically in cities across the world and our awareness of the link between travel and climate change was heightened further still. If in the future we want a safe and healthy environment for our descendants, we will have to move about less. No ifs or buts. We will also have to learn, as we have of late, to find pleasure closer to home. We will have to learn to love our parks.

Fortunately, many of us do already. Before Barack Obama took high office, he let many happy hours slip by in New York City's Central Park. "I just want to go through Central Park and watch folk passing by," he once mused of his former life. "Spend the whole day watching people. I miss that." He simply wanted to be normal, to escape the security ring protecting him after becoming president of the United States. He wanted to *hang out*. No need to whizz around the globe. Just relax in a place he cherished.

The enjoyments of urban parks are manifold, and this book is a celebration of them, wherever they may be. It begins during lockdown in my local park, Richmond Park in south-west London, and proceeds on a world tour in appreciation of parks I have been lucky enough to visit over the years during my job as a travel writer, now in my late 40s and having been around and about quite a bit (going to some of the parks described in this book before Thunberg was born).

In just about every conurbation I have set foot in over the years, I have sought out these oases of green amid the skyscrapers and scrum of city life, be it for a stroll or sometimes for a run. The aim of *Park Life* is to show what joys urban parks offer the world over as well as why we should celebrate, save, promote and create more of these precious green spaces.

The "message" is simple: we should love our parks! Everywhere!

Apologies in advance for such occasional spells of "park evangelism" (I have tried, hard, to keep them to a minimum).

Yet urban parks are not only wonderful places to let the mind wander free while enjoying the fresh air, quiet and greenery. They are also a source of stories galore; secret histories that often shine light on the Big Smoke outside their perimeter boundaries.

It has been a great pleasure to recall the best – and to tell the tales within.

CHAPTER ONE

RICHMOND PARK, SOUTH-WEST LONDON: STAGS, KESTRELS AND A PEOPLE'S HERO

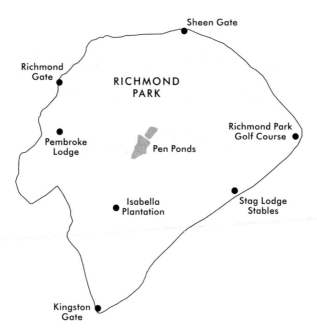

On attempting to enter Richmond Park in south-west London in 1755, John Lewis, a local brewer and lover of the park, encountered a spot of bother.

The gatekeeper, a certain Martha Gray, would not let him in. Lewis, you see, was not in possession of a park permit. Such permits were a new requirement introduced by Princess Amelia, the youngest daughter of George II. This princess had recently taken up residence in a lodge in the park and closed it to all but her friends, who *were* allowed permits. Amelia had been appointed Ranger by her father, a mainly honorific title that did not require actual duties such as looking after the famous royal deer. Underlings could see to that. Her predecessor in the position had been Robert Lord Walpole, son of Britain's first prime minister, who was partial to hunting at weekends. The "job" of Ranger was a plum posting.

Events soon spiralled. Lewis attempted to barge past Gray, but he was held at bay and pushed back. Then the gate (Sheen Gate) was slammed in his face. Affronted, Lewis returned to his brewery in Richmond, consulted his lawyers and took legal action. So began a bitter struggle lasting three years, which Lewis remarkably won, instantly becoming a local hero. The public, fed up with being denied passage across what had always previously been common land, had taken him to their hearts. The mouse had roared! The unpopular princess had been defeated! Free public rights of way were re-established, accessed via stepladders over the walls.

Yet this was not the end of the affair. Princess Amelia, clearly a tricky character, installed stepladders with huge gaps between the rungs rendering them completely impractical to most. Another court case ensued. Lewis won again. But by this time, he had forked out so much on legal fees – and had unluckily during the same period suffered damage from awful floods at his Thameside brewery – he was almost destitute. In stepped local supporters to raise an annuity that saw him through his later years.

Parks have stories – and this one is revealing on several counts. The first is Lewis' obvious, enormous affection for his (and my) local park.

He went to great lengths to establish the right of passage, stretching his finances to the limit. The second is that he was not alone in his enjoyment of the scenery. Witness the rallying around of the local community to support this people's champion. The third is that all this was almost three centuries ago. People have loved parks, in this case Richmond Park, for a very long time.

I love it too. There is something about the wizened old oaks, the dense rolling bracken, the crunch of the grit paths, the mouldering brick walls, the impenetrable brambles, the nervous wood pigeons, the gambolling squirrels, the way the light falls on the wind-rippled ponds, the way the jackdaws cavort in the treetops, the echoes of the woodpeckers, the smell of the foxgloves, the cool hidden corners, the hollows, the bogs, the solitude that is to be had on a quiet morning on the edge of a capital city of 9 million people.

And of course: the deer. Richmond Park has around 600 of them, a mixture of red and fallow deer, spread across its 2,400 acres. This herd is considered the finest in captivity anywhere, with a bloodline stretching back to the days of Henry VIII, who hunted here before the park walls were installed. Each year a cull of approximately 200 keeps numbers in proportion to the size of the terrain. They rut in the autumn; the stags (male red deer) and the bucks (male fallow deer) sometimes fighting to the death. They cast their antlers in February and March. They fatten up on acorns and the leaves of trees, hence the almost perfectly trimmed branches of the ancient oaks. They give birth in May to calves (red deer babies) and fawns (fallow deer babies). They live up to the age of 18 if they are lucky enough to survive the culls; female red deer (hinds) can survive to their mid-20s. They are majestic and ever-present; hazel eyes glimmering in the bracken. As you walk through Richmond Park: You Are Being Watched.

To be able to escape to such scenery, a short walk from the South Circular and the A3, has always struck me as being close to miraculous. In one of the biggest, oldest cities on the planet, somehow this corner of wilderness survives; a lasting testament, if you like, to human beings' understanding of the importance of nature amid all the terraced houses, tower blocks and shopping malls of modern life.

Richmond Park is one of eight Royal Parks in London and the largest in Britain's capital. The city itself is home to more than 3,000 parks covering 18 per cent of the land. This is more than that given over to railways and roads, and plans are afoot to make more than half of London "green" by 2050, says the Mayor of London's office; an honourable, if ambitious-sounding target that makes you wonder slightly where everyone will live. In warrens with skylights beneath fields in place of bulldozed terraces? In marvellous high-tech treehouses? Or, more mundanely (and likely), in giant apartments stretching to the clouds?

During the lockdown, I got to know my local park very well indeed. I walked round with my girlfriend each weekend, starting at 7 a.m. and taking just over 2 hours including a stop for tea at a bench at the top of Broomfield Hill near Robin Hood Gate, and another pause for more tea and a snack by Pembroke Lodge near Richmond Gate. Our movements became set in their ways surprisingly quickly (perhaps this was a Lockdown Thing). After a while it seemed the deer and the squirrels barely glanced at us: *Oh not them again, I bet they're going to go and sit on that bench, yep, look, I told you so, they're on the bench, and yes, yes, the flask is out, they're drinking that strange steamy stuff.*

At the beginning in March 2020, when the trees were bare and antlers were – somewhere – being cast, the paths were almost empty and our breath formed billows of steam on the way out from Sheen Gate, the scene of such high drama in 1755. On those misty mornings, gloriously free of planes heading for Heathrow, an elemental stillness hung in the air, the quietude magnified as though in stunned memory of the city bustle outside the park walls a mere month earlier. Beyond the huddled ducks on Adam's Pond we would go, waiting to see when the first walker would appear on the perimeter path. Sometimes almost half an hour would pass before this "event", long after the sweeping fields of Roehampton, the golf course and the trickle and weeping willows of Beverley Brook.

Nature came and joined us. A great spotted woodpecker swooped, clasped a trunk a few yards ahead and drummed away, the steak of red feathers on its nape a blur. We watched transfixed until a jogger passed, scaring the creature away. Buzzards and kestrels patrolled the skies near Kingston. At first, we could not tell the difference. Then we learned from the wildlife signs by the gates that buzzards have wider tails and broader, moth-like wings. These would sit on dead branches, looking for voles and field mice. We never did see a kill. But we did with kestrels, at least the aftermath of one. Near Robin Hood Gate, a chestnut-brown creature with streaks of mottled brown was up to something on the path ahead. A little creature was about to be devoured. Frozen still, we watched, the kestrel eventually regarding us with mild irritation – we were, after all, disturbing its meal – and flapped away.

Week by week we watched antlers lengthen. By May, almost miraculously, flamboyant new appendages had formed. On the stags, these had a fluffy, velvety appearance and are, I learned, full of blood before they harden later in the year ready for the autumn fights. Bunnies appeared by an oak by the carless road (public vehicles had been banned). Greyish-blue and not seeming to mind us at all, the creatures hopped about cutely by holes dug by the roots. After a few weekends they were, however, gone. Perhaps the work of the buzzards.

We spotted jays in the woodlands; beautiful birds with patches of blue on their wings amid a handsome configuration of pink-brown, black and white feathers. We came to love green woodpeckers, which on first sighting we took to be one of the many feral parakeets that noisily occupy the treetops. Green woodpeckers are far more distinguished, almost haughty creatures, notable for their swift, jagged wing movements and insistent tree-tapping. The flash of red on their heads and their "ha-ha-ha-ha" calls were their giveaways. What with spotting long-tailed tits and witnessing the antics of a pair of nuthatches skipping up and down the trunk of an oak, we were becoming veritable twitchers.

Richmond Park was coming into its own. Woodlands turned the faintest of green as though sprinkled by heavenly herbs before deepening in colour and soon bulging with foliage. Emerald bracken shoots unfurled. The tensions of the week – self-isolation, working from home, Zoom meetings and shuffling off to the supermarket to queue 2 metres apart – were released under clear skies in the clean, fresh air. Yes, it was happening. Pollution, after a mere couple of months of lockdown, was lifting. Air quality monitors were confirming this. With cars confined to garages and planes in hangars, city parks felt greener, cleaner places than ever.

Having become so close to the park, I began to delve into its history. This turned out to be a bag of riches dating from the time of Edward I, who established his court at a riverside mansion in Richmond in 1299. From then on, a local royal connection was formed that led to Henry V building a palace in 1414 followed by Henry VII ordering the more substantial Richmond Palace in 1501. He held the title Earl of Richmond, so he changed the local name from Sheen (also spelled Shene) to Richmond, naturally.

All the while, hunting persisted in surrounding woodlands, but it took a certain controversial monarch to form today's park. That troublesome king was Charles I, who was known to be "extremely partial to the sports of the chase". Having been brought up at Richmond Palace, lived there as a young man and set up his queen and children in residence, he decided to wall off an area of land for his hobby: thus Richmond Park (then "New Park") came into being. Amid much resistance, Charles bullied local landowners into selling properties to expand his hunting grounds, built a big brick wall around it and started killing the creatures within during his spare time.

This was in 1637. By 1649, of course, Charles was dead, beheaded at Whitehall after the English Civil War. And Richmond Park, it would appear, played a small part in this dramatic downfall.

Some local landowners, influential men, had at first refused to sell to the king. Yet Charles would not budge and they were overridden. This was despite Charles' advisors being aware of his rising unpopularity and warning against doing so. Yes, Charles had backed down to allow public access to gather firewood and to cross the park along two newly established rights of way, but his bullish behaviour – he had started to build his wall before legally acquiring the plots inside – ruffled local feathers.

In his illuminating *The History of the Rebellion* (1704), Edward Hyde, the Earl of Clarendon, recounts events: "The building the wall before people consented to part with their land or their common looked to them as if by degrees they should be shut out from both, and increased the murmur and noise of the people who were not concerned as well as of them who were, and it was too near London not to be the common discourse."

By "murmur" read "indignation". By "common discourse" read "gossip" and "scandal". The overall moral of the story being: mess with parks in cities at your peril, even if you're a king.

Add to this history the legend that Henry VIII watched from what is now known as King Henry's Mound, a Bronze Age barrow near Pembroke Lodge, to see a rocket fired from the Tower of London to signal the death of Anne Boleyn on 19 May 1536 (which is almost certainly untrue, as Henry is recorded as having been in Wiltshire that day). Sprinkle in a tale of Admiral Lord Nelson visiting White Lodge, a mansion in the park, shortly before the Battle of Trafalgar in 1805 and sketching his plan of attack against the Spanish in red wine on a tablecloth. Mix in Queen Victoria's stay in that very same lodge in 1861 – and later return for the christening of her great-grandson in 1894, performed by the Archbishop of Canterbury, no less.

Add that Charles Dickens used to dine at Pembroke Lodge, designed by the eminent architect Sir John Soane, when it was home to Lord and Lady Russell (their philosopher grandson, Bertrand Russell, grew up there), as well as at a lodge at Sheen Gate in the company of Sir Richard Owen, the first director of the Natural History Museum. Throw in visits to the park over the years by Prime Minister William Gladstone, Sir Walter Scott, George Eliot and William Pitt the Younger. And with so much going on over the centuries, you begin to realize that the ancient oaks, some 700 years old, have many a story to tell.

This may sound like a lot of historical name-dropping – which it is – but the simple fact is that a great deal has happened in the park and I knew little of it before the lockdown. Being confined to the environs of my locality provided time to poke about. I was loving my local park more than ever: appreciating both the nature within and its hidden histories. I had turned into a tourist on my own block. No need for airport security queues, newfangled coronavirus tests before departure or even motorway journeys for a "staycation". Just wander about in the park for a bit. Cheap, too! Fantastic!

Although, perhaps, I was becoming something of a zealot for "park life", as my girlfriend did begin to suggest.

* * *

As our perambulations of Richmond Park continued, another level of park appreciation arose. We started to make friends. Almost every weekend we would pass two Korean men near Kingston Gate, whom we fancifully took to be the South Korean ambassador and his bodyguard. One of the duo was in his 70s and highly distinguished with a gimlet eye. The other had a sporty build and was in his 30s; something about his step suggested a military background. After so many "pass-bys" we began to wave, nod and smile. When on one occasion the "ambassador" was walking alone, I asked where his friend was to which the "ambassador" replied: "He has flown back to Korea." This is how we knew they were Korean.

Such encounters became a regular occurrence. Joggers and walkers we had seen previously would grin and sometimes say "good morning" or "nice day". This does not usually happen in London, although I have never had a dog and suspect I have been missing out on a whole world of park friendliness coming from possessing a hound.

Our breakthrough friendship was Xue, whom we noticed early on. She wore an emerald-green jacket, face mask and orange trainers. Her walking style was upright with free-swinging arms. Our timings were like clockwork: we would almost always see one another on Broomfield

Hill. After waving and saying hello a few times, we stopped to talk. We soon learned all about her childhood in Shenyang in China's north-east, her work woes, her holiday plans (Sicily, she hoped), her romantic and life aspirations ("I want to meet someone… I do not want children"), her intention to buy a new car, her love of yellow-and-white colour schemes (how she had decorated her New Malden flat), that she likes McDonald's (particularly partial to Chicken McNuggets) and enjoys baking cakes and soda bread. We exchanged email addresses and have been in touch ever since. Soon after lockdown restrictions were lifted the first time, Xue came round for a barbecue.

I explain this here to make a straightforward point: park life is not just about wildlife and greenery. It is about sharing common space with other people. To return to Lewis and his troubles with Princess Amelia back in 1755, it is clear people in this corner of London have long felt this way. To cordon off the parkland is a no-no. A brilliant print from 1755 depicts residents scaling the walls at a breach in their brickwork to assert an ancient right of "beating the bounds" to walk around the parish. It is full-on rebellion! Figures bearing sticks rise over the wall near Sheen Common as though breaking through the battlements of a castle – with Princess Amelia's underlings looking on hopelessly. It is uncertain whether Lewis took part. Probably. His subsequent Sheen Gate showdown was clearly intended to provoke the court case that eventually led to victory for "the people".

During the lockdown, protests echoing those bygone disputes briefly erupted on the other side of London. With a heavy-handedness typical of some local authorities at the pandemic's beginning, Tower Hamlets Council had attempted to close its hugely popular Victoria Park, stating it was doing so to prevent large gatherings and ensure public safety. All hell broke loose, with legal threats soon made by a hastily formed Parks Action Group. This association demanded recognition of citizens' rights to enjoy the east London park, rights that could be traced back to 1845. The sense of indignation seemed rooted in this historical freedom of passage, originally established so the working classes could enjoy "rational recreation" in a clean green space in the increasingly polluted, industrialized city. Tower Hamlets Council's move was deemed "a step too far" and to be "overstepping their legal powers", said protest leaders. Mind your own business! Leave our parks alone!

They soon did. A few days later, Hackney's mayor nervously backed down, saying he had not wanted to shut the park in the first place: "I'm unhappy with it closed and want it reopened by the weekend, but we need to be confident in public behaviour. It was closed for operational reasons. Our park rangers and the police advised that it was best to close because of disorderly behaviour."

Victoria Park duly reopened. "VICTORY FOR VICKY", ran the headlines in the local press, using its local nickname.

Meanwhile, related troubles rumbled on in parks up and down Britain during the early lockdowns: disregard for social distancing, occasional clashes between cyclists and pedestrians, anger over people failing to control dogs (especially with so many new dog owners during the pandemic), overflowing bins, late-night parties or "raves" as the tabloids dubbed them (a few rowdy get-togethers even in the leafy suburbs of Richmond Park). Yet, if anything, these "issues" seemed to galvanize people's love for their local parks further still: *How dare anyone abuse these public spaces that belong to us all!* Condemnation from fellow park-users rained down on social media: *The UK is awash with anti-social, selfish, unempathetic, disrespectful citizens… This nation is becoming one giant waste dump as we emerge from lockdown, disgraceful… Part of me hopes that it pisses down for the rest of the summer if only to ensure the selfish twats who left all of their litter in parks yesterday stay at home.*

Pictures of large gatherings of revellers and litter heaps left for park-keepers to clear often featured on these broadsides. At the same time, some city councils – capturing the public mood and taking a different approach to Tower Hamlets – launched awareness campaigns, occasionally adopting waspish wit. "Why are you tossing litter around here?" asked posters put up by the City of York's council. This question was followed by three statements, each next to a ticked box: "I'm lazy. I don't care about the community. I think other people should pay to clean up after me." The posters ended with a succinct parting message: "Don't be a tosser. You brought your rubbish here, please take it home with you."

All this was, for the most part, a passing phase: lockdown lunacy unleashed. A lot of us live in cities. A lot of us were spending a lot of time in parks. Most – but far from all – of us put this "two plus two" together and quickly calculated the "four": that we were all going to have to get on with one another in our parks, and probably more so in the future than ever. Better to live and let respectfully live than turn just about the only places we had left to venture outside into litter-strewn wastelands.

It was during this period that my mind began to wander and consider parks in general – not just the key part they were increasingly playing in city lives (and my life), but also the ones I had visited in other cities in the UK and around the world. One Sunday, when my girlfriend and I had returned from our park walk, I began to draw up a list of favourites. This quickly grew and a notion began to form: how about "travelling" around them once again – only this time, *in my mind*?

So I did. From the reality of Richmond, I set off on a "park quest" free to "fly" wherever I chose on my list. It was a liberating feeling. First stop? Why not really take to the skies, figuratively speaking? The airfare was cheap: absolutely nothing. The time on my hands was plentiful: everything barring shops selling essentials, after all, was shut. The feeling of wanting to break free was overwhelming. So off I "went" from south-west London to the other side of the planet to the heart of the biggest city anywhere – a green corner of a vibrant metropolis that I had visited a year before and remembered with great affection.

So began a series of happy voyages of the imagination. My park adventures at home amid the ever-busy deer, kestrels and woodpeckers of Richmond, with its proud park history established by Mr Lewis all that time ago, may have been continuing, but across the globe, they had only just started. Bright lights, big cities and some of the world's best parks awaited.

Tokyo: *oresama no tojoda* (here I come).

CHAPTER TWO

JAPAN, NORTH KOREA, CHINA, HONG KONG: SKYSCRAPERS AND ZEN

O K, so you may be wondering how this "journey" was going to work in practice. I was not, after all, *actually travelling anywhere*. To do so, of course, would have been breaking the law for much of the time during the lockdowns.

Instead, as I have said, I hoped that somehow a succession of recollections would emerge forming a meandering trip down memory lane, pausing at parks of many stripes at some of the world's best-known cities, as half-forgotten images, stories and sensations returned. A rather pleasant pursuit when you have a great deal of time to spare while stuck at home, goggle-eyed, watching Netflix in between forays into the finger-twitching world of social media (as so many of us were back then).

And here I have a confession to make. I do not pretend to have a photographic memory capable of reliving moments that happened sometimes a decade or more ago. What I did have, however, were shelves of notebooks and a library of pictures and books to jog the little grey cells. Most of us are secret hoarders of some description. Instead of football programmes, porcelain tea sets or high-heeled shoes, my guilty hoarding habit had always been "travel" – holding on to trips in some form or other that fortunately does not involve too many tacky souvenirs, if you don't count a wooden mask in the shape of an Ecuadorian fox that stares down at me in my study, a Chairman Mao watch bought on the Great Wall of China, a "genuine" Australian boomerang, a "genuine" small fragment of the Berlin Wall and a wooden carving resembling Jamaica with a picture of Bob Marley and keyring hooks. Which was actually quite a lot (and just the tip of the iceberg once I started looking about).

Methods of memory recall aside, my idea was this: to zoom to the other side of the planet to the largest conurbation anywhere – Tokyo, Japan's fascinating, enormous capital – and meander back across the continents, winding through Europe in some of my favourite countries on the final stretch before returning to Britain having completed a "voyage" of many tens of thousands of imaginary miles. Along the way, I would (mentally) drop by at 50 parks (including Richmond Park) and have a little escapade in each.

The hope was that these descriptions of "visits" – short, standalone travel stories – would accumulate to paint a picture of what urban parks mean to communities and cultures across the planet. How parks play an important role in city life just about everywhere. How they provide a common link in the way societies are organized from the Netherlands to North America and even, soon to come in this chapter, North Korea. How the love of parks is a common thread that ties humanity together in all corners of the globe, no matter what the culture or political system. How parks provide pockets of order and sanity in the sped-up, internet-injected lives of those living in twenty-first-century cities as they seemingly inevitably grow and grow.

We all needed a shot of the "exotic", stuck as we had been in our front rooms, with planes grounded and government restrictions banning travel between many countries (sometimes all of them). I certainly did. Hence the choice of "route". Best to start a long, long way from home, before slowly returning via Australia, the Americas, Africa, the Indian Ocean, the Middle East and Europe. So many places, so many memories, so many parks.

Yet Tokyo was not a totally random first port of call. As cities steadily get ever bigger, what was it like in one of the best parks in the granddaddy of them all? Settling down in my study, I began to recall the day I spent at one of its most popular parks. Soon the memories came flooding back... and this "journey" around urban greenery was off on its wandering way.

Down by the lotus leaves
Ueno Park, Tokyo, Japan

When you live in a city with a population of 38 million you need green space. No other conurbation even comes close to Japan's sprawling capital: Delhi has a mere 28 million inhabitants, Shanghai 22 million, São Paulo and Mexico City are tiddlers by comparison with 20 million apiece. Tokyo is simply enormous, mindboggling in dimensions.

Luckily, however, it has quite a few decent parks dotted amid its many skyscrapers. It has to – or else everyone would probably go mad.

To reach Ueno Park, the city's most famous, most catch the Tokyo Metro. If you are doing this for the first time during a period when there is not a pandemic (as I was), this is invariably a memorable experience in carriages that, it is safe to say, would not pass many social-distancing regulations of late. Even getting on is tricky. Without having mastered the knack of swift decisive movement, you may well find yourself (as I did) missing a few trains at the start. This said, you do soon learn the ropes: if not, you won't be going anywhere fast.

On the train itself comes another learning curve. You may not be "packed like sardines", as the cliché surrounding Japanese trains goes. After the boarding experience you may be steeled for this, yet carriages are surprisingly tolerable even in rush hour with a small courtesy gap usually observed, about the size of a book held with its spine held against your chest pointing outwards. So it is perhaps better to say you are "packed like very polite sardines". Which isn't so bad. If anything, it can be far worse on Tube trains back in London.

Ueno Park is in north-east Tokyo. From the Metro station – the journey to which somehow colours your appreciation of the park – it is a few minutes' walk. When I arrived, it was too early for the park's museums. Ahead, however, lay a wide open expanse of curious green plants that looked from afar like a vast crop of rhubarb. Considering this pretty unlikely, I went to investigate.

Ueno covers 133 acres and is Japan's busiest urban park with 10 million visitors each year, although this must have been an off day as the paths were incredibly quiet by Tokyo's manic standards, save for the occasional romantic couple and – somewhat unexpectedly, having seen none whatsoever since arriving in Japan – homeless people wearing little more than rags.

These poor souls had fallen on desperately hard times. Their clothing appeared to consist of grimy old sacking. They were shoeless. Teeth were missing. Expressions were vacant, all hope gone. Ueno Park is apparently where many of Tokyo's destitute sleep rough. Not that any of this features in your average guidebook.

What does figure are its famous cherry blossoms in spring, when more than 1,000 trees bloom and a festival attracts tens of thousands to this candyfloss world of pink. Beer and sake are drunk in copious quantities – visitors bring picnic rugs for parties – and karaoke is performed on portable machines long into the night. What a sight and an occasion that must be (my visit was in October).

Aside from this jovial annual knees-up, attractions at Ueno are many and varied. A zoo takes up a large portion of the park, home to giant pandas, Sumatran tigers and Asiatic lions. An ancient five-storey pagoda pokes above the treetops. Glittery shrines dedicated to shoguns and samurais are tucked in corners. A National Museum of Western Art designed by the French architect Le Corbusier is to be found. As is the treasure-packed Tokyo National Museum (which I intended to visit). There are arts and crafts markets. There are fast-food zones. There are Starbucks. A temple to the goddess of wisdom and fortune (Benzaiten) sits on an island in the wide expanse of Shinobazu Pond.

Richmond Park, eat your heart out! On the evidence of its "things to do", Ueno could give Disney, or many a major European city for that matter, a run for its money.

Shinobazu Pond with its rhubarb-like plants has an almost magnetic allure. The sheer oddity of this large green opening stands out; the stark contrast between its untouched expanse of emerald foliage and the shiny office blocks and smoked-glass hotels beyond is striking, even from a distance. Yet it is only on reaching the edge that you realize this is a marsh-like water and the tangle of leaves must be lotus plants.

It is hard not to be overcome with a deep sense of calm (for me, for the first time since arriving in Tokyo two days earlier). A few minutes' stroll from the controlled chaos of the Metro, a world of tranquillity opens out. The air seems more oxygenated. The city noises no more than a distant blur. Tokyo feels as though it has somehow peeled away. From 38 million people to one: yourself, watching the lotus leaves stirring in a faint breeze. I closed my eyes for a while, blissfully unaware of what was shortly to shake the world in the Chinese megacity of Wuhan (not so far away geographically). No pandemics to worry about back then. No economic crises. No lockdowns – yet.

Shinobazu Pond comes in a sequence of parts. Further on is a bridge near the temple of the goddess, where carp splash in deeper water. Beyond, gaudy pedalos shaped like ducks circle in even deeper water. Further on still is another marshland given over to wildlife. When you put all the parts together, the "pond" is more like a lake.

Ueno Park was founded in 1873, soon after the Battle of Ueno in 1868 that saw the Tokugawa shogunate defeated by imperial forces there, heralding the Meiji Restoration. Some believe the decision to form a park was a copycat move inspired by America's grand opening of Yellowstone National Park in 1872. This period of the nineteenth century – largely because of industrialisation and a growing need for green spaces in cities (as with London's Victoria Park) – was generally a boom time for parks worldwide. Either way, influenced by the other countries or not, the land at Ueno had long been known as a place for "entertainment", famous for its "rendezvous teahouses" with rooms for couples to meet privately (and discreetly). Then, in 1924, Emperor Taisho gifted the entire park to the city of Tokyo to mark the marriage of his son, Hirohito, sealing its future as a place for public relaxation. No snatching back land for imperial purposes after that.

The park is hilly and confusing to navigate. A long road intersects the zoo, with a monorail rising above connecting enclosures. Following this road, feeling relaxed after whiling away time by the lotus lake, you soon come to a residential area on the park's edge with small higgledy-piggledy houses. Washing hangs from balconies. Vines droop from drainpipes. Flower boxes overflow with geraniums. Here, you have unwittingly exited Ueno Park and are in a little next-door neighbourhood quite unlike the concrete jungle of Tokyo in Shinjuku, epicentre of flashing neon lights, bars and kitsch (where my hotel came complete with a giant plastic Godzilla on its roof that roared every half hour, emitting red-light "flames" and watery mists of "smoke").

In this bohemian-seeming quarter packed with little places to eat close to Tokyo University of the Arts, you are one step removed from the neon city. And you may, if you are lucky, come upon a small "traditional Japanese-European restaurant" (as I did). My feet seemed to lead inside, whereupon I discovered a menu in English, American blues music playing (somewhat confusingly), red-and-white lanterns hanging from the ceiling and a map of the vineyards of Burgundy adorning a wall. I ordered roast salmon with a "plenty of vegetables salad" (comprising solely broccoli) and a honey-mustard sauce, accompanied by a "highball" of whisky and soda.

"Please have a good time," said the waitress in perfect English.

It was impossible not to: the food was delicious, the drink punchy and everything just so delightfully different.

After this splendid little "park brunch" – all part of the Ueno experience – I returned to the park proper and made my way to the Tokyo National Museum at the top of the hill of Ueno Park. Here I bought a ticket, entered and found myself face to face with a statue of Edward Jenner.

How unexpected. Yet the Gloucestershire-born physician who pioneered smallpox vaccination in the late eighteenth and early nineteenth centuries, you soon learn, was considered a hero in Japan. At the time of his breakthrough, smallpox killed 10 per cent of populations it affected – startling when you think about it. Were that percentage to apply to Covid, the worldwide death rate would quickly have risen to tens of millions (the coronavirus rate is less than 1 per cent). No wonder Jenner was so revered.

Beyond Jenner, steps led to an elegant modern take on an ancient palace, where the treasures of Japan await at the Tokyo National Museum. These are magnificent. What a superb "park museum": medieval samurai swords; statues of fearsome twelfth-century deities; priceless vases decorated with bamboo and sparrows; delicate seventeenth-century sake cups; Qing dynasty stone lions; fourth-century bronze lions; famous "wave paintings" of sea scenes by Katsushika Hokusai.

After this dose of culture – park life Japanese-style – you may or may not visit the nearby National Museum of Western Art. Or instead, you may (like me) buy some chopsticks from the street market in front of the Tokyo National Museum, before making a pilgrimage to a monument with an eternal flame remembering those who died at Hiroshima and Nagasaki in the atomic bombings of August 1945. After that, I passed back through Ueno and stopped by the lotus pond one last time to gaze transfixed across the impossible-seeming sea of green in the middle of the world's most populated city.

As before, no one else was around. Little birds hopped in the shadows of the lotus leaves. I breathed in the calm, oxygenated air. I breathed out and felt myself relax, even beginning to feel *zen* descend. The Japanese, after all, invented the concept.

Godzillas may have been roaring at my neon-lit hotel a Metro ride away. Down by the lotus leaves, though, all was quiet.

A Democratic People's park
Ponghwasan Park, Pyongyang, North Korea

If you have spent more than a week under the constant supervision of two "guides" in the employ of the North Korean secret services – and feel you have won them over – you may decide the time is right to ask permission to go for a little stroll on your own in the park by your hotel in Pyongyang, the country's capital city.

So I did. My main guide, Mary, acquiesced, asking merely: "Please do not take your camera and do not pass those trees."

She was pointing at a copse in Ponghwasan Park across a bend of the murky-brown River Pothong. On this trip, I was travelling as a "tour operator brochure writer" – not as a journalist, which was what I really was – and my guides had been keeping a close eye on me. Reporters, always closely monitored, are only usually allowed in North Korea during the April–May military parade season.

"Please put away your pen!" Mary had said the day before my walk in Ponghwasan. We had been on a tour of the International Friendship Exhibition, where gifts to the reclusive dictatorship from Yugoslavia's Josip Tito and Libya's Colonel Gaddafi were on display. North Korea was then run by Supreme Leader Kim Jong-il, son of the nation's founder, Supreme Leader Kim Il-sung.

"No one has ever taken so many notes before!" she had added, with great suspicion. By jotting observations in the margins of a guidebook – as though updating observations for my "brochure-writing work" (in reality, notes for an article) – I was clearly putting their nerves on edge.

Despite this episode, my request for an unsupervised stroll had been granted. So there I was, with a spring in my step, walking along a carless street toward a pedestrian bridge across the River Pothong to the park.

By the roadside, a bird-like elderly woman squatted, carefully picking what looked like weeds from the pavement. Nearby, an ancient man was snipping blades of grass. These clippings were "herbs for the pot", as one of the guides had said during an unguarded moment (perhaps not toeing the official Workers' Party of Korea line admitting so to an outsider). Despite the many grand monuments and buildings of Pyongyang, evidence of widespread hardship is everywhere. Six out of ten of the population are estimated to live below the poverty line, although the truth is difficult to know for sure in the reclusive country.

Across the bridge in Ponghwasan Park, a troop of youngsters in red T-shirts jogged by in rows of two, arms swinging in unison. Such regimentation is commonplace. Throughout Pyongyang – population 2.8 million out of a country total of 25.5 million – training and marching seems to be constant as though in preparation for a final showdown with South Korea. "Reunification of the Fatherland" is a state policy designed to clear away the post-Second World War division of North and South Korea along the thirty-eighth parallel, when Russian troops initially controlled the North and the Americans the South. The Korean War of 1950–53 lives strong in minds and the North is, of course, regularly taunting the South with missile tests and provocative language as though about to launch an attack.

You enter Ponghwasan through a gate into grassland and woods. It was pleasant to be free of my guides. A stall sold rice cakes and soda bottles near the entrance. Further on, a group of men was hunched playing cards, one of the players grinned when I looked their way. This felt strange. Since arriving by train from Beijing, I had not interacted with a North Korean unsupervised. Being a tourist in the Democratic People's Republic of Korea is like entering a theatre, as so much of what you see feels staged.

Not so at Ponghwasan Park. A middle-aged man leapt vigorously on and off a bench: a strange exercise that was surely breaking some rule or other (North Korea is not short of pronouncements on what is and is not allowed as your "guides" – all tourists have "guides" – endlessly remind you). Aged fishermen cast bamboo rods in the River Pothong hoping for dinner, perhaps to be served *à la Pyongyang pavement weeds*. There was, however, no evidence of fish being hooked out. Litter was strewn on one side: broken bottles and crumpled Craven A cigarette packets (making me wonder how the obscure British brand had ended up there). The atmosphere was subdued. Life seemed to be going on as "normal" – well, as close to that as possible under the rule of an internationally outcast dictatorship.

Nearby, a game of volleyball was in full swing, the players admirably skilful, yelling encouragement to one another. The way the ball miraculously stayed up as they leapt about was quite a spectacle and it was then I realized something: aside from those at the very top of the Democratic People's Republic, you rarely see an overweight North Korean. Regular food shortages, which country analysts class as "famines" in worse years, do not seem to allow for that.

I kept on along the path. This led to the copse Mary had set as my boundary. Within a clearing cut into the woodland, however, footballers were booting balls. Yes, I was breaking my word, but what harm could there be in watching? I entered the woodland and stood by the side of the pitch, witnessing another show of sporting prowess: shots fizzing at keepers, while others played keepie-uppie, brilliantly flicking the ball about as though putting on a show for a crowd.

What a relief to be unobserved. What a pleasure to be in Ponghwasan Park. How marvellous to be away from all the propaganda posters for founding father Kim Il-sung, who created the strange country in 1948, and his son, Kim Jong-il. After a week, I'd had more than enough of their ever-present white-toothed grins glaring down across squares and boulevards. It was frightening (and impossible) to imagine what this must be like for a lifetime. Only those who have lived it can say – and no one, of course, is allowed to speak out.

A scurrying disturbed my reverie. A short, flustered woman was heading my way: Mary. "Ah, Mr Thom," she said. "I wondered where you were."

It was then I realized I had been followed. My quiet, unwatched corner of the Democratic People's Republic of Korea was no more. Perhaps there is no such thing.

"Sorry, I didn't know you were keeping an eye on me," I said.

"It is my job, Mr Thom," she replied. "I do not want people asking about you."

Maybe she feared I would be picked up by police. In North Korea, outsiders stick out like sore thumbs. I was, just about, the country's only "tourist" (I certainly had not seen any others).

As we walked back to the hotel, Mary – away from my other "guide" for once – opened up. She told me she was studying Chinese and Russian as the English-speaking tourism market was falling off. She said that she was also an English language teacher for children and that she was exhausted from doing two jobs to make ends meet. "There is little time for anything else," she said. Maybe that is how the Kims keep control: everyone is too worn out from work, or hungry, to organize opposition… and fearful of what might happen if they do, naturally.

We passed the card players and I asked Mary whether money would change hands. "No gambling in North Korea," she replied bluntly. Then we left the gate of Ponghwasan Park, where a reproachful woman in a yellow apron glared at me. Mary explained that the woman was upset I had not paid the 50 won park entry fee – about three pence. I had been unable to understand a sign, and Mary had paid on my behalf when following. Secret service guides have their uses.

They also soon set about taking you to other parks if you dare stray into an "unofficial" park. That afternoon, Mary, Lee (my other guide) and I drove to a park on a hill – Moranbong Park – to witness a propaganda-friendly public space. It was as though they wanted to set the record straight, park-wise, in North Korea. This was how parks in the Democratic People's Republic of Korea *really were*. Happy families tucked into picnics on lawns. Students painted pictures of a stream beneath a temple. Copper-coloured acer trees and pink rhododendrons occupied a well-maintained garden. Women in pink robes danced beneath a pagoda, their arms held out sideways and fluttering like branches in a gentle breeze.

Onlookers applauded. A drum beat. A speaker announcement was made ("step it up for the foreigner", I fancied). The dancers' arms fluttered a little more vigorously than previously. There was not a scrap of litter. No one was scratching about for food. It was serene, idyllic and community-spirited, like some corner of park heaven.

From the hilltop, Mary, Lee and I looked down on a bridge across the River Taedong, Pyongyang's main waterway. My impression was they wished to "present" the long sweep of the river, the UFO-like national stadium on an island, the monuments soaring in the distance, the skyscrapers, the great bridges and the unusual water fountains bursting out of the river, casting wide fans of spray. Here you are! Not just a wonderful park: the future of a perfect civilization, too! The Democratic People's Future!

All theatre, of course. All show. Looking more closely once again, the streets were (as ever) empty. Three vehicles crossed a four-lane bridge ahead; the truth being that hardly anyone other than those possessing shiny black sedans with tinted windows could afford a car in North Korea.

Ugly apartment blocks rose in the distance. I had already seen some of these up close, with forecourts in which small piles of charcoal were spread out on sacks for residents to purchase for heating and to cook meals. No electricity or gas installed.

Way down below by the riverfront was what looked at first like a giant car park. Yet, it couldn't be. There couldn't possibly be that many vehicles in the whole capital. On closer inspection, the rows of "cars" turned out to be human beings practising for the big May parades a few weeks hence. On their knees or cross-legged in the big concrete lot, they clutched red flags and awaited their orders.

Meanwhile, the picnic-eaters laughed and the dancers fluttered beneath the pagoda in our perfect Democratic People's park on the hill. A long, long way from home, park life was in full swing, propaganda posters of the two Kims beaming at one another as though sharing a tremendously good joke back by the entrance to the dusty parking lot.

Smog and chi
Ming Tombs Scenic Area, Beijing, China

Back in London, the mayor's target of 50 per cent "green" land by 2050 looks unambitious by comparison with the exuberant goings-on of Beijing's Gardening and Greening Bureau. Officials at the bureau have been busily adding hectare upon hectare of "urban green space" in the form of "urban leisure parks", "urban forests", "small green spaces" and "healthy green ways" over recent years.

Some reports by ChinaDaily.com.cn suggested greenery already covered 46.2 per cent of the city. The Beijing Gardening and Greening Bureau would like this to reach 48.5 per cent soon, according to China.org.cn, another Chinese news source. No exact date was provided for this target, but given that Beijing is already nearly there, the Chinese capital seemed well ahead with things. In the past two years alone, 32,866 hectares of green space had been magicked up – quite how exactly, reports did not explain. When 48.5 per cent is achieved, more than 85 per cent of the city's population would have access to a park within 500 metres.

It all sounded wonderful: images of trees alive with birdsong and butterflies flickering in flowerbeds spring to mind. You may not find it quite that way, however, if you actually happen to go.

At around 20 million residents, Beijing almost equals neighbouring North Korea in population size, though coming nowhere close to mighty Tokyo. On my visit smog was thick: a caramel haze that stung the eyes. Add heat. Add large noisy roads. Mix in the confusion of arriving in such a vast conurbation feeling jetlagged. Amid the hurly-burly and the swirling vapours of a twenty-first-century industrial powerhouse, first impressions for many are understandably: *Help, get me out of here!* As interested as you may be in seeing the Forbidden City and the Great Wall of China, chances are you may feel a touch claustrophobic.

The pollution was dreadful. The World Health Organization's recommended air quality target is less than 10 micrograms per cubic metre of PM2.5 (fine particle matter of 2.5 microns or less), the most harmful small air particles, which are commonly measured to test air cleanliness. Beijing had of late been scoring an average 42 micrograms, while London's latest measure, for example, was 13.2 micrograms. As I was writing, the PM2.5 score in Beijing was a whopping 156 micrograms, according to the daily online Real-Time Air Quality Index. So, pollution clearly remained a big problem – and it may come as little surprise that, as in Tokyo, parks in Beijing are important.

There are plenty of them, many with evocative names: Longtanhu (Dragon Lake) Park, Zizhuyuan (Purple Bamboo) Park, Taoranting (Joyous Pavilion) Park, Tiantan (Temple of Heaven) Park and Shuangxiu (Double Elegant) Park. The latter is my pick of the bunch: why merely be "elegant" when you can be "double elegant"?

The best known is Beihai Park, an imperial garden during the Jin Dynasty of the twelfth and thirteenth centuries, with its beautiful White Pagoda, lake and arched stone bridge. Beihai is said to have been shut during China's Cultural Revolution of 1971–78 so Chairman Mao's wife, Jiang Qing, could enjoy its beautiful grounds in privacy. As with Princess Amelia back in Richmond Park in the 1750s, however, this provoked both a backlash and, eventually, a U-turn. Yet another example of a "people's park" to add to London's Richmond and Victoria parks.

Then you have the magnificent Summer Palace gardens, established during the Qing dynasty of 1644–1912, complete with a lake, islands, bridges and temples. The British burned down the old Summer Palace there in 1860 during the Opium Wars under the orders of Lord Elgin; retaliation for the deaths of two British envoys. Not one of the finer moments in British colonial history (of which there are plenty more to come in this round-the-world park quest).

My favourite park, however, was none of these. On the way back from seeing the Great Wall of China, my tour bus stopped at the Ming Tombs Scenic Area on Beijing's northern edge. For "scenic area" read "park", a lovely one covering a narrow strip of land, no more than a couple of hundred metres wide and about 2 miles long, set around 13 tombs of emperors from the Ming dynasty of 1368–1644.

I liked it (a lot) on several counts. The tombs themselves were ornate with curling terracotta-tiled roofs, stone dragons and the smell of incense. Golden Chinese characters adorned the entrances, where tourists used selfie sticks to take pictures by the resting place of Zhu Di, the first Ming emperor. Close by, steps led to the top of another tomb, which offered fine views across the misty jade-coloured treetops of the park. This mist was not natural... even on the city edge, pollution was heavy.

Yet down a long avenue of trees between the tombs, the air felt cleaner as we soon arrived at a series of peculiar stone statues in the shape of horses, elephants, lions and camels. These dated from the Ming period and looked almost comically big. The elephants were at least life-sized with heads held proudly high and extravagant curling tusks. Next to these splendid, obstinate creatures, the camels were, bizarrely, even bigger, standing alert as though ready to defend the tombs alongside the elephants at all costs. Yet they were by no means *fierce*: the sculptor seemed to have had a dry sense of humour and had finished off the creations with long, mysterious smiles. The overall impression was that the bizarre collection of animals was somehow intended to be very much tongue in cheek. This gave the Ming Tombs Scenic Area, which you might expect to be a grave affair, a wonderfully playful touch.

Wei, our guide, explained that the huge stone statues had been transported in ancient times during the winter, using ice to slide them along as they were so bulky; wells had had to be dug to bring up water to create the icy "paths" every 500 metres or so. After imparting this, he sat at a bench to let us take selfies like everyone else for a while. I joined him.

"Do you understand the internal power energy force?" Wei asked, apropos of nothing. He was looking directly ahead through his thick-lensed glasses as though addressing one of the camels. At first, I was unsure whether he was talking to me.

"The vital force," he continued. "The *chi*. The *Yin Yang*. The good and bad. The hot and cold. The north and south. The east and west."

He turned my way: "Daoism, Taoism. It is in feng shui. It is in tai chi." Wei had decided to teach me some of the basics of ancient Chinese philosophy.

"The *chi*: people cannot see or touch it, but we know it is there," he said. The *chi*, I gathered, was a form of energy. "Acupuncture. Herbal medicine. Meditation. Once you understand this, Chinese culture is easier to understand. Not just people, nature too. The *chi*."

Wei told me to close my eyes and clasp my palms together with my wrists perfectly aligned so my palms touched to my fingertips. When I had done this, he asked: "Which of your hands is bigger? Concentrate!"

I told Wei that my right hand felt larger. "Good," he said. I had in some way – I think – meditated and moved forward in my understanding of the *chi*. This was progress.

Over the minutes that followed, Wei taught me some basic Chinese characters, which I dutifully jotted down. The symbols for a person are like a slightly squashed upside-down "Y". Two of these, slightly leaning forward, are "to follow" or "to be from". Three of the symbols clumped together means "lots of people" or "the general public". A "mountain" could either be three triangles (the ancient way of depicting "mountain") or a long dash with an upward rim at each end and a line sticking up from the middle (the modern way). A "prisoner" is a "person" symbol with a box drawn round it. "Water" is a "greater than" symbol running into a "K", while a wonky "X" with a dash is "fire". I had not expected to learn all of this when entering the Ming Tombs Scenic Area, and my notebook was soon full of squiggles representing "ice", "exit" and "car" (a complicated series of amalgamated "Ls" and "Ts").

After this lesson, Wei encouraged me to close my eyes and join my palms once again to feel the *chi*. This was oddly relaxing (and still comes in useful now and then).

So I will always remember the Ming Tombs Scenic Area, not just for the history, tombs and slightly mad statues, but also for the *chi*.

I had found my *chi*! This does not, let's face it, happen to you every day.

The next morning, I visited another Beijing park.

Early the following day I went for a run in Beijing's city centre. Leaving my hotel, I turned into Tiananmen Square, passing the site of the tragic scenes of 1989 when some believe more than 10,000 protesters were killed by the Chinese Army. Cars with tinted windows drove past the Mausoleum of Chairman Mao and the concrete facade of the Great Hall of the People, close to which a flag-raising ceremony was taking place with hundreds of Chinese tourists watching on. At the northern end of the square, I crossed a road and entered Zhongshan Park, part of the imperial city from Ming and Qing days. Surrounded by trees and pavilions, I made my way to the gates of the Forbidden City, suddenly alone after the crowds of Tiananmen and the many armed soldiers and police.

As in Tokyo by Ueno Park's lotus lake, a sudden sense of restfulness descended. In the centre of this secretive nation expected to dominate the twenty-first century, it was possible in Zhongshan Park to enjoy its capital city of 20 million all to yourself.

How peculiar, yet how satisfying too: a green sanctuary in the heart of smoky Beijing.

Thank you, Beijing Gardening and Greening Bureau.

Keep up the good work!

Tear gas and posh hotels
Chater Garden, Hong Kong

From one park close to an epicentre of political upheaval to another – this one having seen recent action.

Chater Garden is bang in the middle of Hong Kong's central business district, overlooked by the august facade of the Court of Final Appeal and the glistening tangle of metal tubes of the HSBC Building, headquarters of the Hongkong and Shanghai Banking Corporation. Thousands of pro-democracy protesters regularly gather at this small park to campaign against Chinese clampdowns on basic freedoms, which as everyone knows from news reports have gathered pace ever since the British handover of its former colony on 1 July 1997. Recent protests have witnessed police firing tear gas and raising guns as though to shoot live ammunition at crowds lofting banners calling for a "FREE HONG KONG".

How things have changed. My first visit to Hong Kong (and Asia) was a month before the Chinese handover and my lovely hotel room had a lovely balcony facing Chater Garden, across which a lovely breeze blew, ruffling the fronds of a cluster of lovely palm trees.

Everything about this trip seemed lovely. Having been called at the last moment to make up numbers – without a commission from a publication – I was on my first "press trip". I was heading for Australia to write articles about Australian tourism in the company of a press officer from the Australian tourist board, via a Hong Kong stopover. I was just one of a pack of "hacks" (journalists) that included a blasé editor of a men's magazine, a taciturn tabloid subeditor and a veteran freelance food writer with an ironic sense of humour. Everyone got on exceedingly well, most of the time, and it was hardly surprising we did.

We were staying at the amazingly lovely five-star Mandarin Oriental hotel. We were provided with lovely complimentary champagne in ice buckets in our lovely rooms. We were told by a lovely hotel manager that the Mandarin Oriental was Margaret Thatcher's favourite hotel in Hong Kong. Lovely chandeliers and gold fittings glittered. I was on my first journalist "jolly" and it was living up to the name.

This, in case you ever wondered, is how a great deal of travel journalism works.

Taking an evening stroll from the hotel into neighbouring Chater Garden, neon skyscrapers rose all around, while lilac and crimson lights flittered on the inky-black surface of Victoria Harbour. Dizzy from champagne from the business-class flight, the lovely hotel and the press pack's visit to the dimly lit bar of the Foreign Correspondents' Club (copious quantities of free champagne, I was quickly learning, figure large on press trips), I gazed across the dazzling water and continued into the humid park.

Hong Kong seemed so enticing. Fountains splashed and gurgled. Creepers swayed in teak trees. Meandering paths led to the grand Ionic columns of the Court of Final Appeal, home to the old Supreme Court of Hong Kong during British colonial days. Lights on skyscrapers blinked above. The only indication of the massive change shortly to come was a makeshift stall on a corner selling T-shirts bearing the slogan: "WELCOME BACK CHINA. BYE BYE UK" (which might not sell so well now). Taxis honked. Ferries bobbed on the harbour. Couples canoodled on benches. I vowed there and then to return one day.

A decade later, I did. During that interval low-cost airlines had taken to the skies and made travel easier than ever. My flight to the other side of the world had cost about the same as a meal for two at a modest restaurant in Britain and was attracting headlines. Could an airline offering such cheap flights survive? I was sent by a paper to find out.

Chater Garden had stuck in my mind; so, I stayed close by.

Being in town for a few days, I soon fell into a routine of reading the *South China Morning Post* at a bench in the park each morning; a fine way to start the day before the temperature rose and Hong Kong got sticky. There was something about this green space in the middle of the central business district of a major financial capital that was appealing. All around, traders were glued to screens making millions from flickering numbers. Let them make their millions! I would sit beneath the palms and take in the day's news, enjoying the sense of history of the little park, about 100 metres long and 100 metres wide.

And there was plenty of past into which to delve. Chater Garden is named after Sir Catchick Paul Chater, a businessman of Armenian descent but brought up in India, where he was born Khachik Pogose Astwachatoor in 1846. He was a remarkable character, orphaned aged seven, looked after by relatives and shipped to Hong Kong aged 18 to live with his married sister. Soon he was trading gold bullion, planning land reclamation of Victoria Harbour (by taking soundings of water depth), building a power station, establishing a dairy and training horses to race at nearby Happy Valley Racecourse (where he won the Hong Kong Derby 19 times).

He also played cricket for the Hong Kong Cricket Club, being handy with both bat and ball, and often playing on a pitch where Chater Garden is now found. A late Victorian all-rounder, through and through.

Sir Catchick, also known as Sir Paul, was knighted by Edward VII at Buckingham Palace, made a member of the French *Légion d'Honneur* and appointed to the colony's Executive Council. He donated huge sums to his old school in India and left his extravagant house, Marble Hall, and its contents to Hong Kong. His death in 1926 was lead story in *The Hongkong Telegraph*. "Colony's grand old man. Passing of the Right Hon Sir Paul Chater. End of brilliant career" ran the headline, with the reporter describing him as "the most outstanding figure in the history of the Colony, and we are sure that we are voicing a universal sentiment in deeply deploring his demise". The Hong Kong Stock Exchange was closed for a day as a mark of respect, flags flown at half mast and a local group's "bathing trip fixed for this afternoon has also been cancelled".

It is tricky these days to sing the praises of anyone to do with the British Empire, but Sir Catchick does seem to have been both a pretty good egg and uncontroversial, even if the stocks and shares of the Hong Kong Stock Exchange were (perhaps) not exactly cleaner than clean back then. *The Hongkong Telegraph*, at least, really seemed to like him – and a bathing group, too. No public statue was ever erected, though.

Chater Garden is on reclaimed land, as is much of the central business district and Hong Kong in general – at least 6 per cent of Hong Kong is built on such land. Sir Catchick was, naturally given his tendency to have his fingers in many pies, much involved in this process in the early days. His soundings led to 60 acres being added to Central, as the area is known, including the park. A total of 3.5 million tonnes of material was required to do the job, with work finally completed in 1904 after beginning in 1890. If anyone deserves to have a park named after them, someone who created the land on which the park was built fits the bill.

In short, Sir Catchick was quite a personality and, one way or another, Chater Garden has developed a symbolic centrality to life in Hong Kong over the years. It is, after all, the location of its main court. When Hong Kongers protest, Chater Garden is where they so often come. HSBC is next door. So is the venerable Hong Kong Club: "Jacket and tie must be worn at all times in the Red Room restaurant… blue denim and backless shoes are not permitted in the Members' Bar." Ghosts of the cricket games of colonial days seem to float between the palm trees. Ghosts of the workers who toiled to fill in the land that was once the South China Sea do, too.

In Chater Garden one morning, on my second visit to Hong Kong, I had arranged to meet Mr Sam.

Mr Sam of Sam's Tailors was really named Manu, but he told me on the phone he preferred Mr Sam. He called me Mr Tom. He was in his 50s and wore a pink shirt, blue silk tie and a large gold watch. His grey hair had an immaculate side-parting.

We went to my hotel where I was measured for a suit – just as he had sized up the likes of Tony Blair, Bill Clinton and David Bowie. Mr Sam told me how he had trained on Saville Row and that his father had established his business. We shook hands, he bowed slightly and left. The suit, incredibly, would be ready the next day.

And so it was. I had flown to Hong Kong for a long weekend and bought a tailor-made suit, all for the price of a usual fare to Hong Kong. This was the "story" for the paper.

Yet memories of the cool shade of Chater Garden, neon lights flickering and ferry horns blasting on the harbour, stuck. As did my acquaintance with Mr Sam, who called out of the blue three years later and has done ever since after similar intervals: "Mr Tom, do you remember me? I am at a suite at the Savoy and can measure you for another suit, if you require one, Mr Tom." Once I took him up on the offer, visiting his grand "fitting shop" at the five-star hotel, where business cards of Britain's great and good were stacked neatly on his desk.

When pro-democracy protests in Chater flash up at home on TV, thoughts are not just with the activists and their desperate, important cause.

They also turn to a small, peaceful park tucked away in the shadow of the scrapers in a large, humid faraway city.

CHAPTER THREE

VIETNAM, LAOS, THE PHILIPPINES, AUSTRALIA: "CHEAP HAPPINESS" IN BACKPACKER-LAND

Memories of cities tend naturally to be dominated by famous sights, be it the Eiffel Tower in Paris, the Colosseum in Rome, the Empire State Building in New York or the statue of Christ the Redeemer in Rio de Janeiro. Yet beyond these showstoppers, a park or two usually springs to mind as well. That morning stroll to that lovely park around the corner from your hotel you half forgot about, or that little park by the river you paused at for a rest after a day spent pounding round the attractions.

At least that was what I was beginning to discover, ensconced in lockdown London, happy to have torn myself away from an inexplicably addictive and extremely long-running television series about the lives of a family in a motel in small-town USA. I was "travelling" without travelling at all, in between trips to my Sainsbury's Local and circuits round Richmond Park... of course.

As memories began to flood back, it was already becoming a great pleasure to "re-enter" these old haunts and appreciate the often-random qualities of parks the world over. You may meet Mr Sam beneath the palm trees and the shiny HSBC tower. You may learn of the joys of the art of *chi* by a stone statue of a smiling camel. You may be tailed by minders in one of the world's most notorious dictatorships while watching a game of kickabout. Or you may simply fall for the tranquillity of a lotus lake.

Whatever happens, happens, and the great thing was that these buried parks (buried somewhere in the back of my mind) were seeming to throw up surprises, be they big or small, cultural eye-openers or merely *curiosities*. Maybe that was the enjoyment I was beginning to experience. Not just the reward that came from recalling a fine bit of greenery in a big busy city, but also an overriding sense of *what next?*

It was this unpredictability I wanted to capture, with deviations, encounters and offbeat moments thrown in. Pockets of quiet with all their oddities and quirks. Glimpses of green with secret stories away from the "mainstream" of most city life.

With these thoughts to the fore – ahead of striking eastward across the Pacific and snaking up South America to the United States – this imaginary world tour of urban parks was about to take a diversion: curling into the backpacker-land of South East Asia, before zipping down south to Australia.

Consulting the old-fashioned globe in my study, this seemed as logical a way to proceed as any on the "journey" ahead. Why not drop by for a (vicarious) taste of backpacker life once again? Maybe I could somehow "find myself" by dreaming up a local park or two? As unlikely now as it was when I first went, perhaps. But no harm in trying – and was that not what this park adventure really was? A series of daydreams.

It was then I noticed something. Each of the parks in this part of the world seemed to have a common connection. And this shared tie was of colonialists, be they British, French or Spanish, who more often than not seemed to have been involved in dreadful deeds. Where the galleons had ventured, Europeans had hopped off to start ruling the roost while at the same time (often) introducing the European park tradition – places in which to unwind in pleasant scenery after a hard day's work ruling another people's nation, if you like.

So these imaginary "visits" to local parks were often to find themselves touching upon colonial days, as well as other times of outside meddling such as America's involvement in Vietnam... the good, the bad and sometimes the (extremely) ugly.

I had not expected any of this: the subject simply seemed to emerge. At a time when many were taking time out to reconsider the colonial period, there was plenty of food for thought – and some very nice parks, too.

Good morning Vietnam
Tao Dan Park, Ho Chi Minh City, Vietnam

If Vietnam's football team happens to have just defeated neighbouring rivals Laos 9–0, be ready for mayhem in Ho Chi Minh City.

This was how it was on my arrival in Vietnam's second city. A river of bicycles and mopeds draping red flags with yellow stars flowed through the streets. There were honks. There were yells. There were revving motors. It was joyous and it was wild. On the one hand, moving about on foot or finding a quiet spot seemed impossible. On the other, who cared? Join the party!

Not that it was ever exactly peaceful in Ho Chi Minh City. It was not that kind of place. Chaotic exuberance was the order of the day – what a whirlwind of a city.

But there was one hideaway of relative calm in the heart of this metropolis of 21 million people.

Tao Dan Park comprises 24 acres of trees, temples, tai chi practitioners and, between about 6 a.m. and 8 a.m. each day, songbirds.

Early every day, elderly men (mainly) congregate in the park having carefully brought along cages containing their much-beloved songbirds. These cages are promptly hung from hooks on metal frames provided for the purpose by cafes with plastic chairs and tables arranged for the proud songbird owners. Trills, tweets and melodies soon fill the air.

No one quite knows when this tradition came about. It just did. And it is heart-warming to watch.

The men cross their legs and peer up devotedly. Most are smokers. Lost in their admiration, the songbird owners' ash grows on their cigarettes, forming long curls that occasionally drop between drags. The owners hardly notice, being so entranced by the wonderful symphony of birdsong (just like the visitor).

The hope among the songbird owners is that some birds will pick up tunes from the other birds, thus expanding their musical repertoire. A skilful songbird is valuable (some are traded) and confers status on owners. Yet the overriding "purpose" of the gathering is social. Between bouts of avian devotion, owners break out to talk over coffee. Sure, an element of rivalry and showing off exists, but really it is all about having a good gossip.

For newcomers off a plane, there can be few more agreeable places to conquer jetlag and plan a day's activities: a boat ride along the sleepy Mekong River, perhaps; a trip to the Cu Chi tunnels, where the Viet Cong were based during the Vietnam War, maybe.

The hour after the songbird owners have fussily covered cages to protect their loved ones from road fumes, attached them to their mopeds and gone (between around 8 or 9 a.m.) is the perfect time to take a circuit of Tao Dan Park. Down shaded pathways – the park has more than 1,000 trees – you soon come to a replica of the striking red-stone Cham Towers honouring Hindu deities found in Nha Trang, a city on the coast to the north of Ho Chi Minh City. Keep going past sculptures of dragons and tigers, little lotus ponds, aerobic classes, badminton courts (busy) and public gym equipment (ditto) and you arrive at one of the most emblematic sites in Vietnam, if not the whole of South East Asia.

On 30 April 1975 tanks belonging to the People's Army of Vietnam crashed through the wrought-iron gates of what was then the Presidential Palace to complete the "liberation" of the city. As cameras rolled, the armed vehicles crossed the lawns to the front steps where a soldier ran out to unfurl a Viet Cong flag from a balcony. The result was clear for the world to see, after more than 3 million deaths, the Vietnam War and American post-Second World War interference in the country was over. The city, previously known as Saigon, was renamed in honour of the Marxist-Leninist revolutionary Ho Chi Minh. And that, after 19 years of conflict, was that.

The 1960s concrete building is, frankly, ugly. It might pass for an airport terminal. It is on the northern edge of the park and is referred to either as Independence Palace or Reunification Hall. The day before the communists arrived back in 1975 had been frantic at the old South Vietnamese HQ. Around 7,000 remaining Americans and South Vietnamese were forced to flee the country in Operation Frequent Wind, the biggest helicopter evacuation in history (airports had been too damaged to use). Images of queues waiting to board helicopters hit front pages across the globe. "Surrender! Saigon yields unconditionally; end comes only hours after last Americans fly out," screamed the *Daily News* of New York, with a subheading inviting readers to turn to inside pages to read about the "end of the agony".

Independence Palace is now a tourist attraction with information about the war; the building is also used for conferences and as a wedding venue. From the top, with its cafe serving Pepsis, fine views are to be had across the treetops of Tao Dan Park. Meanwhile in the basement, a gift shop sells lacquer pictures and silk prints, while the April 30th Restaurant along a corridor is notable for its unusual slogans: "It is said 'there is no cheap happiness'. However, you can find cheap happiness here. We are proud to bring you cheap happiness." If only all restaurants were so honest.

Back in the park at the songbird cafe, a group of US veterans had gathered. The American soldiers had returned! But they looked bedraggled and fidgety. Louis, a former artillery sergeant in the US army, wore a red bandana and a T-shirt saying: "The Last Great Gunfighters". He hobbled along with a cane and when I asked about his memories of the war, held out his right arm to show me a series of sores.

"Check these out," he said. "I've got loadsa them. Happened when a 40-millimetre round blew up in my hands. Tiny black specks of shrapnel are comin' out to this day."

It was as though he was providing proof he had served. John, one of his companions, looked gaunt. "Vietnam never leaves you," he said. "It always haunts you. Coming back is part of the healing process. I can hear the word 'Vietnam' now and think of a country rather than a war."

They were on a trip across Vietnam, having ventured as far as the Demilitarized Zone, a stretch of land on the seventeenth parallel, about 600 miles north of Ho Chi Minh City, that marked the division between northern Vietnam forces and American troops in the south. While there, they had visited Truong Son National Cemetery for Vietnamese soldiers. Steve, another of the group, said: "One [of the buried Vietnamese] was born in the same month as me – I kept wondering what he'd be doing now if he had lived."

They had come to exorcize demons. Judging by their twitchiness and sometimes glazed expressions, this seemed a work in progress. During our brief encounter, one former soldier left in a huff to stand alone beneath a tree, upset by something that had been said. His companions looked on with sympathy.

They parted and I settled down at the songbird cafe, turning to Graham Greene's novel *The Quiet American*, much of which is set in Ho Chi Minh City and which I had bought back in Britain to read *in loco*.

The Quiet American, published in 1955, is Greene's evocative and perceptive story of American behind-the-scenes interest in Vietnam during the days of French Indochina in the early 1950s, and a great deal of the action centres on the French colonial-era streets near Tao Dan Park. It is in this neighbourhood, now a hotspot of backpacker tourism, that the protagonist (jaded, opium pipe-smoking British war correspondent Thomas Fowler) and his American undercover agent friend (Alden Pyle, the "quiet American" of the book's title) first meet. Much intrigue is soon to play out at nearby cafes and clubs, as well as the Continental Hotel and Hotel Majestic, both of which remain. Turning the pages is like stepping into another era, when Vietnam was ruled by the French, with the Americans lurking in the background.

In the north-west corner of Tao Dan Park the feeling of those cloak-and-dagger colonial days was especially strong. Here you will find the pool of the Cercle Sportif, a Westerners-only sports club during the French days, beside tennis courts and the peeling 1920s facade of the clubhouse that Greene knew well during his visit to the city. Back then, it was home to a billiards room, a reading room and a great deal of gossip.

After the French left in 1954, when the park was known as the Jardin de la Ville, the Americans, as Greene had foretold, soon moved in – with more than 3 million people estimated later to die during the Vietnam War between 1954 and the helicopter lift of 1975. One of the Cercle Sportif club members was none other than William Colby, station chief in Vietnam for the Central Intelligence Agency from 1959 to 1962, later to be appointed director of the CIA and director of central intelligence under Presidents Nixon and Ford. Much plotting went on in Tao Dan Park over the years; much of it, possibly, not so good. The Cercle Sportif club, epicentre of much of this decision-making, remains in its diminished state, known now as the Ho Chi Minh City Labour Culture Palace. Rumours of wrecking balls and shopping malls arise from time to time (but the club seems always somehow to hang on).

Like a backpacker myself, and the songbird owners earlier, I put my feet up and let a lazy hour or so slip by in Saigon's best park; the mad streets of mopeds and bicycles out of sight and mind beyond the temples and tropical trees.

And the next day I was back early amid the symphony of songbirds.

Good morning, Vietnam, indeed.

The last king of Vientiane
Chao Anouvong Park, Vientiane, Laos

After so many megacities, the capital of Laos, Vientiane, is a tiddler: population 820,000. Of the other cities so far, Hong Kong is the closest in size with 7 million inhabitants – that is, if you take the special administrative region of China to be a "city". Hong Kong is officially a "territory" and a very heavily populated one: number four on the table of world's most densely populated countries or dependencies with an estimated 6,781 people per square kilometre (nearby Macau on the Chinese mainland has an incredible 21,158 inhabitants per square kilometre).

Vientiane, however, does not even register on usual "population density" lists. According to one study by the World Population Review, fewer than 31 people live per square kilometre in Laos, ranking the country a lowly 180 out of the world's 195 states. Meanwhile another group, Open Development Laos, puts the number of inhabitants of Vientiane per square kilometre at 209.

Let's just say, the capital of Laos is exceedingly unpopulated compared with Tokyo, Beijing and the others.

It is also exceedingly relaxing, especially in Chao Anouvong Park.

This park is on a sliver of land facing a wide, lazy bend of the River Mekong, not far from the Beaux Arts-style Presidential Palace and a succession of Buddhist temples and stupas dotted around streets of faded French colonial buildings from Indochina days. Laos broke free from the French in 1949, suffered many hardships during the Vietnam War (when Americans bombed the North Vietnamese infiltrating South Vietnam via Laos), formed a rigid communist regime in 1975 and, after an about-turn, began to forge links with the West in the 1990s despite remaining, on paper, Marxist-Leninist. The country does not get many tourists, but those who do visit the landlocked nation are more than likely, after ticking off the Buddhist temples, to take a stroll in Chao Anouvong.

It is a good park for walking, especially at dawn or dusk when the sky ignites in an ethereal blaze of oranges and pinks with great streaks of scarlet and lilac rising above the Mekong. On the other side of the river, in Thailand, low-level buildings line the riverbanks with emerald paddy fields and jungle stretching as far as the eye can see. In the foreground, impenetrable beds of reeds form a blanket of wilderness patrolled by thin white birds. Meanwhile, at the western edge of the park, near a run of bars serving ice-cold Beerlao (a rice beer), a clearing reveals an expanse of silty sand: Vientiane's "beach". On the water, fishermen in conical hats tend nets from low-slung boats in scenes that cannot have changed much in centuries. Looking across the river from Chao Anouvong Park you do not really feel as though you are in a city at all.

The park's highlight is a 6-metre bronze statue of its namesake, who certainly shook things up in these parts, far more so even than Sir Catchick back in Hong Kong.

Park names are often a source of stories. Investigating Chao Anouvong's shines light not just on why Anouvong is so honoured among the lawns and tree-lined paths of the park dedicated to him, but also on wider events in the region.

Chao Anouvong was the last king of Vientiane in the early nineteenth century, a complicated, hot-headed leader who is regarded by many as a national hero for attacking Thailand and asserting Laotian identity in the face of its powerful neighbour. For several weeks in 1826–27 Anouvong's march with his 10,000-strong army towards Bangkok went to plan; he had taken Siam, as the Kingdom of Thailand was named until the mid-twentieth century, by surprise. For this short spell, hopes of a revival of the ancient Lao Kingdom of Lan Xang, which had covered vast tracts of South East Asia in the sixteenth century, were high.

Then it all went wrong. Thailand counter-attacked using weapons secretly bought from the British (that Anouvong had not known they possessed). He turned on his heels. The Thai troops followed. And before long, after fleeing and then returning for an ill-judged guerrilla war-style attack, Anouvong was captured and Vientiane sacked to such an extent the French found little left other than ruins when they stopped by 30 years later to set up their colonial outpost. They were not even sure they had arrived at the ancient city of which they had heard so much.

The tale of what became of Anouvong after his capture, as told by the British chronicler John Bowring in 1855 in *The Kingdom and People of Siam*, is chilling:

The king arrived in Bangkok about the latter end of 1828, and underwent there the greatest cruelties barbarians could invent. He was confined in a large iron cage, exposed to a burning sun, and obliged to proclaim to every one that the king of Siam was great and merciful, that he himself had committed a great error and deserved his present punishment. In this cage were placed with the prisoner, a large mortar to pound him in, a large boiler to boil him in, a hook to hang him by, and a sword to decapitate him; also a sharp-pointed spike for him to sit on. His children were sometimes put in along him. He was a mild, respectable-looking old grey-haired man, and did not live long to gratify his tormentors, death having put an end to his sufferings. His body was taken and hung in chains on the bank of the river, about two or three miles below Bangkok.

Anouvong was aged 62 and, given his miserable fate and legacy, you might question his hero status. After all, his attack, known as the Lao Rebellion, had many implications. Not only was Vientiane destroyed, but the conquering Thai army also enforced a massive resettlement of Laos people to the western – Siam – side of the Mekong, thus weakening Laos as a nation.

This created such instability in the region that Vietnam and Thailand were drawn into conflict. While this was going on, the French snuck in and rebuilt Vientiane while establishing Indochina, with all the implications that eventually had when the Americans attempted to fill the power vacuum of their departure in the mid-1950s. The low "population density" in Laos to this day harks back to Anouvong's actions.

Yet there he stands in his eponymous park, facing his old enemy with a sword tucked under his left arm while his right arm juts forwards in a peculiar gesture that seems to be both an act of defiance to Thailand as well as a suggestion of reconciliation; his palm is half-open, facing upwards as though softly saying: "Greetings." On his golden plinth, the hero is depicted wearing a wide-brimmed hat, baggy trousers and an expression of determination. The statue was erected by the Lao People's Revolutionary Party in 2010. It makes a big, bold yet somehow equivocal statement. In pride of place in Vientiane's number one park lies a mystery.

Plenty to ponder over a Beerlao at the Tipsy Elephant or the Bamboo Bar, after a steaming bowl of grilled prawns and noodles from one of the street stalls on the western tip of Chao Anouvong Park.

This is a restful spot. Colourful tuk-tuks putter by. Backpackers squint at guidebooks. "Sympathy for the Devil" by the Rolling Stones plays. Droplets run down your glass or beer bottle. The sun beats down on the Mekong River as you half pinch yourself that you really are bathed in sunshine by a mighty waterway in South East Asia. Then, a strange skinny westerner with a leathery tanned face and flip-flops may sidle up to your table. Which is precisely what happened to me.

"Are you from Belgium?" he asked inexplicably. There was nothing on my person to suggest I was from the Low Countries (or any country, for that matter).

I told him I was not from Belgium.

"Oh," he said. He looked both extremely disappointed while at the same time not all that surprised. Then he shuffled away without another word. Perhaps he only kept company with Belgians. Perhaps the question was a code: an offer of drugs or something else for sale. *Something* was up and the man had a seedy look that suggested whatever it might have been was probably not on the tourist board website's official list of attractions. Sex tourism had become such a problem in Laos that signs in hotel lobbies warned of a government crackdown; prostitution is illegal in the country. Maybe he was something to do with that. I turned to see if he was soliciting others on their Belgian-ness, but he had slipped away into the shadow of an alley.

Down by the water's edge I dipped my hand in the Mekong as the explosions of colour of yet another glorious sunset in South East Asia slowly faded. A canopy of stars soon unveiled: heavenly flickers in the jet-black firmament that you almost never see in a bigger city with a greater population density. Vientiane's 209 was coming into its own. A jumble of tinny music jingled from the Tipsy Elephant and the Bamboo Bar in the heart of this little-populated, little-visited Marxist-Leninist capital city.

Across the reeds in Chao Anouvong Park, the last king of Vientiane cast a fearsome silhouette. His final days may have been spent as a "mild, respectable-looking old grey-haired man" imprisoned in a torture cage 400 miles south. Now he was back, in the city razed after his adventures, bigger and tougher than ever.

The Mekong flowed slowly by, water lapping on the shores of Laos just as it always has since the days of Anouvong and before. Another Rolling Stones track played as though just for the old warrior: "You Can't Always Get What You Want".

I ordered another Beerlao, toasted the former king – and whatever he may or may not have achieved – listening to the music and the crickets in the reeds.

Dirty old town
Plaza de Armas, Manila, Philippines

During the early days of the coronavirus pandemic, the president of the Philippines, Rodrigo Duterte, launched a "Back to the Province" campaign.

Under the slogan "Manila has reached its maximum", cash incentives were offered to those willing to move out of the big smoke to relieve pressure on public services in what some say is the most densely populated city on the planet with an estimated 46,178 inhabitants per square kilometre. Compare that with Vientiane's purported 209 people per square kilometre and the gulf is enormous. I use the word "purported" and the earlier phrase "what some say" here as statistics vary somewhat depending on who has conducted the research. Other cities such as Male, the capital of the Maldives, Bangladesh's capital, Dhaka, and Tokyo sometimes top such "people per square kilometre" lists.

Lies, damned lies and statistics, some may say. Yet truths lie within them and they reveal the basic picture, quibbles about exact measurements and rankings aside. Just as Vientiane is undoubtedly incredibly unpopulated (and relaxing); Manila is undoubtedly incredibly not so.

President Duterte's offer of 110,000 pesos to move to the countryside, when the GDP per capita stands at 151,000 pesos, was not gesture politics. The Philippine capital city, population 13 million, had reached breaking point… the "maximum". *Provincianos* seeking work in the capital, many living in shanty towns on the city limits, had overwhelmed the infrastructure. Time to return to the country, said Duterte, with a pocket full of presidential pesos.

On the drive from the airport to my hotel, the sense of "maximum" having been reached – and busted – was obvious. From the terminal, beyond the slums, a concrete nightmare unveiled: apartments, malls, flyovers, offices, warehouses, more apartments, more malls, more offices, more, more and more. Concrete, concrete everywhere! And plenty of billboard adverts, too, promoting malls, fast-food joints, sofas, televisions, mobile phones, apartments that will change your life forever just as it has for the happy couple pictured. Repeat, repeat, repeat! The driver swerved between lanes down highways from hell through a Beijing-worthy haze. It was hot and it was awful.

With a day to kill and in search of a touch of tranquillity, after depositing bags in a nondescript business hotel on a busy junction, I went straight out to find a park.

This was surprisingly easy. Not so far from my lodgings was Fort Santiago in the Intramuros district, the old part of town built by the Spanish in the 1570s as their base in the archipelago of 7,641 islands.

Spain ruled the Philippines until 1898 having named the islands the *Felipinas* after Philip II. They had taken their time getting settled in, after an expedition party suffered defeat at the hands of native warriors in 1521 resulting in the death of the explorer Ferdinand Magellan. By the time the Spanish eventually left, the dominant religion was well established as Christianity; the Spanish having converted islanders from Islam. Then the Americans came. Then the Japanese during the Pacific War. Then the Philippines, finally in 1946, gained independence.

Just as in Tao Dan Park in Ho Chi Minh City and Chao Anouvong Park in Vientiane, Fort Santiago feels in the heart of historical action in the capital of the Philippines. That is because it is. The fort is on hallowed land originally the site of a fortification belonging to a Muslim Rajah of Maynila.

To reach the fort, you cross Plaza Moriones, a "square" that is really more like a pretty little park with frangipani trees, palms, lawns and beds of pink and yellow flowers: a veritable oasis leading to a decorative stone archway. This is the fort's rebuilt entrance – most of the centre of Manila was destroyed during the Pacific War – accessed via a bridge above a moat to another pocket of green, Plaza de Armas.

What a revelation. Tucked away near the mouth of the River Pasig, Plaza de Armas offers a corner of Manila in which to breathe, away from the drone of traffic and the helter-skelter goings-on of one of the world's most overcrowded places.

It also offers the opportunity to reflect on the life of a Philippine national hero.

Parks so often seem to have characters lurking in their pasts – first Sir Catchick, then Chao Anouvong. Now José Rizal: novelist, poet, playwright, sculptor, painter, cartographer, journalist, historian, martial-arts enthusiast, fencer, ophthalmologist (his profession) and general genius who called for political reforms during Spanish rule.

His is a tragic story. For daring to speak out in favour of independence, Rizal – who had travelled to Europe to study in Madrid, Berlin and London before returning to the Philippines (by then conversant, it is said, in no fewer than 22 languages) – was labelled a *filibustero* (subversive). He was accused of encouraging rebellion through his writings, imprisoned at Fort Santiago and executed in another park in Manila, now named Rizal Park, in 1896 aged 35. The exact spot where he was killed is now marked by a statue of the polymath being gunned down while suited and wearing a broad-rimmed hat. A grainy black-and-white photograph (of questionable authenticity, but nevertheless said to be accurate in capturing the setting) shows Rizal standing unblindfolded with his back to a firing squad. It is a chilling scene.

It was at Fort Santiago in the days before his death that Rizal wrote a valedictory poem, "*Mi Ultimo Adios*", that was to become an important rallying cry for Filipino independence. Rizal had hidden the poem in an oil lamp in his cell for his sister to find after his execution, and the original copy is displayed in a museum about his life at the fort. It begins:

Farewell, my adored land, region of the sun caressed.
Pearl of the Orient Sea, our Eden lost,
With gladness I give you my life, sad and repressed...

A replica of his family house in Laguna province has been created near the museum, next to another statue of Rizal, who is depicted holding forth an open book. Visitors to the fort can also see the cell where the people's champion spent his final hours. Rizal, who married and had a child who died shortly after birth, must be one of the youngest national heroes anywhere. His charisma and plain brilliance shone so bright that a colonial power feared him: Pearl of the Orient, indeed.

After the grind of the traffic, the haze of fumes and the all-round pandemonium of Manila's streets, Fort Santiago and the greenery of Plaza de Armas feel like hideaways. Somewhere to sit in the shade of a frangipani tree and reflect quietly on a national hero who gave everything to his cause and whose writings went on to mean so much to a country's nationhood.

Is it possible for a park to "rescue" a city? In the case of Fort Santiago's Plaza de Armas, with its birdsong, shadowy palm trees, gentle clip-clop of horse hooves pulling tourist carriages and overtones of history: almost… but no, not really. Not for me at least.

Manila seemed too far gone. Too hectic. Too crowded. Too polluted, even if its heavy smog did have a silver lining. This came in the form of amazing sunsets across the South China Sea, rivalling even those over the River Mekong in Vientiane. All thanks to chemicals in the smog, apparently.

A couple of final park-related notes on Manila.

The first: Plaza Moriones leading to Fort Santiago was dug up not long after my visit. City officials decided to turn the patch of green, which had acted as a buffer between the fort and the city proper, into a parade ground with granite paving. There was no public consultation, officials connected to the Department of Tourism simply decided it was a good idea so visitors could see the gate into Fort Santiago from afar: this sight line towards the old Spanish cathedral seemed to be all-important.

So some of the few lawns and trees in central Manila were removed, prompting a local artist and tour guide named Carlos Celdran to declare that authorities had "paved over my heart". The area had become "flat and anonymous and [it] has nothing to do with Intramuros' character or history".

Somehow news of this came as little surprise. There was something about Manila that screamed: *things have gone very wrong*! As the president himself said, "maximum" seemed to have been achieved. Things were so "maximum" that some of the last trees were being felled to make way for paving stones.

The second note of park/nature-related business: during the lockdown at the height of the coronavirus pandemic, an odd transformation took place in Manila. With little traffic on the highways, locals were amazed to see pollution lift and the Sierra Madre mountains on the edge of the city emerge out of the haze for the first time in years. Levels of PM2.5 in the air dropped by 40 per cent. The Philippines at the time had the dubious honour, according to the World Health Organization, of ranking number three internationally for pollution-related deaths, with 45.3 deaths per 100,000 people, behind China at 81.5 and Mongolia at 48.8 (connected to living in smoky yurts).

As the mountains appeared on the horizon, photographs of what Manila really looked like went viral on the internet. Commenting on the phenomenon, however, a Greenpeace campaigner drily said: "What's happening right now is like an old engine: when you shut it down it won't create any smoke. But eventually, when everything goes back and you turn on the engine again, you're still using the same dirty old engine that will still pollute the Earth. What we're seeing now is just temporary. It's just an illusion, a glimpse of a better society that we can have."

He was right. The lockdown ended and the Sierra Madre disappeared once again. Just an illusion: a glimpse of the mountains already gone.

The dirty old town was back.

A walk from Woolloomooloo
Royal Botanic Garden, Sydney, Australia

When Captain Arthur Phillip, commander of the First Fleet, arrived in Australia in January 1788 he picked the wrong bay.

Acting on the intelligence of Lieutenant James Cook, who had mapped the east coast in 1770 on HMS *Endeavour* in the company of the botanist Joseph Banks, Phillip dropped anchor in Botany Bay.

This was the "right" bay for settlement as far as Cook and Banks were concerned. The duo, who had visited soon after the rainy season, had found a fertile land that seemed perfect, brimming with life as well as botanical specimens.

Yet when Phillip turned up the landscape was parched, with streams running dry and insufficient water. This was not the best start after a journey transporting 775 convicts over 252 days covering 15,000 miles via stops in Tenerife, Rio de Janeiro and the Cape of Good Hope. A total of 40 convicts had died during the long journey.

Something had to be done. So, up the coast Phillip went on an expedition to find somewhere better. After a dozen miles, he turned at a headland and sailed into "the finest harbour in the world, in which a thousand sail of the line may ride in the most perfect security".

One cove in the harbour seemed especially inviting, with fresh water supplies and good moorings. Phillip hastened back to Botany Bay to fetch the others, spotting two French ships on the horizon led by the French explorer Lapérouse. Time appeared to be of the essence. Phillip rallied the fleet and quickly returned to his ideal landing, which he named Sydney Cove after the Home Office minister Lord Sydney, who had dreamed up the plan to relieve overcrowded British prisons on the other side of the planet. On 26 January the flag was raised. The colony of New South Wales had been established.

Mainland Australia has 16,100 miles of coastline. In his rush to set up camp, Phillip had chanced upon such an incredibly perfect spot, just 400 metres across, that Sydney Cove remains to this day at the heart of Australia's biggest and most important city (home to Circular Quay, with its important ferry hub, seafood restaurants, cocktail bars and Museum of Contemporary Art). To put this in perspective, 400 metres works out at 0.000015 per cent of the entire coastline of Australia. Which you might say was quite lucky on Phillip's part, discovered as it was at such short notice with French ships nosing about.

Sydney Cove now is a place where history, commerce and tourism collide. On one side, overlooked by Sydney Harbour Bridge; nicknamed the "Coathanger" for obvious reasons when you see it. On the other, by Sydney Opera House, with cascading roofs reminiscent of the sails of a jumbled flotilla of yachts.

Next to the opera house is the Royal Botanic Garden, one of the world's finest city parks.

Take a look at a map of the city centre and there it is, 74 acres of green with Farm Cove forming a U-shape at the top, where settlers planted first crops of coffee, wheat and barley. From there, the park tapers southward to another pocket of green, named Cook and Phillip Park, which is itself attached to Hyde Park, with its Pool of Reflection and Anzac Memorial to remember Australians who have died in conflict.

Sydney is dotted with parks: Harmony Park, First Fleet Park, Fig Lane Park, Centennial Park, the Chinese Garden of Friendship. And new parks are coming. The latest is Barangaroo Reserve, on the west side of the Coathanger (Sydney Harbour Bridge), on reclaimed industrial land that was previously a shipping container terminal.

It is fair to say Sydneysiders, who admittedly have quite a bit more space, have embraced greenery in a way the people of Manila perhaps have not.

The Royal Botanic Garden is quite simply a very beautiful park, perfect for a city stroll. Down little serpentine paths, borders bloom with curious tubular-shaped flowers in hues of scarlet and lemon-yellow. Lush rolling lawns are lined by eucalyptus trees shedding great peels of bark with mighty boughs soaring way above. Many varieties of eucalyptus have been planted, some with enormous, bulbous trunks and extraordinary bulging roots. Between the towering trees are sweeping beds of tulips, banks of azaleas and secret little sunken gardens with fountains featuring bronze cupids surrounded by purple-headed agapanthuses and neatly sheared box hedges.

Weeping willows cast emerald light beside snaking ponds. Hardy little bush plants grow in rockeries. Tropical palm groves offer shade, the air thick with the fragrance of rainforest flowers. Delicate-leafed jacaranda and acacia trees rustle by the waterfront, the jacarandas alive with purple-pink flowers in spring. Spiky green cacti rise from beds of red earth from the outback, some growing in circular shapes, others upright looking like upturned forks. Aromatic smells waft across from herb gardens. Roses burst into bloom. And all the while staff in khaki uniforms and wide-rimmed hats scurry here and there keeping everything remarkably under control. This is quite the perfect urban park.

Then, there are the views. To the south-west, the gleaming scrapers of the "CBD" (Central Business District), which seem somehow to augment the beauty of the garden – the stark outlines of the towers of commerce in contrast to the pleasant verdant tumble of vegetation. To the north, the dazzling slate-blue water of the harbour, with the sense of promise of passage to the Pacific and beyond.

Ferries buzz and bob past the splendid opera house. The sails of yachts lean in the wind near the Coathanger. Gulls glide above. Sit on one of the benches or rest against the sandstone sea wall on a sunny afternoon and you do not feel in a city at all. Turn around and face the CBD and even then, if your view is not entirely obscured by eucalyptus trees, this hardly seems like a conurbation of 5 million people.

To be in a city centre with this green space waiting just a few blocks away somehow alters your mindset. Greenery is round the corner! As it is in so many of the other little parks and alongside paths beside the bay. No wonder so many office workers can be seen jogging at lunch. No wonder Sydneysiders seem such a fit, healthy, generally cheerful lot.

The Royal Botanic Garden is an old park dating back to early colonial-era Australia, created in 1816 by Governor Macquarie and opened to the public in 1831. As well as being so splendidly maintained, it is the perfect spot to reflect on the extraordinary project Lord Sydney imagined all those years ago as well as the process Australia has been going through in recent years of recognizing and giving proper weight to the fact that when the British came in 1788, they were *obviously not the first people there.*

Far from it. A total of 29 groups making up the Cadigal Peoples of the Eora Nation lived in and around Sydney Cove, which had the name

Warrane before Phillip and the convicts came. "Farm Cove" was known as Woccanmagully, while "Mrs Macquarie's Point" (named after the wife of Governor Macquarie) was Yurong. The wharf where my hotel was based was originally named Finger Wharf (built in 1915), but had recently become known as Woolloomooloo Wharf in recognition of the pre-colonial name of the land.

These names are being slowly brought back to help right many historical wrongs that have included the tragedy of the twentieth-century "stolen generation" of indigenous children forcibly removed from parents to be raised by white families. The importance of choosing culturally sensitive appellations – highlighted by the official change in name of the sandstone monolith in Australia's Northern Territory from Ayers Rock to Uluru – and the need to recognize the pre-colonialist period is far from over. The Royal Botanic Garden itself says on its website: "We would like to acknowledge the Cadigal Peoples of the Eora Nation within Sydney and pay our respects to the Elders past, present and future."

It is believed the first people to arrive in Australia came 70,000 years ago either by land bridges or boat, and that Australian Aboriginals enjoy one of the oldest continuous cultures in the world. When the British came, they were newbies, outsiders known as Berewalgal (people from the clouds), who had turned up in an occupied territory.

The Royal Botanic Garden and environs were at the epicentre of the early meetings of the two peoples. This is where settlers and the Cadigal first clashed, both literally in skirmishes and culturally. This is where Phillip captured locals and dressed them as Europeans, sending one man – Bennelong – on a ship all the way to Britain, where it is said he had tea with the royal family, met Lord Sydney and visited St Paul's Cathedral dressed in a top hat and tails, before returning home. The site of Sydney Opera House is now known as Bennelong Point, while the new Barangaroo Reserve is named after his wife.

All of which confers great symbolic importance to the landscape of the Royal Botanic Garden.

On my visit, I followed paths south beyond the Lotus Pond and the Succulent Garden soon finding myself in Cook and Phillip Park, hardly realizing I had moved from one park to another. In this new park, I arrived at what looked like a cafe built into a small hill, thinking *what a perfect place to take a break with a coffee*. On closer examination, however, this "cafe" turned out to be the entrance to an Olympic-sized swimming pool landscaped beneath the surface of the park. Incredible! Imagine that back in Richmond. From there, it was a short walk onward to the Pool of Reflection and Anzac Memorial in Hyde Park: yet another lovely peaceful space, even if this one is right up beside the skyscrapers.

Keep on walking in Sydney and it is not long before you come to a park.

Just over 230 years since Captain Phillip and the convicts laid anchor, there may be an awful lot of concrete and steel, but there is plenty of green, too. None better than the Royal Botanic Garden with its corners of quiet beneath the old eucalyptus trees down by its sparkling, soul-lifting bay.

CHAPTER FOUR

CHILE, PERU, ECUADOR, COLOMBIA: MOUNTAINS, BEACHES, MORE MOUNTAINS AND *POLICIA*

COLOMBIA

VENEZUELA

Bogotá

Quito

ECUADOR

BRAZIL

PERU

Lima

BOLIVIA

CHILE

Santiago

ARGENTINA

B y now I was getting into the swing of it. The sitcom about life in the American motel had been cast aside and I had not even logged in to Netflix for several days on end. There was no sport on the television (as all sport seemed to have been cancelled). Social media was losing its appeal – how many more "humorous" shots of people working from home with their pets watching on beside their keyboards or coruscating opinions about the finer details of government pandemic policy could a person take, anyway? I was in the "park zone".

My girlfriend seemed to have adjusted with equanimity to this transformation, which gave her free rein in the front room to watch repeats of ballets and operas streamed as though live from various Eastern European concert halls. Most of my time not spent walking in Richmond Park, Palewell Park or Barnes Common – the latter two being close by as well – appeared now to be devoted to massaging my temples in my study, overlooked by my wooden Ecuadorian fox and my old-fashioned globe, while trying to remember overseas parks I had visited once upon a time. It was around then that realized I was, strangely, rather enjoying myself.

In terms of my next "route", this was easy. As I said before, I would "cross" the Pacific Ocean, ignoring islands along the way including those belonging to New Zealand as I had never been there, and "travel" up South America. I was interested in what I might dredge up from the recesses of my mind and slightly concerned that not a lot might be there for dredging. Although in my newly discovered "park zone", I had a burgeoning faith that, as with Charles Dickens' character Wilkins Micawber in *David Copperfield*, "something will turn up".

As it turned out plenty did, with colonialists poking their noses in plenty of times once again and with some extraordinary views from some extraordinarily crowded cities.

Super hilly
Parque Metropolitano, Santiago, Chile

What to do when you have 24 hours in a big, interesting city? Weekend travel supplements overflow with advice: recommended sights to see from dawn till dusk, every moment of the day assigned to touristic enjoyment. Far less onerous and much more relaxing to go for a stroll in a park.

This was my approach in Santiago, Chile's capital – and an easy one.

Parque Metropolitano rises above the city to a height of 850 metres covering 722 hectares; almost as big as Richmond Park (1,000 hectares). The difference is its altitude and its centrality. The *parque* is impossible to miss, making both a fine target for a walk and a vivid reminder to the newcomer that the geography of Chile is different to anywhere else on Earth.

Vital statistics tell the story. While the length of Chile from north to south is 2,670 miles, almost identical to the United States from coast to coast, the country's widest point is a mere 350 miles. On the map, Chile looks a little like a snake standing upright. What is even more extraordinary is that 80 per cent of the land is mountainous, with the Andes forming a natural border with Argentina and Bolivia to the east. The highest peak, Nevado Ojos del Salado, is at 6,891 metres the world's tallest volcano. There are deserts, jungles, fjords and snow-capped peaks. In the far south, you are at the southernmost point on any mainland on the planet.

Parque Metropolitano is not even the highest point in Santiago, that honour goes to a mountain rising 905 metres in a northern suburb, just a few metres short of the United Kingdom's highest mountain yet tucked away in a corner of the city. No big deal: just an enormous mountain in the suburbs. Par for the course in Chile.

On the subject of the country's extraordinary topography, my driver from the airport had been succinct: "We don't have much flat. We're super hilly!"

Then he had pointed to a peak rising ahead. Patchy snow covered the highest slopes.

"Not enough!" he said. "Global warming!"

Yet heavy snow had fallen in the country's Atacama Desert a fortnight earlier, he added.

"*Loco! Loco!*" he concluded. The weather was going through a topsy-turvy patch; just as it seems to be in most places these days.

Reaching super-hilly Parque Metropolitano involves entering an enchanting warren of streets with colourful low-level houses in Barrio Bellavista, where the Chilean Nobel Prize for Literature-winning poet-politician Pablo Neruda (1904–73) once lived. Shelves in ramshackle lapis lazuli shops creak under the weight of the semi-precious purple stone. Tinny, fast-beat music seeps from doorways. Ceiling fans spin in arty little bars and cafes, gearing up (on my visit) for Chile's appearance in the football World Cup later that day; some tables were already taken by connoisseurs heatedly debating the outcome. It is always fun visiting a city on the day of a big match, just as it had been amid the sea of red, also Chile's colours, back in Ho Chi Minh City.

I was keeping an eye open, though. My driver had told me about a recent American passenger who had visited the *barrio* while listening to music on headphones attached to a phone in her handbag. In a dreamy mood she had wandered the busy lanes, so enrapt in the *barrio*'s life that it was only after a while she noticed her music had stopped playing. She looked down and found the wire from her headphones dangling loose. A pickpocket had unzipped her bag, unplugged her phone and made away.

In the leafy foothills of Parque Metropolitano, a peculiar structure with turrets houses the station of a funicular. This little train rises to a giant white statue of the Virgin Mary that can be seen across the city like Christ the Redeemer in Rio de Janeiro. In 1987, Pope John Paul II took the clattering 500-metre journey up in one of the narrow carriages, rising at an angle of 45 degrees, to give Mass at the top. Perhaps the steepest Popemobile ever. Curious, I took a ride.

The history of this funicular provides insight into the *parque's* past – and how Chile's capital gained this wonderful green space. Displays at the station tell of how the mountain was once an ugly quarry providing stone used to pave the city streets and build the city's grand Palacio de la Moneda. That was in the late eighteenth and early nineteenth centuries. A grainy, old black-and-white picture captures scarred slopes of a wasteland staring down on Santiago.

This was when the scouts stepped in. Local scout groups, with a leading politician or two in support, called upon the city to buy the land from private owners and transform Cerro San Cristóbal, as the mountain is named, into a park – a "great lung" for Santiago. Their youthful rallies struck a chord and in 1917 Law Number 3295 was passed, allowing Parque Metropolitano to rise from the destroyed landscape, with only the summit staying out of municipal hands (and in those of the archbishop).

Avant-garde architect Luciano Kulczewski was called upon to create the fantastical castle-station for the funicular near Barrio Bellavista and by 1925 the service was up and running, transporting park visitors to the top for captivating views across Chile's capital.

I joined them, rattling up to the statue of the Virgin Mary and a smaller one of John Paul II.

At the top, it was impossible not to stop and stare.

Looking down at the *centro,* skyscrapers glinted near Plaza Mayor and a carpet of smog unfurled as far as the eye could see. Sounds lifted faintly from the valley floor: the murmur of traffic, the rat-a-tat-tat of a drill, a blast of what sounded like a factory horn. Squares, colonial-era churches and modern offices were crammed by the fast-flowing streak of the River Mapocho. Meanwhile, beyond the *centro* in the outskirts, *campamentos* (shanty towns) arose, makeshift corrugated roofs spilling into the hazy distance. Poverty and the huge gulf in wealth between the haves and have-nots are clear for all to see in Santiago, even if you just go for a day.

From Parque Metropolitano, the extraordinary compulsion of human beings to gather in cities – whatever the circumstances – takes your breath away. All around, the mountains soared, poking into the powdery sky, towering way up above the great swathe of humanity huddled down on the valley floor.

Just about every space seemed filled with construction, grids of streets stretching out far beyond the cupolas, archways and columns of Plaza Mayor. This regulated pattern of roads had been established by the Spanish in the sixteenth century soon after a bloody victory in 1541 against the Michimalonco tribe; a terrifying encounter during which besieged colonialists beheaded prisoners, attaching heads on spikes and tossing others to the enemy outside their fort. The Michimalonco were so horrified they fled. Who could blame them? Barbarians had come from a faraway land to ruin their world. It all happened somewhere down there, near the River Mapocho.

At the top of Parque Metropolitano, your thoughts may be diverted by these grisly historical deeds (colonialists, *outsiders*, yet again on the rampage), but they soon return simply to what your eyes see before them. For those new to South America and its high, crowded capitals, it is a sight that takes a while to get your head round. The view from the top of Parque Metropolitano is both supremely uplifting (the sheer majesty of the setting: the city amid the soaring peaks) and unsettling (the seeming folly of it all).

The view is also a reminder of how cities everywhere need places like Parque Metropolitano. Back in 1541, the colonialists had numbered about 50 in their besieged fort. Today, 36 per cent, or 6.8 million people, of Chile's population of 18.9 million live in the metropolitan area of Santiago, squeezed between the mountains. In 1950, the city had a mere 1.3 million inhabitants. The latest figure of 6.8 million represents a phenomenal growth of 80 per cent in 70 years.

Thank goodness for those scouts getting in a bit of green.

Shaded pathways lined with trees and explosions of pink bougainvillea snaked down from the Virgin Mary to Barrio Bellavista. I took one of the paths, ignoring the zoo, the botanical garden and the lidos along the way. I had another destination.

Just beyond the edge of the *parque*, you come to the cool courtyard garden of a small blue-and-yellow house with a curving balcony: Pablo Neruda's old home, *La Chascona* (tangle-haired woman), named after his third wife, Matilde Urrutia. This is an eclectic building, maintained as it was during Neruda's life. A bar with shelves of spirit bottles lies at its centre, where an audio guide informs you that "Neruda held big parties" before adding that he was "known for his love of romance" (as three marriages suggest).

This guide also tells you that Neruda stood for president of Chile in 1969, was accused of political activism and died 12 days after the dictator Augusto Pinochet took control of the country in an American-backed coup d'etat in 1973. Some have suggested foul play. Chileans lined the streets in their thousands during his funeral in a "popular manifestation against the coup", says the audio.

There is something about Parque Metropolitano that feels tied to Barrio Bellavista. There is something about Barrio Bellavista that feels tied to the hero-poet Pablo Neruda, who sometimes mused on the almost eerie sense of isolation that can be felt in the middle of the cacophony and smog of Santiago. Encircled by the mountains, the "silent geometry" between the peaks, with the ghosts of distant empires in the valley below, had a transfixing hold on the poet.

This "silent geometry" was always there in Santiago and it was what made Parque Metropolitano so magical. Oh yes, and in case you were wondering, Chile was knocked out of the World Cup that afternoon. No parties of red flags in Santiago, sadly.

El Beso (The Kiss)
Parque del Amor, Lima, Peru

Now for something completely different in another big capital city in a mountainous South American country.

Lima is the continent's only capital directly on the Pacific Ocean and it is very crowded indeed. More than 70 per cent of Peruvians live in cities

– already more than meeting the United Nations' worldwide prediction of 68 per cent by 2050 – with no fewer than 9.7 million inhabitants in Lima out of a national population of 32.9 million.

This has grown from 26.4 million in 2000, 17.5 million in 1980 and 8.8 million in 1955. So the capital now has more people living there than the entire country's population of 65 years ago, when it was home to around 1 million residents. To put all this in perspective: in the 1940s, 60 per cent of Peru's population lived in the countryside. I offer these statistics as I find them flabbergasting and also simply to point out that the twentieth and twenty-first centuries have seen incredible change in demographics that are hard to get your head around, in Peru and in so many other places.

Almost inevitably given this rapid mass movement, Lima has dreadful slums – like so many other countries in South America. It is estimated about 30 per cent of the population lives in one, beneath the poverty line with children failing to complete education as they need to work to make ends meet. Healthcare is poor. Living conditions are dreadful, with flimsy housing, mud roads, water shortages, unreliable electricity and inadequate sanitation. Such is the squalor, my guidebook – in a fit of tell-it-like-it-is – warned that tourists may wonder why on earth they decided to come.

This is, of course, the dilemma of modern holidaymaking to "exotic" far-flung nations with annual wages a fraction of those in Europe. The GDP per capita in Peru is £5,182, as I write, compared with £32,049 in the United Kingdom or £46,998 in the United States. The sense of adventure that comes from visiting countries living such different existences almost inevitably verges on the voyeuristic, even when tourist cash really goes to local communities, avoiding the clutches of multinational hotels and tour operators.

Come to see the wonderful ancient Inca remains at Machu Picchu up in the Andes! Come also to see a whole lot else that is not so wonderful, while staying in air-conditioned hotels with 24-hour room service and overflowing buffet breakfasts.

Almost needless to say in a city that has grown so rapidly in recent times, green spaces are enormously important. Luckily, Lima has an especially good one, cherished by locals and tourists alike.

The Malecón (broadwalk) runs for six miles along the crumbling cliffs of the coastline in the central Miraflores district of Lima. Along its twisting pathways, a series of narrow clifftop parks clings to a thin strip of land. When visiting Peru's capital, it is just about impossible not to feel drawn towards these narrow clifftop parks. The appeal is twofold. Firstly, simply the lure of green: of the palms, lawns and flowerbeds away from the busy *centro*. Secondly, the promise of setting eyes on the Pacific Ocean.

There is something captivating about the ocean at Lima, seen from the Malecón. The metallic gleam of the water. The crush and fizz of the waves. The smell of salt rising. The haze on the horizon, where the sea seems to want to join the sky. The feeling of the breeze after the city streets. The gliding gulls. The small birds flickering by the cliffs. The colours mutating up above: milky white, oyster grey, perfect blue.

The little parks through which the Malecón boardwalk winds each have individual names, even though some are tiny, little more than half an acre. So, there is Parque Maria Reiche, named after a German archaeologist, with open grassland backed by apartment blocks. Then there is Parque Grau, named after a nineteenth-century Peruvian war hero of sea battles with Chile and Bolivia and home to a pleasant cafe. Or you have Parque Yitzhak Rabin, in honour of the assassinated Israeli leader, complete with an abstract statue of a figure wearing a halo and steps down to the beach.

Parque de los Niños has a children's playground and a fitness zone. Parque Faro de la Marina comes with a working lighthouse. Parque Raimondi is named after a nineteenth-century Peruvian doctor and is where you can try paragliding. Parque Domodossola features a statue of an eagle honouring Jorge Chavez, a pilot who died attempting a first flight across the Swiss Alps. Parque Salazar is connected to a shopping mall with terraces on which is to be found a statue of Paddington Bear, so famously from "darkest Peru".

In short there are many *parques*. But my favourite is Parque del Amor, next to Parque Raimondi and dominated by a striking sculpture of a couple locked in romantic embrace.

This work, known as *El Beso* (The Kiss), is by Peruvian artist Victor Delfín, who was inspired to create the sculpture after walking along the Malecón in the company of the mayor of Lima. The pair had been ambling along discussing this and that when they inadvertently disturbed a steamy clifftop liaison. With space at home in short supply, especially in shanty towns, the *parques* along Lima's clifftops have long attracted amorous young couples. How about a sculpture to commemorate love, Delfín suggested? The mayor agreed. So was born *El Beso*, which was unveiled on Valentine's Day in 1993 after the surrounding park had been re-landscaped with colourful wall mosaics.

Some reacted angrily to the statue saying it was in poor taste. *El Beso*, based on Delfín and his wife, shows what you might describe as a highly advanced state of kissing. The couple is depicted writhing in a tangle of limbs (*making out* could be another way of putting it). Yet most Limeños loved the statue and the park was soon attracting even more sweethearts than ever. Kissing contests were held on Valentine's Days (longest length of time spent locked mouth-to-mouth deciding the winner). Anniversaries celebrated. Rings held forth. Proposals made.

Quotations from Peruvian writers have been inscribed on the mosaics. *Amor es solo un pajaro que deambula* (love is only a bird that wanders) – Rocío Romina Bances. *Cantor amor desnudate* (sing my love, undress yourself) – Rodolfo Hinostroza. *Me quemo para no ver el sitio vacio de tu cuerpo* (I'm burning to not see the empty space of your body) – Washington Delgado. And: *Te devisto como quien pela una fruta* (I undress you like someone peeling fruit) – Jorge Díaz Herrera. Fruity, indeed. It is noticeable that all the quotes are by men, though perhaps this has changed in the decade since I went.

The flowerbeds seem especially alive with blooms in Parque del Amor. The breeze a little fresher. The sense of relaxation and ease away from the labyrinthine streets of Lima more pronounced. A small amphitheatre next to *El Beso* makes a fine place to sit and watch the ocean at sunset, the golden globe dropping beyond the waves seeming especially golden just for the couples in Parque del Amor.

After seeing a sunset, you may well wish to wander down the Malecón – which some refer to in its entirety as the Costa Verde (Green Coast) – to one of the bars at Parque Salazar to try a green drink in the green setting.

The pisco sour is Peru's national tipple, a concoction of pisco liquor (made from distilled grapes) with Angostura bitters, lime juice, sugary syrup and whisked egg white. The latter ingredient creates a foamy top reminiscent of the waves breaking on the shore below. The "sour" comes from the lime and the bitters. These mix with the sweetness arising from the syrup, which seems to fight the "sour" but never quite win. It is pale green in hue, served ice cold and is a matter of fierce debate in South America. The Chileans claim to have invented the drink, although theirs does not come with egg white and most agree that the pisco sour as commonly known dates from a bar in the Miraflores district of Lima from around the 1920s.

Whatever! After a day's sightseeing and a stroll along the Malecón on your first day in Peru, this is an excellent place to go. For such a large sprawling city to have so much park with so many wonderful ocean views is a blessing that will never go away: that is, as long as developers do not move in, or the cliffs crumble into the sea.

My companions and I clinked glasses and drank our pisco sours. The next day we flew to Cusco to stay at a high-altitude hotel with oxygenated rooms, before taking the *Hiram Bingham* luxury train – named after the American explorer who "discovered" Machu Picchu in 1911 – to see the Inca citadel up close.

A long way from the shanty towns of Lima, up in the thin air of the Andes. A long way from the embraces and sunsets of charming Parque del Amor, too.

Shoeshine Square
Plaza de la Independencia, Quito, Ecuador

Northward from Lima along the Pacific side of South America, Quito is the second highest capital city in the world at 2,850 metres (after nearby La Paz, Bolivia's capital, at a crazy 3,640 metres).

It is so high that hotels, like the ones in Cusco, are stocked with oxygen canisters in case guests feel faint. The highest ski resort in the European Alps is Val Thorens in France at 2,300 metres, which gives an idea of just how far up you are. You notice the altitude immediately, at least I did, though I never needed to use an oxygen canisters. You are also probably quite astonished, as I was, that a settlement of such a size could straddle the mountains that rise all around, with suburbs snaking in every direction, precariously clasping the slopes.

To maintain my ongoing investigation into South American demographics: 17 million people live in Ecuador of whom around 1.6 million reside in Quito. Just as in Santiago and Lima, there is great poverty on the outskirts in shanty towns. A recent World Bank report put the percentage of Ecuadorians living in deprivation at 22.5 per cent – down from 37.6 per cent at around the turn of the century – with a shift in the right direction coming from increased prosperity on the back of a hike in the world price of oil (Ecuador is an oil-rich country). Yet that is still one in five people: a lot.

So, Quito is another jam-packed city – and it is very high up. Partly due to its rugged, sprawling geography, there are many parks including a huge one, Parque Metropolitano. This is to the north of the *centro* and is, like its namesake in Santiago, hilly. Then, even further north, you have Parque Bicentenario, brilliantly fashioned out of the Old Mariscal Sucre International Airport, which closed in 2013 due to being too small for increasingly large aircraft and posing an accident risk in its tight spot between the mountains. Where the Boeing 737s once touched down there are now a thousand trees, a pond and a fitness zone with workout machines. Paths follow the shape of the old runways. Outdoor concerts are held. Greta Thunberg would, you sense, like this park.

There are many others, yet my favourite oasis of green was right in the heart of the city: Plaza de la Independencia, next to the Presidential Palace and a grand cathedral, which I had just visited to take in a version of *The Last Supper* depicting Jesus and his apostles eating a guinea pig (considered a local delicacy). Having been shown round the city at some length by a guide named Mr Chinchin, who lived up to his name by being extremely talkative, there was little I did not know about the life and times of Antonio José de Sucre (a key independence leader who helped defeat the Spanish in 1830 and after whom both the old and the new airports in Quito were named) nor Gabriel García Moreno (a nineteenth-century presidential mover and shaker) nor the methods of the production of chocolate.

I decided I needed a break. So, I sat on a bench and watched life pass by, just like Barack Obama says he would like to do one day in New York's Central Park.

Despite being bang in the middle of town, it was a peaceful place with palm trees, one very tall pine tree, yellow-flowering shrubs, beds of thin pink flowers, lawns, box hedges, a monument to independence heroes and a cluster of octagonal fountains. Almost all the benches were taken and a great deal of gossiping was going on. By the steps of the cathedral, a man wearing a leather jacket and a baseball cap was preaching to passers-by. His calls for repentance and holy living ran in a continuous monologue that seemed co-ordinated with a makeshift band comprising a drummer, a tambourinist, an electric guitarist, an acoustic guitarist and a singer/clapper.

When the preacher had exhausted his latest sermon and needed a rest, he would sit down for a pause to regain his religious energy. At precisely this moment, the band would start up with jolly tunes that attracted the odd dollar or two, Ecuador's currency, to an upturned hat. The band would keep going for several minutes and then decide that it was time *they* took a break. At precisely this moment, the preacher would rise and begin spreading the word of God once again. In this manner neither music nor holy words were ever drowned out. Thus also, background noise of some form or other remained a constant.

The bells of the cathedral clanged at three in the afternoon and soon after, a group of shoeshine boys congregated at the octagonal fountain in front of my bench. They set down their little wooden boxes of polish, brushes and rags and, without further ado, began to wash hands in the fountain. Their day's work was clearly done. Intermittently, after wetting their hands, they rubbed palms on the fountain's rough stone to remove the worst of the polish. A trickle of black ran down on to the paving. After a few minutes, fingers clean, the boys removed their outer clothing of tracksuit bottoms and hoodies to reveal smarter clothes beneath. Then they neatly folded their work clothes and placed them in their backpacks and made off. Their ages were perhaps between ten and fourteen.

Apart from this there was little other excitement in Plaza de la Independencia other than the occasional arrival of a *Policía Metropolitana* officer riding an unstable-seeming two-wheeled vehicle, looking like a moving statue and grinning as though enjoying the ride. In this way, law and order was maintained; a "grin and behave" policing strategy that seemed to work. My breakfast waiter had warned to "watch out for smart alis" in Quito (I think he meant "smart alecs" out to con you), but I never came across any, just as I had not back in Santiago in Chile.

Time slipped away while reading a book and events, such as they were, unfolded. Then I took a taxi up a hill to another green spot.

Seen from Plaza de la Independencia – and just about everywhere in Quito's *centro* – a landmark statue of the Virgin Mary stares down, looking frankly rather odd. This is because the statue is made of aluminium – 7,000 pieces of aluminium – and the figure is twisted with angel wings flapping from either side. Due to this unusualness, there is an element of mystique and drama about the statue, which was unveiled in 1976 and created by a Spanish artist named Agustin de la Herran Matorras; a cut above the one in Santiago back in Chile in terms of quality of large statue of the Virgin Mary on a hill in a city in South America.

The hill, 200 metres high, is known as El Panecillo ("the small piece of bread", as it is shaped like one). The statue is 41 metres tall and you can enter the plinth to admire many colourful panels of stained glass inside, all depicting the Virgin Mary. At the top of a winding staircase, a viewing platform at the foot of the aluminium Virgin Mary faces Quito down below. Just as in Santiago, it is quite astonishing simply to see how human beings on this continent manage to form such huge conurbations up in the mountains. From the statue, it looks as though Quito is a pool of white paint that has spilled between the peaks. By searching for the bell tower of the cathedral with the painting of the guinea pig version of *The Last Supper*, you can pinpoint the whereabouts of Plaza de la Independencia.

By the foot of the Virgin Mary is a little park with benches for picnics and a forest off to one side for hikes: plenty of greenery in Quito.

Walking down through the little park you soon enter lanes of colonial-era buildings. On my visit, marching bands with drummers and xylophone players wearing helmets with plumes of feathers were celebrating college graduations. Bright banners announced the name of each college. A troop of female students in white dresses twirling rods and waving pom-poms marched by. Behind each group of musicians and dancers, proud former college students, some well into their 80s, shuffled along in a great stream of humanity. The roads had been closed and a joyous intergenerational celebration of educational achievement was in full swing.

Women wearing gold-rimmed hats and pink and red dresses spun by. Men in llama-fur trousers and golden waistcoats waved lime-green handkerchiefs. The colours were dazzling. The streets were jammed. The music was upbeat and enthusiastic, with only the odd dud note. It is hard not to fall for Quito, whether you are in one of its many relaxing parks or not. Maybe having so much choice of greenery makes people so happy. Or maybe it is the thin air. Or maybe I just visited on a particularly *buen dia* (good day). Or maybe, just maybe, I was thinking about this too much.

After the procession, back in Plaza de la Independencia, I bought a ten-dollar Panama hat from a stall by the Presidential Palace. Panama hats are originally from Ecuador not Panama, despite the name, Mr Chinchin had reliably informed me during my morning tour. Having been shipped across the world from Panama in the nineteenth century, they became mistakenly known as "Panama hats". They are quite definitely in reality, however, "Ecuadorian hats", Mr Chinchin had declared, somewhat indignant that I might previously have thought otherwise. I put on mine and found an unoccupied old bench amid the chattering Ecuadorians.

The band was still playing but the preacher had left. The musicians had the "stage" to themselves now. A breeze rustled the fronds of the palm trees. The tambourine rattled and chinked. The acoustic guitar twanged a happy tune. A grinning policeman spun by, keeping all smart alis at bay. Up on El Panecillo, the aluminium Virgin Mary caught the last of the afternoon light.

Another lovely green space in another lovely South American city. Another pocket of peace, way up in the Andes.

"In case of emergency: PLEASE KEEP CALM"
Monserrate, Bogotá, Colombia

Colombia's capital has altitude, too: at 2,625 metres it is the world's third highest. At Monserrate, a mountain overlooking the city centre reached by either a funicular or cable car, you are at 3,152 metres. You are also facing one of the most extraordinary expanses of concrete you are ever likely to lay eyes on.

Santiago, Lima and Quito have nothing on the sheer scale and brazen outrageous monstrosity of Bogotá.

Beyond the trees and yellow shrubs covering the mountaintop at Monserrate, a concrete jungle spread out across a vast plain, rolling onward and onward until coming to a halt at a hazy ridge far off in the distance. Boy was it unrelenting. Wow was it ugly. Really, really awful. Dreadful. Downright depressing.

My guide, Luciana, and I gazed down and said nothing for a while. Luciana was showing me around the city on behalf of the Colombian tourist board, which was aiming to change the world's perception of Colombia as a dangerous hive of drug cartels by taking journalists, such as myself, to see the tourist sights. This was all part of a publicity campaign to encourage families to shun the usual Mediterranean spots and the theme parks of Orlando in favour of summer holidays in the much-maligned South American country. Positive articles in the travel sections of newspapers were to relay the message that all was well in Colombia family-holiday-wise.

On day one of my tour, I could feel the campaign beginning to kick in. The ride up to Monserrate on the cable car had been exhilarating. The arrival on the cool mountaintop, after the heat of the streets below, invigorating and refreshing. Looking around the peaks at the forest and the peaceful monastery and the charming old church had me thinking: *Lovely spot this, no sign of drug cartel gangs, plenty of family-friendly holidaymaking possibilities here.*

Then we had turned to look at the big bad city below. Because no matter how you pen the tourist blurb, Bogotá is a big bad city.

Luciana, I could sense, recognized that. And she had decided, with charming honesty and (more than) a slight deviation from the official PR "line", to tell it how it was.

"Unfortunately," she said after looking across the rooftops and skyscrapers for a while seeming almost as transfixed as I was by Bogotá's brutality, "the city has a long way to grow yet, to both the north and the west. It is already too big. I say this: 8 million people live here, and that is 8 million problems! Drugs! Traffic problems! Violence! Until very recently people were afraid of being kidnapped. Problems! 8 million!"

Eight million was the population of Bogotá then (in 2009). The figure was soon to shoot up another 2 million.

Luciana leaned against the wall above the city below and sighed. She wore jeans, Nike trainers, a pale blue polo shirt and a grey hoodie. She had bags beneath her eyes and was in her 30s. She had clearly made up her mind to tear up the usual "script".

"I have been mugged four times," she said, by way of warning in case I went out from my hotel later. "You cannot walk and talk on your cell phone: they will take your wallet. They took my wallet! They will walk behind you. They do this. They take anything from your backpack. Anything! Anything! They do this!"

She paused, as though for dramatic purposes. "But oh my God, how did they do *this*?" she asked, looking at me with deadpan panda eyes before continuing. "One time I was wearing gold earrings. Someone touched the earrings. Then he took them. I don't know how he did it, but he took them. Then he was gone! They were gone! I did not know it was happening. I felt my ears. The earrings were gone!"

Luciana sighed once more. Then she clicked back into her tourist board persona. "It is much safer now in Colombia," she said, watching the pen in my hand and my notebook as though encouraging me to write *this* down no matter what else had been said. "Much! We are trying to alter the perception that our country is dangerous."

She smiled thinly. I did, too. We said nothing further and regarded the view.

During a visit to Bogotá, you get nothing but warnings. Your guidebook tells you to avoid careless displays of money and individuals approaching you with questions or selling something. These may be thieves or con artists. Do not trust anyone saying they are an undercover police officer. Be aware that Colombia is a big cocaine-smuggling route. Watch out for *burundanga*. This is a mysterious drug that comes from a flower that has no taste or smell. Consume it in a drink, however, and your Colombian con artist may take you to an ATM and encourage you to withdraw large amounts of pesos that you will hand over to them willy-nilly, such is the power of *burundanga*. Bag slashers, pickpockets, scammers and backpack snatchers were seemingly everywhere. All of these concerns were heightened at night, when good tourists should keep at their most alert.

My hotel room directory included a "Protection and Security" section in which guests were encouraged in the "In your Hotel" section to lock doors, place "Do Not Disturb" signs on doors and "additionally put other safety systems in place on the door such as chains or pins, whichever the case may be". The "Out of the Hotel" recommendations included guests avoiding talking to people in the streets, not wearing expensive jewellery (unlikely in my case, but echoing Luciana's experience), and using hotel taxis rather than public taxis. The final decree stated: "In case of emergency: PLEASE KEEP CALM." Their caps.

Regarding Monserrate, this beautiful green haven above the con artists, pickpockets and *burundanga* dealers below, advice was strongly given – by everyone – not to walk up or down, especially not in the dark and particularly not on weekdays. Tourists doing so had been relieved of valuable items at both the top and the bottom of the mountain. To cross from Monserrate to a higher peak at Guadalupe was a complete no-no, a seemingly suicidal mission. Or so the guidebooks and hotel notices would have it.

To cut to the chase, it was a dangerous park – a green hideaway where *things were going on*. A far cry from Richmond Park with its oaks, deer, kestrels and dog walkers back home (apologies for so often harking back to Richmond, but it *is* my local park and makes a handy point of comparison).

Luciana had quite a job on her hands. I felt for her. After her earrings story, she turned to me and said: "I don't like you to be alone. I don't want you to be mugged. I want to be a big mamma to you."

Which was sweet. We walked around the small park at the top of Monserrate. A section recreates Calle del Candelero, a street in Bogotá dating from the late nineteenth century. *Policia de Turismo* officers patrolled this fake street in which stalls sold pink and purple pashminas, necklaces, T-shirts imprinted with the face of Michael Jackson (who had died earlier in the year), cowboy hats, sombreros and leather handbags.

Beyond the souvenirs, food stalls offered cheese, sausages, "intestines with the blood of a cow" inside (so said Luciana), sweetcorn and chicken feet. At some stalls, roasted chickens had been propped with sausages hanging from each upper leg as though holding pistols, while each wore a cowboy hat made of potato slices. Even the food had attitude in Bogotá.

Pictures of Christ on the crucifix were also available, as were T-shirts depicting a revolutionary-style moustachioed *Deudor Moroso* (Delinquent Debtor), which were – for some reason I never did fathom – popular. Perhaps dodging bills had a cult following in the Colombian capital.

After seeing the interior of the Basilica of the Falling Lord, with its simple wooden pews, crystal chandelier and pilgrims, Luciana and I went for lunch at the park's main restaurant overlooking Bogotá. This was the Casa Santa Clara Restaurant, and it was in a distinguished whitewashed 1920s building on a cliff's edge above plunging jungle. We took our table, as yet unmugged and with all possessions intact in Colombia's capital. The tourist board campaign to change the outside world's regard for the country was going swimmingly on that front. All safe and sound so far.

I ordered *bandeja paisa*, a tasty concoction of pork stew, kidney beans, avocado, chorizo and black pudding. Piano music played and gilded mirrors in the whitewashed dining room reflected mountaintop views.

As we ate, Luciana returned to the tourist board spiel.

"Security," she said.

"Yes?" I replied.

"Strengthened," she said.

She continued: "Maybe, how do you put it, maybe things are a little disorganized around the edges. But our president got rid of the bad things. The image was that we were corrupt. But that is cleared up. We have a more educated people. Colombia has one of the best education systems in Latin America. Thank God this is changing! Ah, yes, it is horrible that people think they come here and their bags will be ripped open in the streets. The image is that we are all drug dealers. But that is a tiny little minority. In fact, if we were all drug dealers this country would be very wealthy!"

She paused to have a chuckle about that.

"A few bad apples," Luciana said. "A few bad apples mean the whole basket got blemished!"

And with that we (I mean the Colombian tourist board) settled the bill. We caught the funicular down into the city from its pocket of green on the hill, listening to flute tunes interspersed with adverts for Columbian tourism.

"It is changing," said a narrator referring to the quality of the holidaymaker experience in the country. "It is changing."

Everyone kept saying that in Colombia – and, to be fair, I never actually had any trouble and greatly enjoyed my time in the country, especially up in another park, Parque Nacional Tayrona, a joyous wilderness on the mountainous north coast. Plenty of food for thought up on Monserrate, which seemed made for straight talk… and reflection, too.

CHAPTER FIVE

HONOLULU, SAN FRANCISCO, VANCOUVER, NEW YORK, WASHINGTON DC: BRIGHT LIGHTS, BIG CITY PARKS

Amerca and Canada have a rich history of national parks. Deep in the "park zone" now, almost oblivious to the daily dramas of Downing Street press briefings and latest updates on "travel corridors", "roadmaps to recovery" and corresponding "bumps in the road", I began with pleasure to delve into it. With just about everything shut, I had more than enough time to indulge my new "hobby". Metaphorically speaking, this "park quest" had crossed some sort of invisible divide separating normal and not-so-normal-at-all: it was as though I had taken to the garden shed and begun to build extravagant model ships out of matchsticks… except I was in my study dreaming about parks.

My girlfriend by this stage was well accustomed to this growing eccentricity and was, for that matter, starting to display unconventional traits of her very own. In particular, aside from new online live meditation classes led by a floaty voiced instructor in California, she had taken to completing complicated join-the-dots drawing books with marathon-like dot-linking endeavours required, all the while listening to the latest classical concerts performed in obscure Eastern European concert halls. Perhaps I had driven her to it. We were, for certain, living in unusual times.

Such was the situation in which I found myself as I began my investigations into the ins-and-outs of American and Canadian parks.

To begin at the beginning, the United States got the ball rolling in 1872 when President Ulysses S. Grant signed off Yellowstone National Park in Wyoming, Montana and Idaho – as mentioned back in Chapter Two. This is considered the world's first such park and it was not long before Canada followed suit in the 1880s with its Rocky Mountain Parks Act. These were huge places out in the wild; Yellowstone is 2.2 million acres, while Banff National Park in Alberta is 1.6 million acres.

Back in the 1870s, forward-thinking politicians and geologists had been concerned that areas of natural beauty could soon be overrun in the manner of Niagara Falls, which was already attracting thousands of tourists from across the globe. The Falls had become well established as part of the early US "tourist trail", with Charles Dickens, even, going for a week in 1842 and gushing in a letter to a friend: "The first effect of this tremendous spectacle on me, was of peace of mind – tranquillity – great thoughts of eternal rest and happiness." Perhaps that was before Victorian wanderlust, and the crowds, really kicked in.

Natural wonders were steadily becoming "attractions", as we know them now. In an important report to the Senate, the geologist Ferdinand V. Hayden, who had explored and completed a survey of Yellowstone, was – however – just as concerned about mining and deforestation as tourism: "The vandals who are now waiting to enter into this wonderland, will in a single season despoil, beyond recovery, these remarkable curiosities, which have required all the cunning skill of nature thousands of years to prepare." His arguments, luckily, won the day.

National parks had put "greenery" on the agenda, and city parks came around the same time, as planners – partly inspired by urban parks in Britain – recognized the need for green spaces to escape overcrowding during industrialization.

Central Park in New York City took more than two decades to complete, opening in 1876 – after the controversial eviction of inhabitants on the land – and opening on those behind Golden Gate Park in San Francisco, where the very same landscape architect was consulted. Meanwhile, in Canada, Stanley Park in Vancouver was granted park status in 1886, with those north of the border wanting to get in on the act (and also displaying little remorse about moving along those who happened to live there).

Yet the sometimes rather determined foresight of the early city developers means North America has countless first-rate urban parks, so many of which feel integral to local life. After the initial Victorian burst of city parks, North America had taken on the baton of city greenery, establishing the convention of having natural public spaces in the New World.

Well briefed for the next stage of my "journey", I was ready to "fly" on, happy to have moved to a new phase of my lockdown park obsession that seemed to be straying into park buff or, even, *parkspotter* territory.

In this heightened state of being, my route led north-west from Bogotá across the Pacific Ocean to Hawaii, before stopping on the west coast of the United States, slipping due north to Canada, then eastward to the Big Apple and on to America's capital. A lot of wonderful parks awaited.

Aloha!
Diamond Head State Monument,
Honolulu, USA

How do you find yourself in Honolulu amid hula-hula dancers and piña-colada bars having just a couple of days earlier expected to be spending your fortnight summer holiday pottering about at home?

Answer: a whirlwind of impulsive decisions involving Teletext.

This was the period when the "World Wide Web" was new and often so slow you sometimes resorted to faxes. Tempting online travel deals did not exist. But switch on your television, consult a simple information service where holidays were listed (Teletext), book on the spur of the moment and you could be gone the next day: five nights in Las Vegas and another five in Honolulu on a fortnight off. All for a pittance thanks to the beginning of low-cost airlines.

Greta Thunberg (not born at the time): *I am so sorry.*

Bleary-eyed after five late nights in Vegas – blackjack, Budweisers, neon lights, walks along The Strip of gaudy hotels (and no park life whatsoever) – Hawaii was dazzling. The sun beat down on the crashing waves on the ribbon of sand at Waikiki Beach. I hired a "boogie board" and surfed a few breakers, badly, amid the pros.

Then I went up the volcano.

There can be few cities on Earth with such a breathtaking setting. Down by the beach, the fast-food joints, cocktail bars, high-rise hotels and traffic could be stifling. Yet towering above the cityscape, the rim of a magnificent crater arose with gullies and ravines cut into the grassy, boulder-strewn slopes. This was Diamond Head, a tuff cone volcano: a type of volcano with a wide, deep crater. Blinking in the sunshine I set off for the top.

This dormant volcano, believed to be around half a million years old, is overseen by Hawaii State Parks and officially known as Diamond Head State Monument. Originally the giant crater – 1,073 metres across and 232 metres in elevation – was referred to by Hawaiians as *Le'ahi*, a combination of two indigenous words for "brow" and "tuna". The latter is believed to derive from the jagged edge of one side of the rim looking like a tuna fin (which it does). Then the British came along in 1825 and were excited, briefly, by what were thought to be diamonds mixed in the sand on the beach at the foot of the volcano. These were in fact calcite crystals, but the name stuck.

You pay $5 to go up and it is money well spent, as only when you get to the top do you understand Honolulu. Just as in Santiago, Quito and Bogotá, going up – in a park – puts things in perspective.

And the perspective from Diamond Head is jaw-dropping. Beyond the volcanic slopes, the city of Honolulu spreads out. There it is! The apartment blocks, the hotels, the nightclubs, the bars, the malls, the crowded sidewalks, the taxis, the revving Harley-Davidsons, the *everything*. So many hotels. So many condos. So many tourists. The pathways of Diamond Head State Monument were jam-packed with folk in colourful, flowery shirts with cameras round their necks as I went up. People like me, snapping away and grinning inanely, flown in from distant shores on budget planes. I was 7,000 miles away from Britain. I had phoned Teletext Holidays and bought my ticket in a matter of moments on a whim. Greta, really, I am *so, so sorry*.

But no matter how hard Honolulu city planners and the piña colada-drinking crowds may try, there is no getting away from it: Honolulu is beautiful. Jagged volcanic mountains! Palm trees! Sparkling ocean! Sunshine galore! In the park at Diamond Head State Monument, you cannot help thinking to yourself: *What's not to like?* At least, I couldn't. I was a Teletext tourist. I had just "done" parkless Vegas. I was busy "doing" Hawaii.

Given that construction on steep slopes was nigh on impossible, Diamond Head was saved from major development in the twentieth century and was also, in 1968, declared a National Natural Landmark. On a visit, you feel the tentacles of the tourist trap excesses of Honolulu loosen their grip. You also learn why a city was built at this spot in the first place.

It was all about military strategy. America saw the islands of Hawaii as being useful for the defence of its Pacific Coast. So, America took Hawaii in stages, beginning with annexation in the late nineteenth century before adding the islands to the United States in 1959, thus installing Hawaii – 2,700 miles west of Mexico and 3,900 miles east of Japan – as the fiftieth state. But it was Oahu, the third largest of the 137 islands, that was key. This was because of its massive natural harbour, Pearl Harbour, in Honolulu, just across the way. Battlements and a fort, Fort Ruger, were built into the volcano at Diamond Head to protect this position. Tunnels and a pillbox remain at the top for tourists to visit.

Of course, the events of 7 December 1941, when the surprise Japanese attack destroyed so many US Navy ships and killed 2,403 Americans, do not exactly go down well in US military history. The dramatic volcano at Diamond Head and the surfers' paradise of beaches below witnessed one of America's greatest humiliations as well as one of the decisive moments of the twentieth century. Without Pearl Harbour and America joining the Second World War, the fight against the Nazis might have turned out quite differently, and not in a good way.

Plenty to chew on as you hike up and the ocean spreads out in the distance, the aquamarine curve of the planet forming the horizon. Somewhere way down there beyond the haze of clouds lies Australia.

A sense of history hangs in the hot, humid air at Diamond Head. Not only the thought of the Japanese assault, but also of the explorers of old: especially Captain Cook. Before the discovery of "diamonds" on the beach below, Cook came by twice, naming the archipelago "the Sandwich Isles" after his sponsor, the 4th Earl of Sandwich. He was the first European to land on Hawaii. And he never left. In 1779, during an altercation with locals on a beach on Hawaii Island, south-east of Oahu, the man who "discovered" Australia was hit over the head, stabbed and killed along with four marines. His body was then prepared for burial by islanders, who had venerated the explorer despite the deadly disagreement. This involved disembowelment, baking his body to take off the flesh and cleaning the bones for a ritual burial. Some of these remains, however, were also returned to Cook's ship, HMS *Resolution*, so that he could be – partly at least – buried at sea. The dispute that had led to the skirmish is believed to have started after Cook had taken religious idols and fence planks to be used as firewood. This in turn led to islanders stealing a small boat. This prompted Cook to hijack a local king. Then came the angry showdown on the beach.

Quite an ending for the great explorer, though there are two versions of the precise manner of his demise. A painting by John Webber, an artist assigned to the voyage, depicts Cook gallantly signalling to the HMS *Resolution*, ordering the ship to cease firing on the islanders, who were armed only with clubs and spears. This is the "heroic" official version. A perhaps more realistic take, however, was painted by John Clevely, based on sketches by his brother, a carpenter on the ship. This shows Cook attacking the natives with the butt of his rifle – all his shot gone – in a heated bloody battle to the death with bodies of islanders heaped by the water's edge. The painting dates from 1784 and was only brought to light in 2004 after being hidden away in a private family collection over the years. Experts believe Clevely's painting is more accurate. So, not such a hero after all, probably.

Either way, British visitors have been coming to Hawaii for quite some time both for tourism and business. A hike around the crater at Diamond Head State Monument provides plenty of time to dwell (yet again) on colonial meddling. It's also a good workout, with a lot of ups and downs and narrow ways; the most topographically unusual park yet.

After losing myself in matters long ago – but not getting actually lost (the paths are easy to follow) – I returned to Waikiki Beach, rejoining the 390,000 residents of Honolulu and a fair few of its 5 million annual visitors. The population was 23,000 in 1890 when America was first getting interested, by the way.

Then I bought a flowery shirt. Then I ordered a piña colada. Then I watched the sun set across the ocean as Diamond Head turned into a tuna-like silhouette high above.

Just another tourist enjoying tourist excesses a long way from home. But not just another park. Nor is the one to come, 2,400 miles north-east across the Pacific in the closest neighbouring American state.

On Hippie Hill
Golden Gate Park, San Francisco, California, USA

Seen from above, Golden Gate Park is quite extraordinary: a slab of rectangular land, 3 miles long and half a mile wide, surrounded by a tightly packed grid of streets, cutting San Francisco in two.

At one end is a beach with breakers rolling in from the Pacific Ocean, at the other a thin green "Panhandle" of park beyond which the streets slide toward Union Square, the Financial District and the piers with ferries to the former prison island of Alcatraz. It almost seems a mistake: as though city officials in the early days simply never got around to drawing up plans to build on the giant green rectangle. It also looks as if the city surrounding the park is bearing down, besieging this vulnerable natural space.

Golden Gate Park is an example of how competition helped make America great in the first place (never mind a certain early twenty-first-century politician's commandeering of the expression).

Since as early as the 1850s New York had been plotting Central Park in the heart of Manhattan. San Francisco on the west coast was not to be outdone. In 1870 city planners set to work on an audacious scheme to create "one of the beauty spots of the world", at first poaching Central Park's architect, before settling on proposals put forward by William Hammond Hall and his assistant John McLaren, who went on to be superintendent of Golden Gate Park for 53 years. In came grasses from France designed to stabilize the sandy soil. In came pines, cypress trees and eucalyptus trees from around the globe, more than 155,000 in the first nine years. A thousand acres was set aside, 20 per cent bigger than Central Park. As a finishing touch, a magnificent esplanade was built along the oceanfront.

It was extremely popular. The population of San Francisco was 250,000 back in the 1880s and on some weekends a fifth of that number would jump on streetcars (trams) to visit. And it has never stopped being loved by locals, who now number almost 8 million in the dot-com rich San Francisco Bay area.

It is also full of curiosities. One of these is Hippie Hill, where anti-war long-haired hedonists in favour of free love gathered in 1967 during the Summer of Love, smoking dope, taking LSD and listening to live performances by the likes of Janis Joplin and George Harrison. The epicentre of this counterculture movement was in the nearby neighbourhood of Haight-Ashbury, just below the "Panhandle" on the eastern tip of the park. After a good day's counterculturalism, the hippies would go to the hill to relax.

One August day, I visited Hippie Hill, having just been to San Francisco's famous City Lights bookshop to buy some Beat Generation poetry to get in the mood, sadly not managing to speak to the shop's owner, the Beat poet Lawrence Ferlinghetti, who once wrote a poem entitled "In Golden Gate Park That Day" and who was upstairs at the time (no doubt sick of people such as myself requesting to meet him).

At the top of the hill, I sat on a grassy slope, people-watching and eating an orange. This felt appropriate as it was one of the highlights of the "action" in Ferlinghetti's delightfully dreamy-yet-sharp poem from 1958, which describes a married couple walking to the hill; the husband wearing showy green braces and his wife feeding grapes to squirrels. They sit down and eat their oranges in this "meadow of the world". He takes his shirt off and lies on his back with his hat covering his face. She lies down too, staring at birds above, and everything seems so wonderful:

a sunny, happy day in the park. Except for the final disquieting line that goes on to ruin it all, suggesting life is far from perfect for the couple.

The poem, although published much earlier than 1967, seems to capture the contradictions of the Beat Generation that were to afflict the Summer of Love: that it could not last forever; that the party had to come to an end; that reality had to be faced with hard knocks (possibly) coming soon. Yet it also evokes the sheer pleasure of a park on a bright day when you put your worries to one side and live in the moment.

I laid back on Hippie Hill watching gulls in the crystalline blue sky. Then I walked and I walked and I walked for many miles through Golden Gate Park.

From the hill heading in the direction of the ocean, you soon come to Rhododendron Dell, a paradise of pink and white blooms with a statue to the legendary park superintendent, McLaren, tucked in a corner. This statue has a story. McLaren hated statues with a vengeance, believing they spoiled the natural flow of a park. So, he banned them. At least, he tried to. Political pressure was often applied to erect statues in honour of important figures. What was he to do? He decided to let the occasional statue go up. Then he would re-landscape the park to ensure the bronzed bigwig was as unobtrusive as possible.

Yet on one occasion, McLaren was faced with a dilemma. So loved was he by San Franciscans – pleased by his marvellous transformation of the park – that money was raised for a statue in *his* honour, presented to him in 1911. He thanked those responsible, who may have had a mischievous streak, and then, the story goes, simply left it mouldering on the back porch of his house within the grounds of the park near the "Panhandle". There it remained until his death in 1943, after which it was erected in a quiet spot out of view of most passers-by in respect of his statue-sensibility. He is depicted wearing a bow tie and in his left hand he clutches a pine cone upon which he fixes his tender gaze. His feet are grounded in the soil rather than on a plinth to demonstrate his attachment to nature. McLaren is said to have planted more than 2 million trees in California, not just in Golden Gate.

At the risk of sounding like a bit of a park geek, which may well be too late: what an all-round park legend.

Onward from Rhododendron Dell paths lead towards the ocean. It would be impossible to see all there is to see of Golden Gate Park on one visit: the botanical garden, the rose garden, the Japanese tea garden, the dahlia garden, the Conservatory of Flowers, the meadows, the paddocks, the golf course, the lakes. There is even a fine arts museum (De Young Museum) featuring works by Salvador Dalí close to an Academy of Sciences. No doubt superb attractions one and all, but you cannot cram the whole lot in. Drifting is the way to go in Golden Gate Park. Much better simply to idle onward popping into whatever happens to be on your way. Taking this approach, I stumbled upon the Shakespeare Garden and went over to see what was what.

The Shakespeare Garden is said to be complete with every plant and flower mentioned by the Elizabethan playwright: more than 200 in all. A bronze bust of the Bard figures as do bronze plaques with flowery Shakespearean quotes.

From *Love's Labours Lost*:

> When daisies pied and violets blue
> And lady smocks all silver-white
> And cuckoo buds of yellow hue
> Do paint the meadows with delight

Nearby, daisies and violets had been planted.

From *Othello*:

> Not poppy, nor mandragora,
> Nor all the drowsy syrups of the world,
> Shall ever medicine thee to that sweet sleep
> Which thou owedst yesterday.

Nearby, poppies and mandrakes had been planted.

You get the picture. Slightly bonkers, but quite fun.

Beyond is a polo field where as many as 100,000 hippies congregated for music, ecstatic dancing and poetry readings in January 1967, ahead of the Summer of Love. This was referred to at the time as "a gathering of the tribes" and the "first Human Be-In" – and some regard it as the year's true highlight as by summer many of those involved were so zonked on LSD and whatever else they could lay their hands on that much of the idealism of the polo field jamboree had gone. Timothy Leary, one of the poets who spoke at the event, had told the gathering: "Turn on to the scene, tune into what is happening, and drop out!" Perhaps the last part of the message had gone to people's heads by July.

From there, you soon find yourself by the waterfront, watching waves break on the sandy shore as ships roll into San Francisco Bay.

In *On the Road*, the classic 1957 Beat book about driving across America in search of *something*, Beat writer Jack Kerouac's protagonist, Sal Paradise, is at a loss with nowhere else to run when he reaches the coast by San Francisco somewhere near Golden Gate Park. The mad, magnetic draw of the west that had taken him hurtling thousands of miles had come to a dead end. That was it: just ocean, nowhere else to go.

Another place to sit and live in the moment in blissful tranquillity for a while like Ferlinghetti's couple (before they began thinking about things too much).

Of note at the west end of Golden Gate Park are two old-fashioned windmills built by McLaren to pump fresh water from wells by the park's edge. Of note also, since my visit, a recent episode of which McLaren might have approved.

Earlier this year, as part of the Black Lives Matter movement responding to the brutal death of George Floyd in Minneapolis at the hands of police, protesters pulled on face masks and pulled down three statues in the park: one of Francis Scott Lee (the poet responsible for "The Star-Spangled Banner" and a slave owner), another of Ulysses S. Grant (although commander of the Union Army in the Civil War –

and pro-park – Grant owned a slave before the war) and finally a statue depicting Junípero Serra (who mistreated indigenous people at the time of Spanish colonialization).

Down they went, one by one. Scoundrels of the past, gone.

Somewhere up above, if he was watching, McLaren may just have been smiling.

Into the wilds
Stanley Park, Vancouver, Canada

Just as with the Royal Botanic Garden back in Sydney, Stanley Park feels like a spot where things began – and that's because they did.

Stanley is surrounded by water at the mouth of Vancouver Harbour, covering 1,001 acres of land that curl northward out of downtown Vancouver, the largest city in British Columbia. On a map, the park has the appearance of a giant seahorse, with a lake in the middle acting as the creature's "eye", a promontory occupied by a lighthouse the "nose" and a loop by Deadman's Island the "mouth". Meanwhile, downtown as far as Main Street is the "body", where the "tail" is lost in a confusion of junctions near British Columbia Highway 1A.

Maybe this is being a little fanciful; others say the park simply looks like a duck.

It was to Stanley Park and its environs that the European galleons came in the 1790s. Captain José María Narváez, a Spaniard, was first to drop by in 1791, sailing into the Strait of Georgia, the opening to Vancouver from the Pacific Ocean, in search of the legendary North-West Passage linking the Pacific and Atlantic Oceans. For a while, his party was excited they had found the beginning of a mighty waterway to the east coast. But they soon gave up after investigating what is now Vancouver Harbour, and the following year Captain George Vancouver, an Englishman, came under crown orders to charter the Pacific. With Britain in the ascendency in the region, Captain Vancouver duly began naming landmarks, not just after himself, but also his friends and colleagues: Mount Baker (after a lieutenant on the HMS *Discovery*), Puget Sound (after another lieutenant), Mount Rainier (after an admiral with whom he was friends) and Mount St Helens (after another pal, the 1st Baron St Helens).

Despite this shameless name-grab for posterity – and, I suppose, who could blame them, given the opportunity – Captain Vancouver's maps were first rate and used for many years after. Yet British Columbia, as the province was later called, was far from unoccupied and it was at Stanley Park in which Captain Vancouver met members of the Squamish Nation. Few records remain of such interactions although Captain Vancouver describes a friendly encounter close to Deadman's Island, within what is now Stanley Park:

> Here we were met by about 50 [indigenous people] in canoes, who conducted themselves with great decorum and civility, presenting us with several fish cooked and undressed of a sort resembling smelt. These good people, finding we were inclined to make some return for their hospitality, showed much understanding in preferring iron to copper.

Just as in Sydney, Manila and Hawaii, it is extraordinary to imagine these tall ships roaming the globe, laying down anchor and setting to work carving up whatever they could find; local traditions established over many millennia soon pushed aside. Not all that long ago, really, when you think about it.

Stanley Park in Vancouver is so called in honour of yet another Briton: Lord Stanley, 16th Earl of Derby, a former British governor general from the nineteenth century who favoured newfangled parks. It opened in 1888 following a growth in settlement at Vancouver during a gold rush in the mid-nineteenth century.

Lord Stanley had an eye on the city parks popping up south of the border in America. Yet his park is different. Stanley Park is mainly wild forest: a maintained wilderness close to the cut and thrust of commerce. That said, as in Golden Gate Park, there are an extraordinary number of "attractions", almost as though the various park superintendents over the years just could not help themselves despite the plans to keep things rugged and raw.

So today you can find: a rhododendron garden, a rose garden, a rock garden, another Shakespeare Garden (with only the trees mentioned by the Bard, this time), a narrow-gauge tourist train pulled by a replica of a Canadian Pacific Railway transcontinental locomotive, a heated pool, a water park, a pitch-and-putt golf course, tennis courts, a beach or two with lifeguards and cafes; and a major aquarium home to 70,000 creatures including dolphins, sea turtles, seals and – in a section that has nothing to do with sea life – parrots, frogs and three-toed sloths.

I did not bother with any of that. Instead, I went for a jog.

The circumstances in which I found myself in Vancouver again make me regretful – or re-Greta-ful, perhaps, to give a tabloid twist. And I was on a job for one. In 2008, a national newspaper had asked me to fly around the world on low-cost airlines as fast as possible to show, on the one hand, how crazily cheap air tickets had become. On the other, the article was designed to demonstrate how *you, dear reader, could do this, too*. Not that anyone in their right mind would want to dash around the planet on their holidays in 61 hours (the journey's eventual length). It was "stunt journalism" of the first order, from London via Hong Kong to Vancouver and on.

Which was why, with a morning to kill in the middle of the 61 hours, I went for a run; I needed to clear my head after hours cooped up in long metal tubes at 30,000 feet. Stanley Park was perfect as its biggest attraction of all is a 5.5-mile sea wall trail beginning downtown and passing the Lost Lagoon, a man-made expanse of water with geese and herons that marks the beginning of the park proper, before twisting towards the "nose" of the seahorse.

To the right here, pine-clad mountains arise beyond the slate-grey surface of Vancouver Harbour and the feeling of "city" quickly falls

away. Skyscrapers: gone! Busy city streets: out of sight and mind! You
are entering the wilds.

No other urban park has quite such an abrupt effect. One minute you
are in the busiest city in western Canada. The next you are imagining
grizzlies padding out of the woods and roaring after you with claws
aloft (there are none, however, slightly disappointingly). The sonic
disturbances of a city – the revving engines, sirens, alarms, blaring
music, voices, whistles, yells, the accumulated sounds of urban life – are
replaced by the breeze through the trees and the trill of birdlife. Salty air
blows in off the Strait of Georgia. The scent of pine trees and wild herbs
drifts across the sea wall track. It is as though you have stepped through
a door marked "end of city" and entered a heavenly green hideaway.

No wonder Canada, one of the world's least populated countries,
so consistently comes out near the top of "quality of life" studies. No
wonder Vancouver always ranks highly in the Global Liveability Index
compiled by *The Economist* Intelligence Unit. There is so much nature
it almost spills into its major cities. Thoughts of emigration may soon
spring to mind when you visit Vancouver (they did for me).

The sea wall trail is glorious, gripping the foot of steep slopes as it
bends round the coast. The wall was finally completed in 1971 after
the project was begun in 1917, giving an idea of the huge engineering
task required to establish the trail at the trickiest remote spots. Each
mile took an astonishing 8.72 years to complete, and this did not come
without a cultural cost.

It is estimated that around 200 people lived in the area when park
status was first granted in 1888, most in a village named Xwayxway. But
over the years, development, first the cutting of simple roads through
the forest, then the sea wall, meant settlements moved or were destroyed.
One local historian, J. S. Matthews, interviewed a man named August
Jack Khatsahlano, who was a boy when the developers came. Speaking in
1934, Khatsahlano said: "We was inside this house when the surveyors
come along and they chop the corner of our house when we was eating
inside. We all get up and go outside see what was the matter. My sister

Louise, she was the only one to talk a little English; she goes out and asks Whiteman what he's doing that for. The man say: 'We're surveying the road.' My sister ask him: 'Whose road?'" His family were forced to leave.

Moving inland from the sea wall near Brockton Point, a haunting collection of bright First Nations totem poles pays tribute to the indigenous people of British Columbia who predated Narváez and Vancouver – and Stanley Park.

From there the trail winds around the top of the head of the "seahorse" and you begin to see the skyscrapers of the city once again. Another chance to marvel at having quite so much green bang in the centre of a city.

It was to this space that Vancouver's very own hippies, inspired by the Human Be-In in San Francisco in January 1967, held their very own Be-In a couple of months later, prompting Vancouver's straight-laced mayor, Tom Campbell, to refer to the wild-haired revellers as "parasites", "scum" and "lazy louts" who:

> …contribute absolutely nothing to the welfare of the community, but expect hospital care when they take bad trips and police protection when they get into trouble – and yet when the police are around they shout 'fuzz'… They don't want to pay taxes. They want to take everything and give nothing… We have a scum community that have organized and decided to grow long hair… Half of them are American draft dodgers, who will not even fight for their own country and who are up here for protection. If they were in their homeland they'd be in gaol. They are first-class troublemakers.

Mayor Campbell did not like hippies much. Yet as with so many parks, the feeling was that Stanley belonged to the people. Have a Human Be-In and let your hair down! The park was for everyone to do whatever they wanted! So they did, even if the mayor blew a gasket or two.

One final Stanley Park-related matter.

When Captain George Vancouver, aged 37, returned to Britain he visited Richmond Park and especially enjoyed the view from Richmond Hill. He decided to move to Petersham at the foot of the hill, near the Thames, dying in obscurity of what is believed to have been a kidney complication only three years later. What had happened? Surely he was a returning hero? Not so. Despite his many accomplishments, Vancouver was far from celebrated by all on his return. Rather the opposite, as he had upset a certain Thomas Pitt, a prominent cousin of William Pitt the Younger, then the prime minister, by disciplining him and sending him back to Britain while on the expedition. Thomas Pitt held a grudge. He challenged Vancouver to a duel, which he declined, not wanting to escalate the feud. But Pitt remained livid. He stalked Vancouver and eventually assaulted him with a cane in Mayfair, administering many blows.

This was society news and a humiliation, captured by the prominent cartoonist James Gillray. A legal dispute followed, adding to other complications Vancouver was already facing over his handling of staff during the exploration of Canada. He had become something of an outcast, and it is strange to imagine the great explorer living out his final days tucked away avoiding his enemies by the gentle-flowing Thames after rounding the globe on the high seas.

Another Richmond Park fan, though – it *is* a lovely park.*

"Are the green fields gone?"
Central Park, New York City, USA

Barack Obama's love of Central Park gets to the essence of park life: the enjoyment of simply watching the world go by and "being" for a while. Just like the hippies of 1967 (without the weed).

---

* Vancouver is buried in St Peter's Church in Petersham, close to one of Richmond Park's gates. His grave is by a brick wall on the right at the back. I visited to pay my respects yesterday for the first time on a sunny Saturday. Not another soul was about.

On a bench near the park's iconic Bow Bridge over the Lake, the stretch of water level with 73rd Street in New York's immense grid of streets, I sat transfixed. All around autumn glowed in explosions of copper and gold, mauve and rust-red. Bursts of emerald and lime blended to form a canopy of colour completed by flickering shafts of ethereal yellow. The trees up above seemed to be having a party. Dappled sunlight filtered across pathways. Ducks quacked as though sharing jokes. Gossiping New Yorkers on office breaks idled by. Others made phone calls or pecked at mobiles. Others, like me, rested on benches, legs outstretched, and watched.

On the cast-iron bridge, couples, perhaps tourists, posed for photographs to capture shots of the skyscrapers of Fifth Avenue and Central Park West. Gothic towers reflected in the still water. Distant taxis honked and motors revved, the sounds echoing faintly across the Lake. Not obtrusive, quite the opposite: the noise was almost comforting. New York City was getting on with things, but I was not having to. The sensation was of lying in at home on a day off during the week. I was taking it easy. Why not? That's what parks are all about, aren't they?

The city hummed with activity. New York was living up to its reputation for manic madness; the city that never sleeps was wide awake and going full tilt that autumn day. All was calm on my bench, though. I hummed a tune, peering up at the towering concrete-and-glass skyline beyond the dreamy-coloured trees.

This was when the roller skater arrived. Her age was difficult to determine. She could have been 60. She might have been 80. She wore grey Nike tracksuit trousers ("sweatpants" in the local lingo), pink woollen leg warmers above her roller skates, a grey Nike hoodie and a pink woollen bobble hat. She had hazel eyes, freckles on her cheeks and an incredibly elastic body.

Not far from my bench she placed a stereo, pressed a button and funk-soul music softly played. A guitar twanged. A bassline thumped. A sweet melody rose above the beat. And the woman in the grey Nike tracksuit was off: performing a sudden, tight backwards twirl on her roller skates before dancing.

Her movements were mesmerizing. She began with a rhythmic glide that looked as though she was skating on ice while somehow always remaining exactly on the same spot. She was moving but somehow not moving; speeding up and slowing down as if hypnotized by the music. It was brilliant. It was weird. She had fallen trance-like into the groove, her dance matching the beat to perfection, arms twisting with abandon.

The woman in the grey Nike tracksuit was performing for anyone who cared to watch, not for dollars. She was also, clearly, doing it for herself. Her face was almost expressionless as she jived, calmly relishing every moment. A little backwards circle or two was followed by a low spin with an outstretched leg, then a serpentine body shake. The fluidity and control were magnificent. She was at one with the music in a big park in a very big city. No matter what anyone else was getting up to just then.

New York was casting its spell in the way only New York can. Its sheer energy already had me addicted from the neon glamour and shows of Times Square to the bustle and intrigue of Little Italy, the dimly lit cocktail bars of the Meatpacking District and the crazy spill of commuters amid the grandeur of Grand Central Station. And Central Park was not letting the side down. You do not get many boogying, possibly octogenarian roller-skate dancing divas in parks back in south-west London. Not in my experience, anyway.

So, an hour slipped by in America's greatest urban park – in Obama-time, if you like.

Although the United States has many first-rate parks in cities, Central Park has a special place in the scheme of inner-city American greenery. This is because it was one of the country's first, certainly the first major city park, with plans dreamed up in the 1850s and the grand opening in 1876.

At the time it was in dire need. New York's population had tripled to 700,000 between 1820 and 1855. Industrialization and dense, ramshackle housing were getting out of control. Herman Melville, author of *Moby-Dick*, who lived in New York then and was in the middle of completing his masterpiece, wrote: "The 'Whale' is only half through the press; for, wearied with the long delays of the printers, and disgusted with the heat and dust of the Babylonish brick-kiln of New York, I came back to the country to feel the grass, and end the book reclining on it, if I may." Overcrowding and overdevelopment in his hometown were clearly one of the author's hobby horses. At the beginning of *Moby-Dick*, Ishmael, referring to Manhattan, asks simply: "Are the green fields gone?"

City planners back then were coming to the realization that such complaints were justified: green fields were needed again. Parks had been opening to relieve inner-city problems in cities in Britain since the 1840s. New Yorkers looked across the pond and quickly grasped the benefits of spaces open to the public for free, away from the noise and soot of mills, factories, docks and Babylonish brick-kilns.

Land was set aside, requiring the eviction of 1,600 impoverished residents, mainly African Americans and Irish immigrants living in shacks in the centre of Manhattan: 770 acres of territory covering two and a half miles in length and half a mile in width was marked out. Then a competition was held to win a contract to design the park, with Frederick Olmsted (a New Englander whom San Francisco initially called upon for Golden Gate Park) and Calvert Vaux (a recently arrived Englishman) winning with their joint submission.

The English influence here was key. Vaux clearly understood the value of parks, while Olmsted had visited Liverpool on a transatlantic jaunt and – the story goes – popped across the River Mersey to see Birkenhead and have a snack at a bakery. At this bakery, the baker told Olmsted he must visit the recently opened Birkenhead Park. This park provided a free area of meadows, lakes and winding paths for dockers and other industrial workers. Olmsted strolled over and was extremely impressed. Then he returned to New York a "city park man" through and through.

He wrote:

> The time will come when New York will be built up, when all
> the grading and filling will be done, and when the picturesquely-
> varied, rocky formations of the Island will have been converted
> into foundations of rows of monotonous straight streets, and
> piles of erect, angular buildings. There will be no suggestion left
> of its present varied surface, with the single exception of the Park.
> Then the priceless value of the present picturesque outline of the
> ground will be more distinctly perceived, and its adaptability for
> its purpose more fully recognized.

Bravo! Another park hero to add to John McLaren back in San
Francisco – not to forget Vaux, his right-hand man (as some do). All
had stood up against business developers who wanted to make the
most of what would soon become prime Manhattan land, without
too many blades of grass likely to figure in any of their projects. This
was a turning point for urban USA. Central Park became a template
for what was possible, with other cities taking note of Olmsted and
Vaux's successful blocking of suggestions to have a grand avenue cut
down the middle of the park. They stuck to their countryside-in-the-
city scheme thus preventing "erect, angular buildings" coming in later
along such an avenue. Both went on to design many a municipal park
across the United States, adding green touches to cities throughout
the nation.

Imagine what New York would be like without Central Park…
skyscrapers filling that great green gap.

Imagine also another (happier) version of history. From Bow Bridge
and the roller-dancer, it is a short walk to Strawberry Fields, a 2.5-acre
memorial within Central Park dedicated to John Lennon, who was
murdered, aged 40, outside the Dakota Apartments overlooking the
park on 8 December 1980. Fans of the Liverpudlian musician – who
would no doubt have visited Birkenhead Park in his youth – flock to the

circular black-and-white floor mosaic with "IMAGINE" written in tiles in the centre. Yoko Ono, Lennon's wife, helped fund the memorial along with contributions from countries across the globe.

Lilac flowers had been scattered in the shape of a peace sign and no one was playing a stereo or roller-dancing; Strawberry Fields is an official "quiet zone". Trees and shrubs had been planted from around the world there, and the feeling of peace and of sadness hit home, especially if you are a lover of his music (as I am).

The saddest moment of this park quest.

After paying my respects I walked and walked and walked, just as in Golden Gate Park, but with 20 per cent less land to cover.

It was still a good long way round. To the North Woods, past softball pitches and scampering players, fountains and flower beds, arbours and acacia trees. To the Jacqueline Kennedy Onassis Reservoir, with scrapers casting long mottled reflections. To the gothic extravagance of Belvedere Castle on a rocky outcrop facing Turtle Pond. To the winged splendour of Bethesda Fountain, where hippies cavorted in the 1960s and where anti-war protests were held. To the sloping grasses of Sheep Meadow. To the gaudy old-fashioned carousel. To the gates of the zoo, where snow leopards, penguins and lemurs lurked.

Central Park famously fell into decline in the mid-twentieth century, becoming dangerous to visit at night. Graffiti covered walls, windows in buildings were smashed, plants wilted and landscapes eroded. Restoration to save Olmsted and Vaux's vision kicked in later in the century, and by 2000 the green was back. Crime fell. New Yorker pride in the park returned, as did the joy of visiting the nation's number-one city park with 38 million visitors a year.

To go and to stroll and to sit on a bench and to do nothing and to watch a roller-dancing disco (if you're lucky) and then to stroll on again in the quiet in a long rectangle of green in a city of 8 million people: that is something to look forward to.

Some people love New York. I do. Some people also have a soft spot for Central Park. Just like me.

Park of dreams
West Potomac Park, Washington DC, USA

On a stage close to the Washington Monument obelisk built in West Potomac Park in honour of George Washington, America's first president, a preacher wearing a tan-coloured long coat, sunglasses and a trilby was busy honouring another famous US politician.

"We praise you in the name of Jesus, Lord God! When people said there would never be a black president, we kept believing, Lord God! Thank all nations!" The preacher paused and swept his hand towards us (a small group of tourists). "Thank all nations! All faces! In the name of the Father and the Son and the Holy Spirit." The preacher paused to gather breath, holding his microphone to one side. He continued: "Lord God! Sisters! Lord God, you heard our prayers! Lord God in the name of Jesus! We say amen, amen, amen!"

The onlookers by the open-air stage burst into spontaneous applause. It was January 2009, a week before Barack Obama was to be inaugurated as the 44th president of the United States and the nation's capital was in a state of excited anticipation. More than 2 million tickets for the inauguration parade had sold out in a minute; some were now fetching ten times the face value on eBay. Metal barriers and scaffolding were already in place by the domed US Capitol building – home to Congress – at the far end of the National Mall, an area of green flanked by museums running eastward from Washington Monument that saw anti-war protests during the Vietnam conflict.

Pop-up gift shops sold President Obama mugs, President Obama number plates, President Obama hoodies, President Obama badges (some featuring First Lady-to-be Michelle Obama, others Vice President-elect Joe Biden). T-shirts ran the campaign slogan: "Yes we can!" as well as "Yes, we did!" On one, a quote from the 44th American leader-elect said: "I am not asking you to believe in my ability to bring about real change in Washington. I'm asking you to believe in yours."

There was electricity in the air. Change, real change, seemed on its way. It was an intriguing time to visit Washington DC and see its most prestigious park.

West Potomac Park offers a lesson in American history. It also sometimes sends shivers down your spine. The history comes in the form of the many monuments to great figures of the past as well as those who have died in conflict. The park's official boundary runs from Washington Monument, down a long, thin pond (the Reflecting Pool) to the Lincoln Memorial, beside the churning River Potomac. Within this space are to be found the Franklin Delano Roosevelt Monument (honouring the 32nd president), the Jefferson Monument (remembering Thomas Jefferson, the third president), plus memorials to the soldiers of the First and Second World Wars, the Vietnam War and the Korean War. Since my visit, a granite memorial in honour of Martin Luther King Jr has been added (in 2011), known as the Stone of Hope in recognition of a line from the civil rights campaigner's 1963 "I have a dream" speech: "Out of the mountain of despair, a stone of hope." More of which to come.

Confusion about what constitutes the park's exact boundary is understandable as the National Mall officially ends at the base of the giant obelisk to George Washington, although many locals consider the Mall to continue all the way to the Lincoln Memorial, a distance of 3 miles. This does not really matter either way as everything blends together and the net result is a whole lot of green in the heart of the government of the world's most powerful nation.

Washington Monument, however, is key, acting as the centre of a "cross" with a long horizontal middle with the Capitol on the right and the Lincoln Memorial on the left. Meanwhile, the White House is at the "top" of a short vertical section that leads down via the Monument to the Jefferson Memorial and the Tidal Basin. This Basin is surrounded by a path beside cherry trees that come alive in gorgeous blooms each spring.

The overall setting is wonderful, and this is not by mistake. George Washington himself approved the land, formerly part of the state of Maryland, as capital of the new nation in 1790 (after seeing off the

British in 1781). The government came first in George Washington's thinking. This was to be the seat of power for a mighty new nation. The politicians would have pride of place in fine surroundings in the new District of Columbia.

Initially, the state of Virginia had also offered land for the new capital, on the other, western side of the Potomac. But then race politics (or you might just say racism) kicked in. With some northern politicians in favour of abolition of slavery, those in Virginia – many of whom were slave owners – were unhappy. Their land was returned, leaving all of Washington DC within what had been Maryland, 68 square miles in all. For this reason, if you look at a map the city shape is an imperfect square. The US Civil War of 1861 eventually settled the huge dispute that divided America in favour of the northern abolitionists, of course, with a certain Abraham Lincoln, the 16th president, at the helm.

A lot of history, as I said, in West Potomac Park.

From the stage with the preacher in the trilby by the Monument, the Reflecting Pool follows round to the marble, fluted Doric columns of the Lincoln Memorial, with the great president staring down with a steady gaze, looking gaunt and determined and wearing a bow tie while sitting in his giant throne-like chair. On the top of the steps to his statue is where shivers set in.

The history of race relations is entwined with the history of the United States, and nowhere do you feel it more strongly than from this vantage point. On one wall of Lincoln's memorial, completed in 1922, are his famous words from the Gettysburg Address, after the defeat of southern Confederacy forces in Gettysburg in the state of Pennsylvania in November 1863: "Four score and seven years ago our fathers brought forth on this continent, a new nation, conceived in Liberty, and dedicated to the proposition that all men are created equal…" On another are words from his second inaugural address in March 1865, just before the end of the Civil War: "With malice towards none, with charity for all, with firmness in the right as God gives us to see the right, let us strive to finish the work we are in, to bind up the nation's wounds."

Yet the most famous speech given on the steps of the Lincoln Memorial itself was 100 years after Gettysburg. An inscription on the floor marks the spot where Martin Luther King Jr delivered his "I have a dream" speech to a quarter of a million civil rights supporters in 1963. With the Reflecting Pool lined with crowds ahead of him, King paused and launched into his immortal oration about the nation rising up one day to fulfil the American dream of equality that Lincoln had triumphed and which remains as important today as ever (witness the Black Lives Matter movement not just in America but across the globe).

To visit West Potomac Park and to ascend the steps of the Lincoln Memorial is to follow in the footsteps of American giants.

From the Lincoln Memorial it is a stroll to the haunting cloaked figures of soldiers at the Korean War Veterans Memorial. From there, another brief walk delivers you at the Franklin Delano Roosevelt Memorial, showing FDR, who was paralyzed by polio and could not walk, seated beside his beloved dog. A nearby tableau depicts a Great Depression era breadline; designed to highlight the dilemmas FDR faced as president when he introduced his New Deal to deliver national economic recovery (something the whole world could well do with now).

Onwards from FDR, you come to the Jefferson Memorial, all elegant marble steps and columns by the Tidal Basin. Up the steps, inside, is the tall bronze statue of yet another American giant, the principal author of America's Declaration of Independence in 1776. His words, to which King had referred, are inscribed in the monument's dome: "We hold these truths to be self-evident: that all men are created equal, that they are endowed by their Creator with certain inalienable rights, among these are life, liberty and the pursuit of happiness..."

After seeing the memorials, with their inspirational words at every turn, you may decide to find a bench beside the choppy water of the Potomac.

I did. The river here can be forbidding: swirling currents, whirlpools and eddies pulling along driftwood, old tyres, plastic barrels and tangles of rope. After the perfection of the monuments, it can be rough and "wild".

On my bench, I thought back to my morning.

It had been a memorable one. Before coming to West Potomac Park, I had stopped at U Street to try a bowl of chili from Ben's Chili Bowl restaurant, a famous fast-food joint about a mile north-east of the White House. As I was about to cross the street from the metro, though, a series of cars with tinted windows had pulled up outside the restaurant and armed policemen and men wearing bulging suits – presumably armed security officers – had leaped out. A cop had held out his hand and made me turn back.

A wave of rumour broke out on the sidewalk. Obama had arrived! Or so it was said. A policeman would tell us nothing, but his look confirmed this was true.

Obama had come to indulge in one of his favourite snacks, just a few days before the big day. From across the street I snapped a picture of president-elect (well, the very top of his head) when he left Ben's after 15 minutes. The feeling all about U Street, one of the epicentres of civil rights marches in the 1960s, was ecstatic. There were cheers. There were cries. There were tears. There was happiness all round.

After the cavalcade left, I entered Ben's Chili Bowl and ordered some chili. The small restaurant was in disarray. Waiters were dancing. Customers were dancing, some with the waiters. There were smiles and laughter. Jermaine, who had served Obama, was waiving the $20 bill he had been given and doing a jig. The president-elect had ordered a half-smoke hotdog with cheese and an iced tea, tipping Jermaine $6.50.

"I'm never gonna spend it! Never!" he said.

In his autobiography, *Dreams from My Father*, Obama describes how when he was a mere senator he would jog around the memorials of West Potomac Park, often ascending the steps of the Lincoln Memorial to imagine the crowds and the "mighty cadence" of King, who had, along with Lincoln, dedicated their lives to "perfecting an imperfect union". Whenever Obama stood there his heart, he said, filled with joy.

Just as hearts had been that morning on U Street. Just as hearts seemed to be across Washington DC that January day.

Sitting by the River Potomac near the Lincoln Memorial there is always plenty to ponder (in perhaps my favourite overseas city park of all).

CHAPTER SIX

CUBA, HAITI, BARBADOS, ST HELENA: DAIQUIRIS, BOGEYMEN, "LOBSTERS" AND NAPOLEON

Havana

CUBA

HAITI

DOMINICAN
REPUBLIC

Port-au-Prince

Caribbean Sea

Bridgetown

BARBADOS

SOUTH
AMERICA

To
St Helena

As I have mentioned, if these stories of park life feel a tad offbeat, well that's because they are meant to be.

Parks can be enjoyed in many ways: some may prefer a brisk walk, others a lie down on a lawn perhaps with a picnic, others still to kick a ball or hurl a frisbee. You may like to poke your nose into local history. You may simply wish to breathe the fresh (or fresher) air. You may decide to meet people. You may not. You may seek a mix of all the above. Then again, what takes your fancy could just depend on how you feel that day.

These reimagined park visits were delivering snapshots: glimpses of urban glens that were by no means "guides". Parks can be many things to many people. Places of release and relaxation. Places of gatherings. Places of protest, sometimes. Places to step away from the ever-turning wheel of city life. Places to cherish the quiet. Places to let your hair down (but not too much in case the Mayor Campbells of Vancouver get upset).

I was beginning to become increasingly contemplative and even a touch philosophical about parks. At home, deep in the lockdown with hardly any planes now flying into Heathrow above my terraced flat in south-west London, I would sit in my study, watched by my Ecuadorian fox, and increasingly *think parks*.

This thinking was soon to move me onward from the Americas, down south on a short tour of the colonial-era-ravished Caribbean before heading to one of the most isolated (and peculiar) spots on the planet, deep in the South Atlantic Ocean on the way to Africa. In the middle of nowhere, a lovely little park in yet another colonial outpost (this one still going) awaited.

Greene-land 1
Parque Central, Havana, Cuba

On the way to Parque Central, I was scammed.

A man on a side street stopped me to ask my nationality. "Are you Canadian?" was his opening gambit – taking a different approach to the shifty man back in Vientiane in Laos. Apparently, a lot of Canadians visit Cuba. He seemed friendly enough, with a slight nervous twitch and a warm smile.

His next move, as though this were part of a chess game, was to explain that his sister had a "friend in Manchester" and, if I had a moment, could I write a postcard to this friend on her behalf as his sister's English handwriting was poor? I agreed: what harm could there be in writing a postcard? The man with the twitch, who gave his name as Eduardo, led me to a cafe on a smaller street close by, where I was introduced to a woman wearing a miniskirt and a red satin top bearing the words: "AMERICAN GIRL". We sat at a scuffed wooden table and I waited for a card to be produced. It was not. Instead, a round of mojitos was delivered. *Oh, what the hell,* I thought, *why not?* We clinked glasses and drank. Still no card.

At a scuffed wooden table in a corner, I now noticed, a portly red-faced European was sitting with a tattooed woman on his lap. She was drunkenly whispering in his ear. He would occasionally squeeze her. She would giggle and whisper some more. They would drink. Then the pattern would begin again. It looked as though they were well set for a long day's whispering, giggling, squeezing and drinking.

The twitchy man made his third move.

"Look into my eyes," he said. So I did. "We are very poor. I live with my wife," he indicated the woman in the red satin top, who smiled suggestively at me. "And our two children and my grandmother. We cannot afford soap. We are allowed one bar of soap a month." All part of the rationing of the regime of Fidel Castro, then still alive, aged 82. This was 50 years after the revolution and around town posters on billboards declared *ANIVERSARIO 50 DEL TRIUNFO DE LA REVOLUCIÓN* beside pictures of the revolutionary.

"I am a mechanic, but I work on the streets. I can get you things," he said. The woman in the satin top smiled suggestively once more. I indicated that I did not wish to go down the path of the portly red-faced European.

This induced move number four. "Can you give us some money, Mr Tom?" he said. "Look into my eyes: we have no money, Mr Tom." I got up to leave, rapidly bringing move number five, the final move. This came in the form of a bill for the drinks that was much more than it would have been at Hotel Nacional, one of the city's finest, where I was staying overlooking the choppy waters of Estrecho de Florida. Checkmate! I talked the figure down slightly, paid, Eduardo grunted, folded the notes away, looked with extreme displeasure at me, and I left around the corner to Parque Central.

In Havana it always seemed that a lot was going on, especially around Parque Central – and it was with Eduardo's unsuccessful scam playing through my mind that I first set foot in this unusual city oasis. This *parque* was really little more than a small square with a marble statue of José Martí, a nineteenth-century Cuban independence writer, a few trees with bushy-leaved branches and the odd palm. Yet it was a veritable hive of action. On the streets, old yellow Chevrolet taxis with sagging suspension crawled by, trailing fumes. Traps pulled by skittish little horses rattled along, the sharp-eyed drivers seeming to take in every pedestrian's customer potential at a glance. Ancient Buicks and Pontiacs rolled past looking as though they might collapse in a heap at any moment; bumpers and panels on some held together by tape. Just like the taxis, they were from the 1950s before Fidel's 1959 revolution against the dictatorship of President Fulgencio Batista.

In one convertible Cadillac of similar vintage, a bride to be sat upright on the top of the back seat, her head way up above the level of the windscreen. She was grimacing slightly and hanging on, looking like a swan as her lacy wedding dress billowed in the humid air on the way to matrimony: a grimacing, billowing swan. Meanwhile, empty tricycle taxis slowed in front of the distinguished facade of Hotel Inglaterra, hoping to pick up a fare. Then strange little three-wheeled vehicles painted yellow like the Chevrolets would slide by, so small the red-faced European would struggle to squeeze in, especially with his whispering friend on his knee. There appeared to be a great many ways of getting about in Havana.

The Inglaterra is Havana's oldest hotel, from the nineteenth century and with an open-air rooftop bar providing fine views of Parque Central. This was of interest to me as it figures in Graham Greene's hilarious 1958 novel, *Our Man in Havana*. As with *The Quiet American* in Vietnam, I had brought along a copy to read on the trip. It is about a vacuum-cleaner salesman named Mr Wormold who is recruited to MI6 as a spy and invents all sorts of contacts so he can file fake "intelligence" back to Britain. This "work" provides him with extra cash, which he needs to pay for his teenage daughter's expensive tastes. His deceit drags him into the underworld, much against his wishes and to great comic effect. All around Parque Central features in the book and some of the clubs and bars were still around: Sloppy Joe's, the Tropicana, the Floridita. The novel captures the heady excesses of the daiquiri-guzzling pre-revolutionary days and is the perfect accompaniment to any visit.

But there was no time for reading in Parque Central. In one corner of the square, beyond the statue of Martí, a group of men had gathered and they were in fervent discussion about something or other. Could this be a counter-revolutionary cell? After 50 years was Cuba, then under the control of Castro's younger brother Raul (then aged 77), about to turn once more? It seemed an uprising was in the offing.

No, they were discussing baseball. The park is, I later learned, one of the favourite places for groups of men mainly of a certain age, with some younger fans mixed in, to meet and argue with one another about how *their* Cuban baseball team is better than their conversational sparring partner's baseball team and how certain players for *their* team are better than their rival's certain players of note – *absolutely no question about it, not the slightest beginning of a shadow of doubt, I feel sorry for your soul that you feel differently*. This was amusing to witness: the sheer passion of it all. Fists were shaken, vigorously. Insults were hurled, with venom. Expressions of incredulity at the abomination of nonsense that their ears were having the indignity to receive were clear from across the *parque*. How could their rival baseball follower have the audacious temerity even to broach such an opinion? This heated disputation is so common across Cuba that it has a name: *esquina caliente* (hot corner).

The American influence may have gone – Batista was US backed – but America's favourite sport had stayed. As had, on the south-west corner of Parque Central, an extraordinary, large building called El Capitolio.

This is an almost identical version of the United States Capitol in Washington DC, facing West Potomac Park, complete with dome and steps up to an august entrance flanked by Ionic columns. A carbon copy of the home of America's Congress, although Cuba's is – apparently – 1 metre wider, 1 metre taller and 1 meter longer. *Touché* Havana! The structure was completed in 1929, while America's dates from 1800.

Inside is a shiny marble-floored chamber with a large diamond embedded in a panel, apparently marking the centre point of Cuba's road system. A giant golden statue known as La Republica depicts a figure holding a spear and a shield glaring down upon visitors. This is, apparently, the third largest indoor statue in the world, one of the two bigger statues being the one of Abraham Lincoln at the Lincoln Memorial. There are a lot of *apparentlys* about El Capitolio, formerly home of Cuba's parliament and president's office.

From the top of the steps of El Capitolio you have a good view across Parque Central, beyond the angel-topped tower of Gran Teatro de la Habana (home to the national ballet) and the Teatro Payret cinema showing *El Cuerno de la Abundancia* (*The Horn of Plenty*) on my visit, a comedy about families seeking a fortune from an inheritance and getting up to all sorts of mischief. A visit to watch a film at the lovely, old Payret, with its enormous dusty auditorium and almost 2,000 seats is a highlight of Parque Central: the first *parque* so far with a cinema! If you count a building next door.

Another highlight is a visit, a stone's throw away, to El Floridita bar, where its legendary daiquiri cocktail was invented, apparently (yet again), and Ernest Hemingway often visited while staying in Havana, definitely. His preference was for El Floridita's daiquiri without sugar, but with double shots of rum, rendering it effectively "rum and lime", which became known as a Papa Doble after Hemingway's nickname "Papa".

A bronze of the writer sits at his favourite place by the bar at El Floridita, which, with its pink walls and neon signs, is impossible to miss. I took a bar stool next to him with a Papa Doble amid a cacophony of afternoon drinkers in La Casa del Daiquiri ("Home of the Daiquiri", as a sign on the bar informs you). The chatter floated across the fancy, fanned room. The glasses clinked. The alcohol took effect. The mood became mellow – the run-in with Eduardo forgotten by then.

A *parque* with palm trees and baseball lovers, hustlers, literary stories, films, buildings with diamonds in its floors and rum cocktails... Parque Central in Havana is another good one.

Greene-land 2
Place Toussaint Louverture, Port-au-Prince, Haiti

In Haiti our guide, a former missionary turned tourism representative, said there were nine words she would prefer me not to report. These were: "Haiti is the poorest nation in the western hemisphere."

It was the bicentenary of the formation of the nation, founded by slaves who revolted against French colonial rule, and hopes were high that the country was about to turn a corner and become a major tourism destination cashing in on the sun, sand and palm trees of the Caribbean after decades of dictatorship and bloody misdeeds. To put this anniversary in historical perspective, the date it was founded – 1804 – was 60 years before the US Civil War, more than half a century before Lincoln's groundbreaking "all men are created equal" Gettysburg Address in America.

Haiti was ahead of the game. Yet this proud history has been tainted by a messy recent past. Turbulence at the top over many years had led to great hardship at the bottom over many years, too. In 2004, when I went, the gross national income per capita was $440 and life expectancy for men was 49 and for women 50. Those living in the neighbouring Dominican Republic, a few hours' bus ride away, could expect to keep going 15–20 years more. The description "poorest nation in the western hemisphere", sad to say, was apt.

Troubles were ongoing. United Nations troops and an interim government had occupied the National Palace after a coup earlier in the year that had seen President Jean-Bertrand Aristide flee to South Africa. Aristide had introduced a paramilitary force called the Chimeras to maintain control after being democratically elected a few years earlier. The Chimeras, named after the monstrous fire-breathing creature of Greek mythology (which gives a hint to their behaviour), were just the latest such paramilitary outfit to install a reign of terror in Haiti and it was no wonder, really, that our guide was jittery; she had already warned us not to go out after 5 p.m. as this "might not be good for your health or your wealth".

The most infamous government "enforcers" before the Chimeras had been the Tonton Macoute under the terrifying rule of François "Papa Doc" Duvalier from 1957–71. They were known for their dark glasses, straw hats, blue denim shirts as well as their inscrutable, intimidating bearing and vicious means of getting what they wanted. They carried machetes and guns. They were named after "Uncle Gunnysack", a Haitian mythological bogeyman who whisked children away in gunnysacks and fed them to people for breakfast. They were, unsurprisingly, greatly feared.

During their rule, a certain novelist turned up to poke his nose around.

The regime of "Papa Doc" forms the backdrop of yet another Graham Greene tale from a hot distant clime: *The Comedians*, published in 1966, whose main character, Mr Brown, ran a hotel in Port-au-Prince named Hotel Trianon (in real life, Hotel Oloffson). This hotel, where the plot takes off with a discovery of a body by the pool, was where I was staying, my room adjoining the very pool. Above the terrace of the whitewashed, fretted facade, there was also a Graham Greene Room in which the author is said to have stayed. First, *The Quiet American* in Ho Chi Minh

City, then *Our Man in Havana*, now *The Comedians* – following in the footsteps of Greene can take you around the world to some unusual spots (not that I was doing that, it just seemed to be happening).

To the astonishment and concern of our former missionary turned tourist guide, myself and Doug, a photographer, decided to go for a walk without her and her driver keeping an eye on us in the Haitian capital.

This took us down a hill to Place Toussaint Louverture, a park beside the National Palace, named after the revolutionary general François-Dominique Toussaint Louverture. It also took us completely by surprise.

The National Palace was magnificent: a long, grand whitewashed building with domes and columns with hills rising behind. It was almost unbelievably perfectly white and well maintained, gleaming in the furnace of heat of downtown Port-au-Prince beside the palms of Place Toussaint Louverture. Too pristine. Too perfect. It looked almost as though the building had been transported from another nation altogether, tied by ropes beneath helicopters perhaps and dropped down in the city centre.

Doug and I paced around Place Toussaint Louverture, admiring the setting and recalling the tragic end to the revolutionary's life: Louverture had been tricked by the French into a meeting and then imprisoned in France where he was so poorly fed and watered he died in a roofless cell in 1803, just before the French were sent packing. Yet he had set in motion the revolution in Haiti (then called Saint-Domingue) in the name of *liberté, egalité et fraternité*, much to the displeasure of Napoleon, and is regarded as the father of the nation.

A statue of Louverture holding a sword in one hand and a telescope in another, with a cloak slung over his shoulders, stands in pride of place before the National Palace in the square/park named after him. His look of defiant pride says it all.

On a far corner of Place Toussaint Louverture, artists sold fading paintings of beaches and sunsets lined up against a fence. Doug and I went over to take a look. The artists were both extremely pleased to see "tourists" and extremely disappointed we did not buy anything. I got the impression we were the closest approximation to holidaymakers in Haiti. Yes, there were plenty of other outsiders, but they zoomed about in shiny, brand new Nissan sports utility vehicles marked "UN".

Our guide had been withering in her assessment of these United Nations representatives and their vehicles: "There'll be 6,000 or so troops out here by the end of the year. But they're not doing anything. They've spent a fortune on vehicles – which is very nice for all the rich people here who sell Nissans. But you don't often see them on the streets. They're supposed to be keeping the peace, but people have been shot in front of them and they've done nothing."

Whether this was true or not, it was hard to say. Truth seemed to lie in the possession of whoever happened to speak it in Haiti, as it had been since the time of Greene, Papa Doc and the Tonton Macoute.

The slums of Cité Soleil are not far from the Presidential Palace, which had to be pulled down after an earthquake in 2010 (so Place Toussaint Louverture no longer enjoys what was once its prize possession). These are some of the worst slums anywhere on Earth: a corrugated-roof hellhole without proper sanitation, healthcare, education, electricity or water supplies. Gangs rule the streets, with guns and kidnapping part and parcel of everyday life. Around 400,000 people are crammed in and those few tourists who visit Haiti, usually on swanky cruise ships, go nowhere near it. The closest we came was flying out of Toussaint Louverture International Airport, with the impoverished commune at one end of the runway.

The guide had been very clear on the point when we had left on our stroll: "Do not go!" This time we listened. Besides, it would have been voyeuristic to turn up at Cité Soleil without so much as an invitation from a local. The impoverished commune's existence so close to the pristine palace, however, was yet another reminder of the nine words we had been forbidden to speak.

After one last turn around Place Toussaint Louverture on the way back up the hill to Hotel Oloffson, Doug and I had an encounter. This was nothing to do with being relieved of our wealth and all to do with meeting one of the people upon whom Graham Greene based a character in *The Comedians*.

At an art gallery on Rue Chile, we met Issa el Saieh, a then 85-year-old Haitian-Syrian who Greene turned into Hamit, a Syrian shopkeeper who provides a room for Mr Brown's adulterous affair in his novel. El Saieh's gallery was within an echoing white mansion and we were his only visitors. What did he think about the coup earlier in the year? "Terrible, just terrible: if I was a tourist, I wouldn't bother coming here. I haven't sold anything for months, not that I really give a damn."

In better times, Issa had sold Greene a painting for $50 and become friends: "He was a nice guy, but he could also be a pain in a way. If he didn't like you, you'd better watch out. He'd bad-mouth people."

Issa's art is vivid – realism mixed with abstract works – but he would not mention prices. "I've got one foot in the grave and one on a banana peel," he told Doug as he showed him one picture, "so I only want to sell if you're really interested." When we left, Issa, who shared Greene's quizzical eyes, cried after us: "Make sure you tell tourists to come and see me: I need somebody to lie to!"

Our stroll to Place Toussaint Louverture had taken us into the pages of Greene.

Quite a walk in the park – and we were back before 5 p.m. like good tourists in Port-au-Prince (all in one piece).

"We've got the suite"
Independence Square, Bridgetown, Barbados

Independence Square is a quiet spot in the centre of Bridgetown, the capital of Barbados, the most easterly Caribbean island – and quite different to Cuba and Haiti, which are in turn so dissimilar to one another. Visiting the West Indies can feel at times like entering a series of parallel worlds.

On one side is a statue of Errol Walton Barrow, the country's first prime minister after the country broke free from the colonial control of Britain in 1966. Next to Barrow is a yard with the blue and yellow colours of the Barbadian national flag decorating the surface of the flagstones, a small fountain surrounded by neoclassical columns and scattered palm trees on a lawn.

On crossing a bridge to reach this little corner of green, I made a friend. A skinny man with a whiskery grey beard swayed into view, squinting with watery eyes. He was clutching a brown paper bag with an open bottle protruding. He wanted to impart some information. Using his bottle-free hand in a swiping motion as though flagging down a taxi, he gestured for me to come over.

I followed his instruction. "Best prime minister we ever had," my new friend said, looking dreamily across at the statue of Barrow. He was pointing at the statue to make sure I knew to whom he was referring. We both stared at Barrow for a while. The politician is captured in mid-oratorial flow with one arm raised and the other tucked behind his back, extolling the benefits of freedom from Britain, no doubt.

"Our best PM, oh yes!" he repeated. Then the skinny man winked a glassy-eyed wink, added "Oh yes! Oh yes!" and teetered on his way.

He was heading in the direction of a stone archway on Chamberlain Bridge, which spans River Constitution, a waterway dividing the heart of Bridgetown. This archway commemorates the 21st anniversary of the independence of Barbados and on the far side of the bridge is "Little Big Ben", a replica of the original at Westminster, though less than half the size. Barbados is nicknamed "Little England" because of Britain's close historical associations to the Caribbean island dating back as far as the 1600s. The island's judicial system is based on Britain's, cars drive on the left (that ultimate sign of Britishness), the country is within the Commonwealth and Queen Elizabeth II remains head of state, though moves are afoot to cut all colonial ties by appointing a home-grown political figurehead.

Independence Square is both at the heart of Bridgetown, while also feeling one step removed. Catamarans belonging to some of the

Caribbean's plushest five-star resorts may be moored near Chamberlain Bridge, while across the River Constitution holidaymakers bustle in and out of souvenir stores selling knick-knacks, tobacconists with shelves of cigars and diamond-and-emerald jewellery boutiques pitch at high rollers. Yet Independence Square is usually tourist free, a pocket of normality away from the rum-punch world of the island's many all-inclusive hotels.

This may well come as something of a relief. It did for me. For a week lobster bodies had been getting redder and redder (and bigger) by the day at my all-you-can-eat-and-drink fun-in-the-sun hotel. From your balcony you could watch these fellow guests, who sported a wild array of tattoos, rise periodically and slide into the courtyard pool to cool off. They would not be in for long, just enough to leave an oily trail of sun cream, before padding to the poolside bar to order more "free" cocktails. This was a cycle of behaviour so reliable that you could almost imagine David Attenborough lurking behind one of the palm trees whispering a commentary: ... *and here we can see the early twenty-first-century sunseeker, his body temperature stabilized, gathering daiquiris to return to his resting mate.* The consumption was startling. The lack of desire to do anything else striking. Thousands of Barbadian dollars had been disposed of and thousands of miles flown for a fortnight of sizzling and sozzling, and they were making the most of it, around sunset dancing to reggae on the terrace as the day's accumulated drinks kicked in. They were clearly, to be fair, having a ball.

Independence Square, if you like, offered a holiday from this holiday. No free drinks. No middle-aged Europeans and Americans, slightly unsteady on their feet, increasing their chances of skin cancer while happily overdoing it. None of that. Just a shady spot by the river, where the best thing for it was to find a bench, sit back, breathe in the fresh air away from the main road – and be nosy. Why not? That's part of the appeal of parks, after all, as Obama says so fondly of Central Park back in New York. Stretch out your legs, slip into the rhythm of local life and be nosy, unashamedly nosy for a while as you watch folk pass by.

"Boyfriend! She said she got a boyfriend! Boyfriend!" said a woman in a green top gossiping to a woman in an orange top as they shuffled by my bench. "Boyfriend! Oh! Ha! Ha! Ha!" It was clearly in their opinion highly unlikely indeed that their acquaintance had a boyfriend. Their voices drifted away.

"Trini are hard to get over," said a man to his son in great seriousness. They were talking cricket: the Barbados Tridents were playing Trinidad and Tobago that evening at Kensington Oval in Bridgetown. Cricket is the island's number one sport and taken extremely seriously indeed, the island having produced many of the game's greatest players. "It should be a good one. Tight! Tight! Tight!"

They moved off towards the bridge. A fierce man with a goatee beard strode by and then stopped by the riverfront talking on his mobile. He seemed in the middle of some sort of dispute. "I am sorry but I cannot accommodate you!" he boomed. "Sorry! No! You can't just call and ask that!" He clicked off his phone and paced onward muttering.

Then another man sauntered by, this fellow with a monkey on a leash, smiling to himself as though monkey-walking was quite natural. A local eccentric going for his constitutional by the River Constitution. No one else paid much attention.

Then a younger man in a Michael Jordan basketball shirt passed and stopped to ask my name, to which he replied: "Mr Tommy-man – give me a knock, man!" To which we touched fists in a "fist bump".

He moved on. Before long another younger man sidled up: "My man, my man, you want ganja?" Seeing he did not have a customer, he shrugged and slipped away.

Welcome to park life Barbados-style. In half an hour or so, plenty of people-watching (and listening) is to be had, though no roller-skating dancing divas materialized à la Central Park. At last count, the population of Barbados was 287,000. The feeling at Independence Square is that if you sat there long enough you might meet the lot. The island is a mere 21 miles long and 14 miles wide, after all, and everyone seems to have business in Bridgetown.

Take a tour of Independence Square and chances are you will encounter even more Barbadians. A group of men played cards on an upturned box by one of the other benches. "You wanna join us, man? There's room." I was tempted, it looked a convivial enough way to while away an afternoon, but not knowing the game I declined, almost immediately regretting the decision.

This was because, on the edge of Independence Square you come to a bar with a balcony and a fine view across the square. I entered, with an eye on a free balcony table and with the thought of an ice-cold Banks Beer.

A group of holidaymakers from one of the all-inclusive hotels was at the next-door table (plastic wristbands for the buffet and free-drinks bar being the giveaway). They were Scottish and evidently a few days into their holidays having already turned an eye-catching, almost luminous lobster red. From snippets of conversation, I gathered, they were regular visitors to Barbados, hence their confidence to leave the poolside bar and *drink rum punches somewhere else*; a phenomenon that Attenborough, were he to take up a study of certain holidaymakers in Barbados, might well devote a cutaway segment: ...*now we can see the early twenty-first-century sunseekers as they break from the "nest", seeking new sources of sustenance and exploring the outer reaches of their territory.*

They were talking about coat hangers. "They never have any coat hangers," said one, sounding peevish, to another. By "they" she was referring to the people who ran her hotel. "So, I always have to bring my own," she said, in a tone that suggested: *isn't it so typical.* The way she used the word "they" seemed almost a throwback to colonial days ("white man's burden" in the twenty-first century).

One of her companions expressed sympathy although *she* was not having any coat-hanger issues. "We've got the suite," she said as if by means of explanation. "We've got coat hangers in the suite." She sounded super pleased about this. Her friend took a sip of her pink drink, looking pensive for a while.

One-upmanship of this sort, you soon notice, is common among some of the island's all-inclusive hotel holidaymakers.

Then the woman who brought her own coat hangers turned, gazed briefly and appraisingly at me, swivelled once again with an ashtray in her hand, placed the ashtray on a corner of my table and adjusted her body so she could smoke and flick ash into the ashtray on my table so the smoke would not bother her friends. This, she seemed to consider, was quite OK as I happened to be at a table for four and there was space.

If only I had stuck with the card players down on Independence Square.

Not just Napoleon
Castle Gardens, Jamestown, St Helena

St Helena must be one of the strangest places on the planet, and Jamestown, its capital, is the strangest place on St Helena. Which makes it extremely odd, but in a rather wonderful way.

First there is the setting – of the island itself and of Jamestown within the island. St Helena is part of the British Overseas Territory of 14 former outposts of the British Empire and it is incredibly remote, deep in the South Atlantic about 1,200 miles west of Angola and 2,000 miles east of Brazil. This is so out of the way Napoleon was exiled to St Helena for six years until his death in 1821. Partly due to its inaccessibility the population is tiny: 4,500, with a mere 629 people living in Jamestown.

The island is 10 miles wide and 5 miles long, about half the size of the Isle of Wight, and was settled by the British in the seventeenth century after an earlier tenure by the Portuguese, who had discovered it uninhabited. With the Cape in South Africa held by the Dutch, for many years St Helena's fertile land and fresh water made a key staging post for the East India Company; until the Suez Canal opened in 1869, that is, providing a much quicker route and beginning a decline among the Saints, as locals are known.

Jamestown is squeezed between volcanic slopes rising to 300 metres in a narrow gully occupied by colourful Georgian houses running along

Main Street, Market Street and Napoleon Street (there are not many other streets). To give an idea of its narrowness, the opening to the ocean is about 400 metres wide, with "downtown" jammed into the land beyond a breakwater that leads to a tiny "harbour".

From the oceanfront walking into the gully, you immediately come to a defensive wall with a decorative archway, a small castle (from where British governors run affairs) and a gaunt church next to a miniscule prison, after which Jamestown progressively thins until about a mile later all buildings come to a halt by a waterfall. Seen from the top of Jacob's Ladder, an incredibly steep set of 699 steps rising to the top of the western volcanic slope above town, Jamestown looks like a river of terracotta roofs surrounded by rocky slopes.

Not many tourists make it to St Helena. Until 2018, a visit required a five-day journey on the RMS *St Helena*, a cargo ship with a few berths. This was when an airport, built at huge expense on the flattest land, finally opened after initial unexpected trouble with wind shear.

The attractions for those who do come are many: a dramatic interior of subtropical forests and ravines alive with rare birds; great hiking trails; visits to Napoleon's abode, Longwood House; and snorkelling beside whale sharks. Then there is the history of British involvement explained in a fine museum as well as simply the island's other-worldliness and timelessness. You might be in the 1600s or 1700s on Main Street or the 1800s at Longwood, although the overriding feel across the island is of 1950s Britain: when life was simpler and slower and people stopped to chat and say "good morning".

Oh yes, and St Helena has a lovely little park.

Castle Gardens, next to the castle, is an oasis of green shaded by ancient trees that cast ghostly shadows on a lawn with a fountain. Pink and white flowers cascade from well-maintained beds. Scarlet blooms ignite the branches of an aptly named flamboyant tree. And all the while black-and-yellow streaked mynah birds screech for all they are worth, strutting among the highest branches and generally causing a commotion. The birds were introduced to St Helena to pick ticks off cattle and although the noise is at first distracting, their racket soon becomes almost comforting, the calls rising and falling at certain times of day.

The word "oasis" might seem to be over-egging matters in such a sleepy-sounding place some distance beneath the equator deep in the South Atlantic. Why should an oasis be required, anyway? Isn't the whole place an oasis? Yes, that might seem to make sense, but downtown Jamestown, where so many of the shops, the market, the bars, the harbour and the government buildings are to be found, can be cacophonous. From Monday to Saturday the pavements are almost always jammed with folk nattering away; Saints are inveterate natterers. From across the island, cars roll in at around 9 a.m. – and the nattering begins.

Despite being on such an unpopulated island, it is often tricky to find a parking space in this "metropolis". This does not, however, hold for the governor himself, who has his own spot for his shiny Jaguar. The governor can often be seen striding by Castle Gardens with his ramrod gait, wearing a suit and tie and carrying a battered-looking black leather box containing the island's documents.

Castle Gardens – once part of the island's East India Company gardens (adjoining the site of a former house belonging to a park superintendent, where Napoleon spent his first few nights on St Helena) – is a place to unwind, despite the raucous mynahs. It is also the perfect spot to reflect on St Helena's history, suitably raucous itself, at a bench in the humid shade. Back in the sixteenth and seventeenth centuries Jamestown was a hive of bars, brothels and brawls. After days at sea sailors would let loose, so much so that St Helena's cathedral was built on a hill to be kept away from the bedlam below.

"All those sailors, bars and brothels, it was an awful place," said Basil George, a local historian, who joined me at the gardens one day. Basil was in his early 80s with twinkling eyes, a walnut-crushing handshake and a mischievous streak. He wore a sleeveless jacket with pockets from which he would occasionally dig out a dog-eared document or photo and launch into a vivid story of dastardly bygone days.

"Oh, they were a rough lot all right," he said of his ancestors. "I'll tell you what's what, warts and all."

He began with a dark past. "This island has an awful history of slavery," he said. "Slaves were left in wills as property and they were listed lower than cattle. At one point the slave population outnumbered the settlers."

He paused, fiddled with a pocket as though about to reveal some evidence, appeared perturbed that he could not find what he was looking for, and continued.

"How have we all come to be integrated with a common identity?" he asked rhetorically: descendants of slaves and landowners from the early days, many of whom came to seek new lives after the Great Fire of London in 1666, still live on the island. "It's isolation. We have to rely on each other: that's why!"

Basil had a theory: "Without St Helena, the East India Company would not have thrived. All the wealth that fed into Britain when Britain was booming. This island helped lay the foundations of rule in India. Oh, there's more to St Helena than Napoleon, you know."

In one corner of Castle Gardens is a column known as the Water Witch Monument, dedicated to those who died in the employ of the *Water Witch*, a Royal Naval vessel that was deployed to capture slave ships around St Helena in 1839 after Britain abolished slavery. During this period as many as 30,000 liberated slaves, most from between Sierra Leone and Angola, came to St Helena. The majority were sent as freemen to the Caribbean while some remained on the island. Yet the horrific conditions on board slave ships meant many corpses were found by Royal Naval interception vessels, while others died during rescues, and as many as 9,000 are buried on St Helena. While building a road for the new airport, skeletons were discovered.

A ship's report of one interception made by the *Water Witch* in 1840 offers intriguing insight into their work:

At 3 p.m. on this day chase was given to a suspicious looking Brigantine under the land who then made all sail to gain a small bay, on entering which at 4.30 p.m. she ran on shore under all sail, the crew immediately deserting her by boats. On boarding the said vessel I found a large number of slaves on board, a great many in the water who had attempted to swim on shore but the distance being too great many were drowned in the attempt, some regained the vessel and others were saved by the boats of the *Water Witch*; on mustering the slaves immediately on getting the vessel afloat, there appeared to be 245 left on board of whom five died immediately after taking possession.

St Helena and the waters surrounding the island must have witnessed many such tragic scenes. Upon being discovered and chased by the Royal Navy, some schooners would jettison slaves to lighten loads and hasten escapes. It hardly bears thinking about. Horrific tales from the high seas less than 200 years ago.

Near the Water Witch Monument, by battlements facing the sea, Basil stopped and pointed. "See that archway," he said. There was a small arch in the defensive wall. "When Napoleon came, he went through there."

The former emperor was then marched up (subsequently named) Napoleon Street to be held first at a private house and then at Longwood House, further from the harbour, thus making escape trickier.

Basil and I shook hands, bone-crushingly, and parted. What luck that such local historians exist (even in such remote places).

Then I went to visit Anne's Place, a cafe/bar/restaurant draped with sailing flags within the grounds of Castle Gardens, where I can recommend the chicken curry and where the waitress, a former journalist for Saint FM radio station, will ask, if she sees you taking notes: "I hope you are writing good things about St Helena!"

"Of course," I replied. "Of course."

I needed no prompting. Castle Gardens, so different from West Potomac Park back in Washington DC, is one of my favourite little parks with its ghostly ancient trees, screeching mynah birds and sense of being *a long way from anywhere* – and Anne's Place is one of my favourite little park cafe/bar/restaurants, too.

Deep in an ocean so far from home, the volcanic slopes rising and a breeze sweeping up from the sea along the lane, Napoleon, disgraced and dispatched, once trod.

CHAPTER SEVEN

SOUTH AFRICA, SUDAN, ZANZIBAR, THE SEYCHELLES: AFRICAN DREAMS

EGYPT

Khartoum

SUDAN

CHAD

SOUTH
SUDAN

ETHIOPIA

KENYA

THE
SEYCHELLES

Stone Town,
Zanzibar

Mahé

TANZANIA

SOUTH
AFRICA

Cape Town

To another continent, to more great parks. Ground was really being covered now, great tracts of the planet traversed. I looked at the big, dusty land mass ahead on my study globe, coolly considering its park potential like a seasoned "park dreamer". Where had I been? Oh yes: there, there and there. Which cities… which parks? And soon I was off on another series of mini-odysseys, imagining being somewhere far away while stuck in the middle of what had become a global lockdown. Hardly anyone, anywhere could by this point legally travel abroad – aside from government officials, epidemiologists and pharmaceutical CEOs – no matter what country they happened to live in. And even when rules were relaxed in the UK, optimistically for short periods between lockdowns, airlines had long ago cancelled most flights and, anyway, people were wary of the need for endless Covid tests and quarantines as well as fearful of last-minute regulation changes preventing trips and necessitating painfully lengthy refund claims. Unless you were extremely determined, and preferably in possession of a private jet, travel overseas of any sort was off.

So "visiting" Africa had an almost illicit allure. It also began, mainly because of my first African park, to get me thinking about parks and walking. Which seemed a rich seam of "park thought". After all, Richmond Park to me was not just a wonderful park because of everything in it and its interesting history, but also because I enjoyed walking around everything in it while thinking about its interesting history.

What did the great thinkers and writers have to say on the matter? I looked up a few, starting with an "ancient". Hippocrates is reported to have been of the opinion that "walking is man's best medicine". A touch sexist, perhaps, although to be fair to Hippocrates, some now believe he never even said this in the first place (hence the use of "reported"). Whatever. I liked the "best medicine" take: parks do have medicinal qualities, especially in the depths of a lockdown, when we were all in need of a bit of soothing. Meanwhile, the German writer Thomas Mann believed that "thoughts come clearly when one walks". With which I could only agree; walking has always, in my experience, seemed to shuffle ideas into order. Yet another German, the philosopher Friedrich Nietzsche, went a step further, declaring that "all great thoughts are conceived while walking". I wouldn't perhaps go that far: I've had a few in the shower (and the pub). But I got where he was coming from.

Virginia Woolf revelled in the "delight and wonder" that walking offers, allowing her to step into the minds of passers-by as though becoming, if only momentarily, another person. Which was an insightful way of looking at it, and perhaps another way of saying "being nosy". Woolf also believed that "to walk alone in London is the greatest rest". I got this too, although I tend (not always) to enjoy company. And finally, the great writer and walker Charles Dickens, taking a slightly melodramatic slant, once opined: "If I could not walk far and fast, I think I should just explode and perish."

I particularly liked this last one: it fit the lockdown mood.

Anyway, I was thinking about the nature of parks a bit more and what we do in them. With such ideas percolating, from St Helena my feet were to lead onward to one of the great parks, sights and walks in Africa before zooming up to a little-visited country to the north-east (Sudan), dipping down to a small island with an astonishingly rich history (Zanzibar) and travelling 1,000 miles east into the Indian Ocean to the Seychelles, home to some of the finest beaches on Earth. Many more park stories lay ahead and, at risk of repetition, the days of former "masters" from European countries were to come to the fore once more. Visiting parks around the world and delving beneath the surface a little, you cannot avoid that… and nor would I want to. It was about time all of us in the West faced up to the history of the past few hundred years, as an old newspaper colleague of mine, Sathnam Sanghera, had just written in his excellent, partially lockdown-written book *Empireland: How Imperialism Has Shaped Modern Britain*. Not just Britain, of course, plenty of other nations too. Although Britain was to figure in some of this chapter's parks, one way or another.

"Beacon of hope"
Table Mountain National Park, Cape Town, South Africa

Impossible to miss, impossible not to admire, impossible not to gaze upon in wonder, Table Mountain is simply captivating.

It is also eminently walkable. Trails snake up through the jagged contours of the sandstone mountain, so named for being famously shaped like a table and often covered by a "tablecloth" of clouds that spill over the edge and ooze prettily down the slopes.

On other, clearer days the gargantuan silhouette takes on the appearance of a slumbering giant with its face up to the heavens, eyes closed in the bulbous "head" at the ocean end as though in disapproval of the five-star hotels, bars and shops, shops, shops of the Victoria & Alfred Waterfront marina below.

On the very best days, at dawn or dusk, the cliffs blaze with golden colours and the whole mountain looks like a promised land.

Table Mountain National Park dates from 1998, although nature reserves of various names have been given to the mountain and its environs since the 1930s. It is vast: 85 square miles stretching as far as the Cape of Good Hope, Africa's most south-westerly point. Within the park's boundaries is part of the wider fynbos region of endangered flora and fauna that includes more than 8,500 plant species, most of which are found nowhere else. On Table Mountain alone 2,200 species exist, more than in the entire UK.

So, Table Mountain National Park is not really an "urban park" taken as a whole. But the bit above Cape Town feels like one, the top of the mountain at 1,084 metres, usually accessed by a rotating cable car, with fine views across the city to the ocean beyond and waves breaking on Robben Island, where freedom fighter Nelson Mandela was held for 18 of his 27 years in captivity.

We shunned the cable car and decided to hike up.

"We" in this instance being myself and a motley assortment of noisy English cricket fans known as the "Barmy Army". They were in

Cape Town to watch a Test match against South Africa being held over the New Year and I was writing about them for a paper.

One of the "rules" of this "army" was that everyone seemed to require a nickname. So there were the "Captain" (their leader), "Bagpuss", "Whispers", "Sade", "Kiddy", "Duty Free", "Slackers" and "Dopey Barrie". Each nickname had a justification: "Sade" was considered a "smooth operator" with women after the soul song of the same name by Sade, "Kiddy" was from Kidderminster, while "Dopey Barrie" was simply dopey. My nickname, rather uncharitably, was "Sunday Sport" even though I was writing for another paper.

As you might imagine, we made quite a spectacle ascending Table Mountain. As you also might imagine, there was not much interest in the variety of fynbos plant species. Quite a few routes are possible, but we had selected the easiest, naturally, following a sign marked "Contour Path/Platteklip Gorge".

In 1503, the first recorded ascent of the mountain was made at this gorge by the Portuguese captain Antonio de Saldanha, the earliest European to set foot on the land that was to become Cape Town. Now the city is home to 4 million people, most living in sprawling government-built neighbourhoods on the outskirts of the centre dating from the Apartheid era of racial segregation from 1948 to the early 1990s. Mandela's release in 1990, of course, acted as a catalyst for change to democracy.

One of the reasons for Saldanha's ascent was simply that he had become lost, as his ship had been on numerous occasions already skirting Africa's west coast on the way to Cochin in India, his eventual destination. He was hoping to locate Cape Point by the Cape of Good Hope, a rendezvous spot for his and two other Portuguese ships. He did so. And after naming his conquest "Table Mountain" and scouring a great cross in part of a rock formation close to Table Mountain known as Lion's Head, Saldanha scampered down and went on his way.

Not that there was much concern among the Barmy Army about any of this, either. What was most pressing in their minds was *getting up*. Members of the Barmy Army are not, usually, early risers, especially while

Portrait of John Lewis, eighteenth-century Richmond Park hero, by T. Stewart, a pupil of Joshua Reynolds, at the Old Town Hall in Richmond, south-west London

Tribute to John Lewis at Sheen Gate, Richmond Park, London

Red deer at Richmond Park, London

Shinobazu Pond, Ueno Park in Tokyo, Japan

Moranbong Park in Pyongyang, North Korea

View across the River Taedong from Moranbong Park in Pyongyang, North Korea

Ming Tombs Scenic Area in Beijing, China

Independence Palace by Tao Dan Park, Ho Chi Minh City, Vietnam

Royal Botanic Garden, to the left of the Sydney Opera House, from across Sydney Harbour, Australia

View from Monserrate in Bogotá, Colombia

Statue of the Virgin Mary in Quito, Ecuador

Central Park in New York City, United States

View from the Lincoln Memorial in West Potomac Park in Washington DC, United States

Parque Central in Havana, Cuba, taken from the steps of El Capitolio

National Palace (prior to the earthquake in 2010) by Place Toussaint Louverture in Port-au-Prince, Haiti

Castle Gardens, Jamestown, St Helena

Meeting of the White and Blue Nile rivers by the Al Mogran Family Park in Khartoum, Sudan

Independence Arch by Independence Square in Bridgetown, Barbados

Cable car station to the top of Table Mountain in Table Mountain National Park, Cape Town, South Africa

Seyyid Said bin Sultan, picture in the House of Wonders, Forodhani Gardens, Stone Town, Zanzibar, Tanzania

Forodhani Gardens in Stone Town, Zanzibar, Tanzania

Coco de mer tree in the National Botanical Gardens in Mahé, Seychelles

Resting on jolies *(public chairs), by Hiyfaseyha Maidhaan park in Malé, the Maldives*

Abhayagiri Stupa in Anuradhapura, Sri Lanka

Rhino at Chitwan National Park in Nepal

View from Rani Jhansi Park in Shimla, India

Cargo ship passing the French Garden at Suez in Egypt

Statue commemorating Israeli settlement at Umm Rashrash park in Eilat, Israel

Seahorse Fountain at Green Square/
Martyrs' Square in Tripoli, Libya

The Aghlabid Basins in
Kairouan, Tunisia

The Panathenaic Stadium
by the National Garden
in Athens, Greece

Mount Srd overlooking Dubrovnik, Croatia

Ferris wheel at Prater
in Vienna, Austria

Schleusenkrug beer hall on the edge
of Tiergarten in Berlin, Germany

Apartments facing Victory Park in Minsk, Belarus

Palace on the Isle in Łazienki Park in Warsaw, Poland

Frédéric Chopin statue in Łazienki Park in Warsaw, Poland

Author on a pedalo on the River Limmat by Quaianlagen in Zurich, Switzerland

Jardin Darcy in Dijon, France

Hotel room facing Oosterpark in Amsterdam, the Netherlands

Jardín del Turia in Valencia, Spain

The city's coat of arms fashioned out of plants at Jardín del Turia, Valencia, Spain

Chinese pagoda at Victoria Park in east London

Sign for a pub at Victoria Park, London

Dog statue, Victoria Park, London

Author next to the lake, Victoria Park, London

"on tour" and with no cricket play that day. Our ascent was in the full heat of the day, a faint breeze off the ocean providing a smidgeon of respite. The usual time taken to hike up is about 2–3 hours. We made our way along a dusty zig-zagging track surrounded by boulders and unidentified endemic plant species, with cliffs soaring above. Sometimes the track simply comprised higgledy-piggledy boulders, where each step up felt like ascending a broken escalator. Often the steps were larger than that.

Soon our "regiment" was well dispersed, smokers and the more hungover lagging way behind. "Sade" and I were the first to the summit by a good half an hour, enjoying perhaps the finest view of any city park anywhere. Better even than Sydney's Royal Botanic Garden.

Below, Cape Town looked like a Persian carpet laid down neatly to fit the contours of the coast. The "carpet" was coloured faint pink (rooftops) and white (apartments) with swirls of green (trees), edged along the coast by a wavy line of vivid white (breaking waves), the "carpet tassels", if you like. A smoky cloud clung to the cliff directly below, where contemplative brown pigeons with peculiarly long necks stood on ledges regarding the vista like avian holidaymakers about to pop down on the cable car and continue on a mini-bus tour of the wine region. Conveniently, the smoky cloud was so tight to the cliff face you could see far beyond Robben Island in one direction and towards the Cape of Good Hope in the other. The ocean was as still as a bathtub, the curve of the Earth traced on the horizon.

What a view! As if to cap off the glory of it all, a tame-looking fluffy brown creature with adorable hazel eyes, similar to a guinea pig, joined us. This was a dassie (or rock hyrax), a regular near the cable car restaurant and a distant relative of the elephant even if they look like rodents. In millennia gone by, a hyrax the size of a horse once existed. In recent years, however, since my Barmy Army ascent, the numbers have fallen away badly on Table Mountain and no one is quite sure why.

This is a park of all parks: 2,200-plus species of plants including bright spiky petalled proteas, bugle lilies (tall, thin plants with clusters of orange and white flowers) and *Disa uniflora* (crimson orchids also known as

Pride of Table Mountain); mind-boggling seascapes; its own weather system; awesome sandstone cliffs; even cute little creatures related to elephants hopping about all over the place.

Yet the enjoyment is somehow enhanced if you hike up like Saldanha, the very first tourist all those years ago, rather than take the cable car. For a start, there is the sense of achievement: you have earned some satisfaction. But there is more to it than that. Climbing the boulders seems to empty the mind of small things. At least it did for us. Two nights earlier some of us (including me) had had possessions stolen from our rooms in our basic student digs and all of us had been moved to an apartment subsequently found to be rat infested and home to a brothel. This was our "upgrade". This was also touring Barmy Army-style.

But at the top of Table Mountain after a hike, who cared?

As Hippocrates had supposedly said, walking is usually the "best medicine". And as Thomas Mann had said, too, "thoughts come freely when one walks".

In this instance: thoughts about Cape Town. From above, Cape Town looks carefree and as picturesque as any city anywhere. Below is a riviera to equal any riviera, sun-kissed and blessed by the glories of nature. You peer down and think: *What a heavenly place to live.*

Yet you know only too well that on the other side of Table Mountain it's not quite like that. Each day in Cape Town a glance at almost any issue of *The Cape Times* revealed stories of the infamous gang-ridden neighbourhoods of the inland Cape Flats where theft and murders were rife, drug abuse widespread, fear a part of daily life and water shortages and power cuts commonplace. Each day horrors and hardships were reported, sometimes as tiny items. Sure, there was plenty of cricket news. Plenty of much else as well.

So the view from Table Mountain seems to tell two stories. Yes, there it is: the perfect tourist world straight ahead of the V&A Waterfront, the penthouses, the five-star hotels and the beachside clubs. This was the world into which the cricket fan was delivered, whether a Panama hat-wearing member of the Marylebone Cricket Club or a baseball cap-wearing Barmy Army supporter. Yet also, however, there is the *other side* of poverty and crime so many years on from Apartheid – the racist regime and legacy of colonial times evolving from British and Dutch rule.

On the top of Table Mountain you cannot help but have another thought, too.

What must it have been like for Mandela to gaze across at this magnificent mountain for close to 20 years in his prison cell out at sea?

The answer to this is known. On his release, Mandela said: "To us on Robben Island, Table Mountain was a beacon of hope. It represented the mainland to which we knew we would return one day."

Table Mountain and its park – so glorious, so naturally wondrous – seem somehow to represent so much.

By a big river
Al Mogran Family Park, Khartoum, Sudan

The Grand Holiday Villa Hotel in Khartoum had some grand claims and an unusual take on "royalty". It was, according to its promotional buff, where "royal visitors of the past" had included Queen Victoria, Thomas Cook and Winston Churchill. Safe in the knowledge of such a calibre of former guests, new guests could be assured of "five-star conveniences" including a barber's shop, a billiard room, a steam bath and two pools (male and female). Sudan is an Islamic country, hence the bathing division and why the list of royal-standard facilities did not include a bar.

While Queen Victoria never ventured out of Europe and Cook and Churchill may not quite count as "royals", it is possible at least that the latter two stayed.

Churchill visited Khartoum on a tour of Africa in 1907, when the hotel existed, nine years after taking part in the Battle of Omdurman during which the British defeated local forces using machine guns in a bloody conflict that saw 12,000 Muslim warriors armed with spears and swords killed. Now, just over a century on, the Grand Holiday Villa Hotel is home to a Churchill Ballroom next to its sumptuous marble reception with its brass chandeliers and tiger-print armchairs. Deeds on the battlefield put to one side.

I mention all of this as it was here that I met Mr A, who was about to take me to a very interesting park. He was middle aged, wearing shades, a pristine white polo shirt and an enormous diver's watch. He was to be my guide for the day and he looked nervous. This was because he had seen me talking to a hotel manager while jotting notes. Mr A whisked me to his car, saying: "The government does not like journalists. They check in at the hotels. It's not a big deal, but try to avoid problems by saying you work for the tour operator."

At the time of my visit in 2017, Sudan had been ruled since 1989 by a dictator, President Omar al-Bashir, whose "elections" were widely deemed rigged and who was wanted by the International Criminal Court on charges of genocide and war crimes.* A long-running tribal conflict in Darfur, a region in the west of the country, had seen 2.5 million people displaced and 300,000 killed. Meanwhile, in 2011, after a bitter struggle, the independent state of South Sudan had become the world's then youngest country. The ongoing civil war had seen 4 million people displaced and 400,000 deaths. The division of Sudan and South Sudan had been the result of religious differences: the south being mainly Christian and animist, while Sudan is 97 per cent Islamic.

Not exactly your average holiday destination, you might say, although the Foreign Office had given the thumbs up to go to Khartoum, the capital, and to visit the pyramids and other antiquities in the north-east.

---

* President al-Bashir was deposed in a coup d'etat in 2019 and convicted for corruption in Sudan. At the time of writing, the International Criminal Court is pushing for him to stand trial in The Hague.

Mr A slid the gear of his Toyota Land Cruiser into first and we purred away along the banks of the Blue Nile passing the hideous bulbous tower block of the Corinthia Hotel.

"People call it Gaddafi's Egg," said Mr A, explaining that the hotel had been financed by Libya when Colonel Gaddafi was in charge.

Just beyond Gaddafi's Egg, Mr A turned right and pulled into the deserted car park of the Al Mogran Family Park.

The park was closed. The metal main gate was padlocked and a guard sat in the shade of a tree smoking a cigarette. Mr A approached and spoke some words of Arabic, his hand meeting the guard's momentarily.

He returned, grinning; his edginess gone now we were away from the hotel. "This is the key to the confluence," Mr A said triumphantly, holding up a key on a keyring with a long leather strap.

He opened a creaky gate and we were in, crossing dusty lots with empty children's playgrounds and a Ferris wheel. Nearby were rows of shuttered stalls, beyond which we walked beneath acacia trees to the point where the Blue and the White Nile rivers meet, the two main tributaries to the Nile, the world's longest river.

"This park is now abandoned," said Mr A. "For more than one year now: abandoned. It was ceased for maintenance. That is what is being said. Maybe the land is being sold. Something hidden is happening."

Was it usual to offer a bribe to get into Al Mogran Family Park? "Yes, I did this many times in the last year," he replied. "There is a military compound on the other side. They don't want people to come here as someone could shoot accurately from this position. The parliament also is over there."

He pointed vaguely towards the city centre. We had almost reached the end of the park, where a rusty gate opened to the confluence of the rivers. "Remember, look like a tourist," he said as we went through; this was just in case any binoculars were trained on us. "There is a big phobia of journalists, especially because of Darfur and the International Criminal Court."

The Blue Nile originates in Ethiopia and the White Nile begins in a spring in Rwanda, before entering Lake Victoria and flowing

4,130 miles to the Mediterranean Sea. What is remarkable at Al Mogran Family Park is that the tributaries live up to their names: the Ethiopian water is indeed an inky-blue while the water from Lake Victoria is a milky coffee colour. Where the two meet a water battle of sorts goes on in the form of eddies and currents. The White Nile seems to win this fight, mainly because the clearer-looking waters of the Blue Nile are inevitably compromised by its muddier flow.

Across the swirling water, several hundred metres wide here, the minaret and dome of the Al-Nilin Mosque rises. In the foreground is an unoccupied island covered in reeds. A few fishing boats are usually bobbing about, while a murmur of traffic floats across the water from a metal-framed bridge crossing the White Nile in the direction of Omdurman. Not much else was going on.

What is extraordinary is how unsung it all is. Ahead, the rivers meet to form the mighty Nile, yet there we were on a mudbank at the end of a path overgrown with weeds. An empty chair stood in a patch of shade beneath an acacia tree, presumably belonging to another guard. A discarded car bumper was heaped by a crumbling wall, perhaps deposited during a high river. A shuttered Coca-Cola cafe with a ripped awning and vegetation overgrowing the old fridges looked forlorn and forgotten.

Al Mogran Family Park is eerie in its solitude, uplifting for the magnificence of its location and almost mythical when you consider the importance of the Nile to the ancient Egyptians.

Waters flowing from here kept the pharaohs in business 5,000 years ago, the flooded plains bringing the irrigation of crops and the abundance upon which a whole civilization grew. Off the proceeds the pharaohs and their queens smothered themselves in gold to indicate wealth in life and impress the gods in their tombs. Hieroglyphics were invented. Great temples to the deities arose: Isis, Horus, Osiris, Amun, Ra. So did the pyramids. So did the mysterious Sphinx.

It was at the confluence overlooked by what is now the Al Mogran Family Park that the Scottish explorer James Bruce's heart sank back in 1772. Bruce had believed he had discovered the elusive source of the Nile at Lake Tana in Ethiopia and he had followed the Blue Nile northward to Khartoum where he encountered the White Nile. At a stroke his hopes were dashed and it was to be a century before the source of the White Nile was discovered.

Most likely, Churchill would have come to this spot on his 1907 visit. During that trip, he had been impressed by the "steady and remarkable progress" of British colonial rule since the Battle of Omdurman, which included the construction of a railway between Khartoum and Cairo.

Churchill's thoughts during that trip must also have been on the events of the so-recent conflict. The Battle of Omdurman had been prompted by the decapitation of the Victorian war hero Charles Gordon, whose fort in Khartoum was sacked in 1885 after Gordon had decided to take charge of Sudan under the name of the British rather than simply evacuate after coming under attack (his orders from London). Nevertheless, his death sickened Victorian Britain, with Queen Victoria herself furious that backup troops had not arrived in time.

The 1898 assault was revenge and it had been a bloodbath, although Churchill had not fired the machine guns. Instead, he was in the heart of the action on a cavalry charge during which he killed four men at close range using a pistol. One of his shots was taken so close that his gun struck the enemy soldier. At the end of the battle where the cavalry charge had taken place, men of both sides lay all around bleeding from terrible wounds with faces slashed to ribbons and spears through torsos.

Yet during the Battle of Omdurman a total of 48 of the British/ Egyptian force had died compared with 12,000 Sudanese, as mentioned previously. General Kitchener, in charge, described the result as "a good dusting".

After this, it was not until 1956 that the British granted the Sudanese independence.

Mr A and I walked back though Al Mogran Family Park, handed back the key and returned to the Grand Holiday Villa Hotel.

From my balcony that evening, I watched the Blue Nile flow to the confluence so close by. What a location. What a long way still to the sea.

Bohemian rhapsody (of green)
Forodhani Gardens, Stone Town, Zanzibar, Tanzania

When Freddie Mercury was a boy he would have played beneath the mango trees and palms in Forodhani Gardens, with Indian Ocean waves lapping on the shore and Africa looming on the horizon across the glittering sea.

Until the age of eight, Mercury, born Farrokh Bulsara and destined to become the flamboyant frontman of the rock group Queen, was raised close by amid the labyrinthine lanes of Stone Town, the old part of Zanzibar's capital. His Zoroastrian Parsee parents had emigrated from India and his father, Bomi, worked as a civil servant for the British at the prominent House of Wonders facing Forodhani Gardens.

This office lives up to its name: a mad-looking whitewashed building with cast-iron columns, high ceilings, verandas and a bell tower. All built in 1883 for the Sultan of Zanzibar, who wanted to show off his wealth. The "wonders" included the island's first electric lights as well as East Africa's first lift, designed by a British engineer.

Mercury was sent to boarding school in India though he returned aged 17 to finish his schooling in 1963 when Zanzibar gained independence from Britain. However, just a year later, political upheaval saw the ruling sultan overturned. The Bulsaras fled to England, settling in Middlesex where Mercury went to Ealing College to study graphics and met his fellow members of Queen. He never went back.

Yet images of Stone Town and Forodhani Gardens must have been ingrained in the musician's imagination. It is such an evocative setting. On one side, the high damp walls and fortifications of the Old Fort built by Omani Arabs after the Portuguese were expelled in 1699. Next door, the House of Wonders lit up at night and brimming with chandeliers, grandfather clocks and gilded portraits of sultans. Across the way, the mouldering facade of another old palace, now a museum with arabesque battlements.

Throw in the curve of a sandy beach lined by palm trees, the fishing dhows rocking gently in the bay, the hidden archways into alleys leading who knows where, the ancient teak doors studded with spikes – and it all makes a heady mix. The spikes on these doors once prevented damage by passing elephants transporting both people and goods. In 1295, Marco Polo wrote that Zanzibar had "elephants in plenty" (although there are none now). The enormous entrance to the House of Wonders, it is said, was constructed so the sultan could ride an elephant through his front door.

For Stone Town had once been the trading capital of Africa's east coast, rising to its pinnacle during the rule of the powerful Seyyid Said bin Sultan of Oman in the early nineteenth century. Tiny Zanzibar, 35 miles long and 12 miles wide, was known as the "metropolis of East Africa" back then and Forodhani Gardens was the home to rambling customs sheds full of spices to be bagged up and shipped across the globe. Cloves were the biggest export. Zanzibar and the other islands in its archipelago, comprising around 50 in total with Pemba, Unguja, Latham and Mafia the principal among them, were collectively known as the Spice Islands.

Other trades went on too: ivory and slaves. Both were big business. British involvement had grown steadily in the region in the nineteenth century – with pressure put on the sultanates to end slavery – and when Zanzibar was made a British protectorate in 1890, effectively adding the island to the British Empire, Royal Navy ships were already patrolling the waters of the archipelago in search of slave dhows.

For Mercury, Ealing must have come as quite a culture shock.

Walking round Forodhani Gardens does not take long. It is a pleasant little well-kept park with gardeners usually hard at work mowing lawns or tending potted plants. On my visit, the park was home to an assortment of cats that prowled near the Coca-Cola cafe by a jetty during the day and switched allegiance at around 6 p.m. to another area with food stalls open in the evenings. Everything was neat and tidy, not a single piece of litter. A small sign said that the gardens were gifted US$2 million by the Aga Khan Trust for Culture. Evidence of this splurge was all about.

A high flagpole had been installed at the opposite end at the food stalls. From this the blue, black and green flag of Zanzibar fluttered in a soft breeze. Zanzibar is a semi-autonomous part of Tanzania and has its own slightly different flag to the mainland 25 miles away (as well as its own religion in Islam, while the mainland is principally Christian). A road runs along the top of the gardens and now and then a vehicle playing boom-boom music would pass by with "LOVER BOYZZZ" painted on the window or the name of the driver's favourite Premier League football team: Chelsea and Arsenal well represented.

My guidebook had warned of *papaasi,* untrained fast-talking guides who hustle visitors into buying souvenirs or excursions, some being "outright crooks" involved in crime and drug dealing. *Papaasi* translates as "ticks" or "parasites". Perhaps they were waiting for richer pickings than me, though, as I never saw any.

Forodhani became a park in 1936 to commemorate the rule of Sultan Khalifa, with a domed bandstand built in the middle. This is a popular spot where locals hang out, some lying out enjoying a snooze, others cross-legged fingering worry beads. Across a lawn is a concrete archway built in honour of the arrival of Princess Margaret in 1956 (so said another small sign). It is a perfect place for a pause after sightseeing.

Forodhani as a whole is delightfully restful and the temptation is to take a nap, just lie down in the shade like the others and drift away for a while… perhaps imagining the bygone days of Victorian explorers of Africa.

Because Zanzibar was the epicentre of so much of that.

The discovery of the confluence of the Blue and White Niles in Khartoum by James Bruce back in 1772 had set off a frenzy of curiosity and wanderlust. Where was the source of the mighty river? Where?!

The Royal Geographical Society and others in London wanted to know. Grants were dished out and the explorers set forth, coming to Stone Town for the convenience of the location as a stepping stone for launching into the interior. A house by the beach by Forodhani bears a circular plaque: "This building was the British Consulate from 1841–74. Here at different times lived Speke, Burton, Grant and King. David Livingstone stayed here and in this house his body rested on its long journey home."

And it is from Forodhani, that one of the most unusual tales in the history of British exploration unfolded.

In 1858, the British explorer John Speke arrived in Zanzibar in the company of swashbuckling fellow countryman Richard Burton. They spent six months organizing a caravan of 130 men and 30 animals to see them to the source – Burton learning Swahili during this period – and sailed across from Stone Town. Sometime afterward, however, Burton fell ill with malaria. Speke decided to push on, leaving Burton to recover. And it was not long before he came upon a large lake, which he named Lake Victoria. He had done it! At least he imagined so. Speke felt sure this was the source of the White Nile, although he had no proof of a river flowing off the lake.

He returned to the ailing Burton and they discussed the matter. The pair agreed it was still not absolutely certain that Lake Victoria was the source. They departed together by ship to Britain, but Burton's health waned and he was dropped off at Aden in Yemen for further recuperation.

Speke, promising Burton he would not claim to have found the Nile's source, returned to Britain leaving Burton to recuperate. On arrival in London, however, Speke changed his mind and put it about that the source had been discovered. He was championed by the Royal Geographical Society, which funded another trip and Speke selected a different exploring partner (he had never really got on with Burton). They were soon off, missing Burton's return altogether.

Burton, of course, was furious and when their paths eventually did meet, with Speke having failed once again to establish conclusively the Nile's source, temperatures rose and a debate between the pair in Bath was scheduled to settle the matter. Tickets were sold out, the showdown eagerly anticipated.

Then came a further twist. The very day before the debate, Speke was killed in a hunting accident. He had managed to shoot himself while climbing a wall; many believed he had committed suicide knowing that he had been in the wrong. The announcement of his grim death was made at the hall where the debate was about to begin.

It does not end there. The debate's adjudicator, a Scottish physician and explorer named David Livingstone, was then sent off to Africa – via Stone Town – to resolve the issue for himself. But he soon lost his way, so much so that nothing was heard of him whatsoever for six years.

His disappearance was a big mystery of the times. Where on earth was he? *The New York Herald* sent a reporter to find out. So it was that Welsh-American journalist/explorer Henry Morton Stanley discovered the long-lost Scot settled in a remote village, greeting him with: "Dr Livingstone, I presume?" Then Stanley and Livingstone went on together to prove Lake Victoria was the source of the White Nile. Job done and dusted, finally! Although Livingstone died soon after.

There is a Swahili saying that goes: "The patient man will eat ripe fruit."

Well, Livingstone, with the help of Stanley, had (eventually) lived up to that.

All beginning from Stone Town and Forodhani Gardens.

Close your eyes on a bench by the bandstand – Mercury's first stage? – and the past comes flooding back.

"Sexy seeds"
National Botanical Gardens, Mahé, the Seychelles

It is possible to spend an entire visit to the Seychelles beside a private plunge pool in a private villa bothered only by the arrival of your private "butler" on an electric golf buggy delivering room-service meals.

The Indian Ocean archipelago of 115 islands suits seclusion and escapism, geared as it is toward honeymoons, anniversary celebrations and weddings. Celebrities, billionaires and royals seeking to shake off the attentions of paparazzi flock to the upmarket resorts and spend, spend, spend. On a visit to North Island, the Duke and Duchess of Cambridge are believed to have forked out £9,000 a night for a villa with a four-poster bed, pool and access to a remote strip of white sand beach.

Given that the GDP per capita in the Seychelles is £12,700, this is (more than) quite a lot. Yet this is the highest GDP per capita in the whole of Africa (the islands, despite being so far away, are granite remnants that drifted from the continent 200 million years ago). Because the population is so low, at 97,000, and because there is at least some trickle down of cash from wealthy visitors, the standard of living is higher than on mainland Africa.

Based on my visit, not many tourists, however, go to the Seychelles National Botanical Gardens on the edge of Victoria, the capital city on the main island of Mahé. All those private villa-dwelling millionaires with their plunge pools and occasional trips to the spa – anyone for "anti-ageing full-body caviar massages"? (£475 a pop) – are missing out.

The gardens are a treat, like entering a perfectly arranged jungle. Beyond a green metal fence, you find yourself immediately ensconced in a tropical heaven of palm trees, shrubs and exotic flowers, each species carefully name tagged. Lawns lead to lily ponds sprinkled with purple-and-white blooms and little aquatic plants that look like banana trees. Silvery dragonflies dart about here and there; little bright flashes in the equatorial light.

Cacti with tennis racket-shaped appendages and aloe vera grow in clusters by granite boulders that seem to tumble out of the landscape just about everywhere in the archipelago. Endemic screw-pines with roots fanning out like hideaways built by cub scouts arise, thick with plumes of spiky fronds and large cones. All around, beds of pink and yellow shrubs spread out beneath the canopies. Nutmeg, allspice and cinnamon trees fill any gaps, completing the perfection of this little jungle idyll.

The highlight of the Seychelles National Botanical Gardens, however, is the country's endemic palm trees, of which the Seychelles has six varieties – each with a story to tell.

You soon learn *a lot* about Seychellois palm trees at the Seychelles National Botanical Gardens. It is safe to say you will never afterward gaze upon palms on the island, or anywhere for that matter, merely thinking: *There's a palm tree.*

The showstopper, if a palm tree can be referred to as such, is the coco de mer, billed on a gushing information panel as: "Giant of the plant world. A sexy seed. A sexy male inflorescence. Is it any wonder that humans have woven myths around this palm?"

You may well wonder what on earth all this is about. I did. It transpires that within the husk of the fruit of the coco de mer the largest seed in the world exists, weighing as much as 18 kilograms. Not only is it the largest seed in the world, it is also shaped, as some botanists describe, "like the hips of a woman". The name coco de mer comes from the seeds (or nuts) of the plant being washed ashore as far away as Sri Lanka and India, where people once believed the giant seeds came from the depths of the ocean.

The reason for this was that husks from beachside palms had tumbled into the sea and sunk to the ocean floor. Eventually these husks would deteriorate, allowing the suggestive seed, filled with fermented gas, to break free and rise to the surface. Mariners who witnessed this believed the seeds were from a forest deep beneath the waves. Word got around that they had healing and aphrodisiacal powers, and those lucky enough to find the seeds on distant shores soon discovered their sell-on value was enormous. The Holy Roman Emperor Rudolf II paid 4,000 gold florins for his.

To add to this intrigue, the species has a male tree and a female tree, with the male tree's flower producing large amounts of pollen on long, phallic-looking stems to ensure the female blooms are pollinated. All other palms on the Seychelles are hermaphroditic with the male and female reproductive organs on the same plant. Another ancient myth is that the coco de mer physically mate on stormy nights, although anyone who witnesses this will go blind. The trees can grow to 30 metres, live to 1,000 years old and are quite beautiful, especially the female version with its clumps of bulbous fruit.

In short, it is quite a palm tree.

Yet this is just one of the six endemic palm trees of the Seychellois archipelago.

Then you have the Seychellois thief palm. This palm has 2-metre-long, orange-rimmed leaves that collect water in pockets where geckos reside. The fruit is orange-red and tiny, so you may safely walk beneath, unlike with the coco de mer's female tree. A sample of a thief palm was transported to the Palm House of the Royal Botanic Gardens at Kew in London in the nineteenth century, whereupon the palm was stolen in 1857. Hence the name.

Meanwhile, there is the Rocheria palm, with wide, deep-green flamboyantly drooping leaves that look like brush strokes on a painting. The palm is named in memory of Albrecht Rocher, a young German explorer who set off from Zanzibar in 1859 to investigate the interior and, like so many others, discover the source of the Nile. After joining an Arab slave caravan and reaching Lake Malawi he was tragically murdered at the age of 24, possibly because the slave traders believed he would inform on their activities.

Another palm, the cabbage palm, has the scientific name: *Deckenia nobilis*. This 40-metre specimen is named after yet another German explorer, Baron Karl Klaus von der Decken, no less: the first European to attempt to climb Kilimanjaro, although he only made it 4,300 metres up the 6,000-metre mountain. He also died young in horrific circumstances, murdered in Somalia aged 32 on a remote stretch of the Jubba River. There seems once to have been a fad to name Seychellois palm trees after stricken German explorers.

The two final endemic palm trees are in honour of distinguished nineteenth-century Belgian horticulturalists, neither of whom died in tragic circumstances.

The *Verschaffeltia splendida* (or stilt palm) has long leaves, reddish fruit and stilts at the base of its trunk, with its scientific name deriving from Ambroise Verschaffelt, a counsellor to King Leopold II. While the *Nephrosperma vanhoutteana* (no anglicized name) derives from Louis Benoit van Houtte, who travelled far and wide and was famed for his knowledge of orchids, which he cultivated in an enormous nursery in Ghent at the height of "orchid mania" in the mid-1840s. The local,

Creole name for the palm is *latanier millepattes* because the leaves undulate in a breeze in the manner of a crawling millipede (in English-speaking countries it is referred to as Van Houtten's palm). Its fruit is especially favoured by tufty-headed bulbul birds as well as Seychelles blue pigeons, peculiar creatures with royal-blue wings, long white feathered necks and crimson heads.

There you have them: the endemic palm trees of the Seychelles. Your head may be swimming with endemic-palm tree knowledge on departure from the Seychelles National Botanical Gardens. You may possibly be considering putting your name down for Mastermind with the endemic palm trees of the Seychelles as your chosen specialist topic. You would stand a decent chance of progressing a round.

But the gardens are not all palm trees. In one corner is a glasshouse containing many delicate endemic *orchid* species. In another is the botanical garden's big draw for those interested in fauna rather than flora: a pen full of Aldabra giant tortoises, which, on my visit, lay around slumped with their legs spreadeagled as though having collapsed after a banquet involving a great deal of red wine. Some weigh up to 250 kilograms, living to 150 years old, so perhaps their lack of mobility is understandable.

Most tortoises on the Indian Ocean islands were exploited by European sailors of old for their meat and shells. Fortunately, the Aldabra Atoll, 700 miles south of Mahé but still within the Seychelles, escaped the worst of their attentions as well as British plans for military development in the twentieth century. After the French first got hold of this slice of paradise in the 1700s, naming the islands after Jean Moreau de Séchelles, a minister of finance under Louis XV, the British came and took them away under the threat of attack in 1810. Independence was eventually granted in 1976.

The Seychelles National Botanical Gardens has its very own "park hero": Paul Evenor Rivalz Dupont, who created the gardens in 1901 and went on to become director of agricultural services in the Seychelles.

He had at first planted crops gathered from Asia (his passion), but then turned to other species as the 15-acre gardens slowly developed their character with native plants introduced, too. He worked tirelessly to keep up the gardens until his retirement in 1934, establishing the principle of conservation in the country. So, another "hero" to add to John Lewis back in Richmond, San Francisco's John McLaren, and New York's Frederick Olmsted and Calvert Vaux.

His tiny park is like a dream of green, complete with some flying friends. Look up at the treetops at the back and it is not long before a fruit bat flaps out and swoops sinisterly between the branches.

No butlers delivering room service to royals, just a few bats, some old palms with some very large, unusual nuts and some ancient tortoises having a snooze.

Just nature putting on a (Seychellois) show.

CHAPTER EIGHT

THE MALDIVES, SRI LANKA, INDIA, NEPAL: OCEANS, MOUNTAINS, TEMPLES AND TIGERS

INDIA

Shimla

New Delhi

NEPAL

Kathmandu

Mumbai

Anuradhapura

SRI LANKA

THE MALDIVES

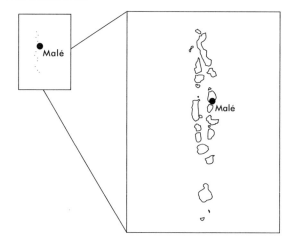

Malé

Malé

My intention by now was unashamedly to champion the world's urban parks. To step off the rapidly revolving conveyor belt of twenty-first-century life – as we were all having to thanks to a virus beginning with "C" – and give city parks of all stripes their due.

I was, looking back, beginning – quite regularly – to get on my high horse about the subject. *So often we seem to take for granted the green places in cities*, I would say to anyone who cared to listen during this phase (including my girlfriend who appeared perfectly capable of simultaneously listening, nodding and texting friends). *How short-sighted of us! How unfair! After all*, I would say, adopting the manner of a statesman addressing a national assembly, *remove them and imagine what we would be left with: desolate urban landscapes! Imagine the sense of claustrophobia! The feeling of being stifled. Surrounded by concrete! Stuck!*

My conversion to the "park cause", having thought about them a great deal (and even dreamed of them at night), was deepening further still. From park lover to park buff, parkspotter to park philosopher, park thinker to park evangelist or even park junkie… if parks had been alcohol or hard drugs, I would have been checking into a rehabilitation clinic at around this point. I was in deep, immersed in foliage amid the big-city bustle and fumes, seeking sanctuary in all corners of the globe.

It had become amazing to me – if not something of an international scandal – that tourist boards and guidebooks did not make more of their urban parks. Most city guides, to which I have previously alluded, focused on "attractions" such as museums, galleries, palaces, castles, cathedrals, marketplaces, zoos, aquariums, riverboat rides, beaches, restaurants, hotels and bars. Yes, parks would get the odd mention, but usually they were of secondary consideration (Central Parks and Stanley Parks aside). *Nothing wrong with that*, I supposed, after much reflection. *Be reasonable*, I said to myself, *"attractions" are what most people go to see.*

Yet as I was experiencing time and again, parks could take you away from the clamour and the crowds of obvious "sights" and offer another, subtle or at least less obvious take on city life: park life, that is.

I consulted my old globe. Onward from the Seychelles, 1,350 miles north-east to the Maldives, another archipelago famed for its white sand beaches and opulent hotels awaited. Then north to Sri Lanka, India and the heady heights of the Himalayas in Nepal, I would "go"... in search of park life.

"Irony: the opposite of wrinkly"
Hiyfaseyha Maidhaan Park, Malé, the Maldives

Resting on a *jolie* chair made from piping and string in Hiyfaseyha Maidhaan Park on the capital island of Malé is a good way to get to know the Maldives as few holidaymakers at the main island resorts ever do.

Jolies may be rudimentary but they are also extremely comfortable. On a scorching day in the middle of the Indian Ocean you will find no better place to be.

There is a tried and tested way to "do" a *jolie*. First, stretch your arms behind your head. Then cup your head in your hands. Next, nestle your back into the strings. Then slip off your flip-flops and rest your feet on the frame with your knees up. You may then close your eyes. Chances are that an enormous sense of satisfaction will swiftly descend. After which, you may well fall fast asleep.

Sitting in a *jolie* beneath the shade of a mango tree, listening to waves break on star-shaped concrete blocks protecting the shore from storm surges and doing nothing whatsoever is somehow (indefinably) good for you. This is a place to let your thoughts drift and, if you remain awake, idly people-watch as locals take turns along the coast.

Malé is one of the most intense cities on Earth, though you would not guess so in Hiyfaseyha Maidhaan Park. Population density measures vary, but Malé usually tops – or comes very close to the top – of the worldwide list with no fewer than 23,002 people per square kilometre. This is more even than Macau at 21,158 and blows away lovely quiet Vientiane in Laos with its paltry 209.

The result of having a fully formed city on an island designed for no such thing – the island is about a mile long and a mile wide with a population of 200,000 – is a great commotion of traffic and a huge number of people, most of whom (most of the time) seem bizarrely intent on going from one side of the island to the other.

This is the HQ of an Islamic archipelago of 1,190 islands stretching around 500 miles from north to south, many of which are classed "tourist islands" where extravagant resorts with water villas on stilts have been constructed and alcohol is allowed. On non-tourist islands where locals live, such as Malé, booze is banned. The entire population of the Maldives is 516,000, spread out far and wide beyond the equator to the south.

When flying into the international airport on neighbouring Hulhule island and seeing Malé from above for the first time, you can hardly help blinking and wondering: *Is this for real?* After many hundreds of miles across empty ocean, an oval-shaped Manhattan of concrete apartment and office blocks suddenly rises from the water. It is almost impossible to imagine such a place exists.

In Hiyfaseyha Maidhaan Park, however, you are one step removed from the madness of the watery metropolis. Not much usually goes on. Sitting on your *jolie,* which are provided in place of public benches, you may regard Maldivians purchasing "power juices" designed to "boost your systems" from a cafe across the way. You may guess at the occupation of those passing by: schoolteachers with satchels of classwork, government officials with pens in top pockets, airport staff on their way to shifts? Teams of joggers who may be footballers or police or soldiers in training pace by. Rebellious-looking teenagers who look like they may be skipping lessons saunter along in pairs.

Your fellow *jolie* companions will probably be either fast asleep, almost fast asleep, on the point of descending toward the point of almost falling fast asleep, merely extremely sleepy or wavering between entering extreme sleepiness or simply remaining a normal level of sleepy. *Jolies* can have this effect on you. None of my *jolie* companions were women.

It seemed to have been the elderly man's hour on the *jolies* in Hiyfaseyha Maidhaan Park when I went. No other tourists. Apart from day trips to see the main mosque and the port-side market or hotel stays before or after flights, holidaymakers do not really hang around on Malé.

A little way beyond the cafe was Malé's Artificial Beach, where a narrow gap in concrete defences against sea surges had been allowed so waves could gently enter on to a little crescent of sand beyond which, across the water, you could see the tail fins of planes and the radar tower of the airport. On Artificial Beach families splashed about happily in the shallows most of the time, playing with balls and practising strokes. Mothers and girls wore headscarves and full-body waterproof costumes while men took to the water in T-shirts.

It is a pleasure to hang out by this "people's beach", with the tower blocks of Malé rising inland between which mysterious lanes lead to endless corner cafes and little, higgledy-piggledy family-run shops. If anything, hotels in the Maldives, away from Malé on its main, self-contained tourist islands, are even more expensive than those in the Seychelles; the them-and-us even starker. Before my visit, David and Victoria Beckham had recently stayed at the One&Only Reethi Rah in the North Malé Atoll, where they had booked four of the best suites and flights for £250,000 over 11 nights. This worked out for the ex-footballer and his fashion-designer/ex-pop star wife at precisely £15.78 a minute. With the per capita GDP of the Maldives at the time being £3,925, their holiday was 64 times the annual Maldivian wage.

You have time to think about such matters on your *jolie* in Hiyfaseyha Maidhaan Park. The "them and us" of luxury holidaymaking seen up close (especially when you are not part of it) is so often mind-boggling.

Behind the *jolies*, with their pleasant palm-tree shade and parade of characters striding by for exercise along the main coast path, you soon come to a dusty lot where kids play football and a stage with yellow banners at the far end near a memorial to those who died in the 2004 tsunami in the Maldives. More than a hundred people perished as the waves struck; the country being incredibly vulnerable as the average elevation above sea level is a mere 1.5 metres with the highest "mountain" at 5.1 metres. If water levels rise across the globe due to melting ice caps, as so many predict, a large number of islands in the Maldives will be submerged. This is a concern taken so seriously that a 2-metre-high artificial island using landfill connected to the airport island has been created at great cost, effectively an "emergency island" for the future.

Pondering this while resuming people-watching, you may notice that Maldivians have a penchant for clothing with messages. "WISH I AM THERE", says a T-shirt worn by a teenager, playing on the traditional postcard message "Wish you were here". "GAME OVER", says another written in the graphics of an old-fashioned computer game and with an accompanying picture of a newlywed couple. After this, "LICENCE TO BITCH", then the rather fantastic: "YOU'RE NOT YOUR JOB. YOU'RE NOT HOW MUCH MONEY YOU HAVE IN THE BANK. YOU'RE NOT THE CAR YOU DRIVE. YOU'RE NOT THE CONTENTS OF YOUR WALLET. YOU'RE THE ALL-SINGING, ALL-DANCING CRAP OF THE WORLD." Although my absolute favourite is: "IRONY: THE OPPOSITE OF WRINKLY."

It takes some effort to raise yourself from a *jolie*. When you do, it is a pleasant walk along to the tsunami memorial via the yellow stage. The sea breeze is invigorating. Kids scamper after footballs. Graffiti scrawled on the sea wall says "NO JUSTICE, NO PEACE", while another is inscribed: "COPS = PROSTITUTES. MALDIVES SOLD FOR $$$" – making you wonder if all is well in paradise.

Despite the island's hallowed status in honeymoon travel brochures and regular appearance on the covers of glossy travel magazines, an undercurrent of unrest appeared to fizzle in Malé. At least it did when I went, in 2013: democracy then seemed to be under threat from powerful new leadership. That was the picture painted by the Maldivian Democratic Party at the time – the yellow banners on the stage were their colours.*

---

* In 2018 free and fair elections were held, ending this shaky period of politics in the Maldives, although tensions remain behind the scenes.

Beneath a cluster of mango trees a group of activists in yellow T-shirts was embroiled in a heated discussion when I passed. We got talking. Vote-rigging and a clampdown on opposition voices were both big problems, they said. One woman in the group had been arrested and taken to Dhoonidhoo, the Maldives' notorious "prison island", where she was slammed in a cell with 20 others for "obstructing police activity". She did not quite understand what she had done wrong and the police had eventually admitted the same, releasing her without charge after six days. Another woman said: "I was arrested once at the airport, handcuffed and walked away by the police. They told me I was a 'danger to society'. It was scary but I found it quite funny. They went to all that trouble, just for me! I was held for two hours."

"You are sitting next to a terrorist, by the way," said the first woman in yellow. This had been yet another of the charges against her that had not stuck. "Yes, you have two very dangerous people here. One terrorist: that's me. And one assaulter of the police." She pointed to her friend, and they both burst out laughing.

Not the kind of pool talk you get all that often at the One&Only Reethi Rah, one suspects.

This corner of Hiyfaseyha Maidhaan Park feels like a Maldivian "Speakers' Corner", about as far removed from the tourist islands as you could imagine.

Waves lap on the shore. Mopeds buzz by. And after talking politics, you may just be tempted to find another *jolie*, remove your flip-flops, rest back and close your eyes for a while in one of the most densely populated cities on the planet... Maldives-style.

A game of cricket
Abhayagiri Stupa, Anuradhapura, Sri Lanka

Sometimes an image sticks in your mind that makes a park special. A glimpse that forms an indelible memory that stays tucked away somewhere up in the little grey cells. For me in Anuradhapura, the Buddhist pilgrimage city in north central Sri Lanka, it was a game of cricket.

In the shadow of the hulking red-brick dome of the ancient Abhayagiri Stupa (or Dagoba), near the lot for tour buses, was a tiny park beside the jungle where a dozen teenagers were playing cricket in the afternoon. One of the batsmen wore an AC Milan football jersey with "99 RONALDO" written on the back. Another wore baggy cut-off jean shorts and an equally baggy T-shirt. The ragtag of fielders were all similarly attired with various football teams represented and loose-hanging shorts. Some of the older players sported gold neck-chains that flapped about as they ran in the field or sprinted between the wicket. Collectively they looked as though they might be about to visit the beach for the day.

It was a fierce contest. The bowlers sprinted in to hurl the ball with all their might in the direction of the stumps. This was just a patch of lumpy park grass, not specially cut for a cricket wicket. The result of the uneven surface was that when the ball bounced it could jag away from the batsmen at the last moment. Or keep dead straight. Or leap up. Or stay low. Or do anything it damn well pleased. This sudden movement (or not) meant the batsmen had to be extra vigilant, especially as the ball was moving with such speed.

No holds were barred. The bowlers were giving it all, knowing they had the upper hand. The ball arrowed in at velocity, ready to explode off the lumpy pitch. But what happened next was what was so remarkable: the batsmen held their nerve and, with lightning adjustment, swift foot movement and a flash of the bat, played each ball with shots that might have graced Lord's. You could just imagine old boys in one of the members' stands, between sips of champagne, murmuring: "Oh, very well played! Jolly good shot!"

But we were not at Lord's. We were on the edge of the jungle in Sri Lanka's ancient capital. White-robed pilgrims flocked to Abhayagiri. Tourists stopped by on bicycles, a convenient way of seeing the other Buddhist stupas at Anuradhapura. Nobody paid any attention to the little park, where I sat for a while waiting for my tour group to gather, simply admiring the fine cricketing skills on display.

Great cracks of bat on ball sent fielders scurrying into the undergrowth of shrubs and the creepers of the jungle. Yet very often there were screams of delight as a catch was taken or the stumps of the wicket flew. It was hardly surprising given how tricky the conditions were that batsmen were regularly "out", whereupon they would drop the bat in great shows of disgust, kicking the dusty turf in frustration. Yet this kept the interest of the game going as each of the ten players soon got their chance to hit the ball and would not have to wait too long once "out" to have another go. It was a circular movement of players, each having a try bowling, wicketkeeping, chasing balls or batting: well-organized, rules obeyed.

The scene was striking on many levels. On one, there was the sheer enjoyment of the game, thrown together with little more than a bat, a ball and the three pieces of wood for the stumps. The look of intent on faces showed that each player was engrossed, focused on every delivery. On another, the skills being honed on this rough patch of park would make playing in "normal" conditions where the grass was not so uneven much easier. The players were being faced with a challenge and were rising to it in style. Not only that, the players clearly understood the game was especially tricky and, despite displays of disgust when "out", really knew that this was bound to happen sooner or later.

On another level still, seeing the contest made me think of how often I could remember watching a thrown-together game like this back home: teenagers, who were perhaps aged 14 to 18, racing about enthralled by the joy of the intricacies of the sport, having raised an ad hoc "team"… all were playing at full tilt. Sadly, I could not. Perhaps that was why the cricketers had stopped me in my tracks. This was a slice of park life that was fresh and alive: the love of the game obvious at a glance. No wonder Sri Lanka's national team, not so long ago world champions, often punches above its weight compared with cricketing nations that have larger populations.

All the while the awesome outline of the dome of the Abhayagiri Stupa loomed through trees hung with creepers like wild strands of hair. This was where King Vattagamani Abhaya built his enormous stupa in the first century BC to form a centre for the practice of Mahayana Buddhism. It was said once to be more than 100 metres high, though now, with the loss of its pinnacle, the height is 70 metres: still extremely tall for a 2,000-year-old structure.

The stupa has a story. Before it was built, the king had lost his throne to Tamil invaders and had been forced to flee. As he did so he was mocked by a Jain Buddhist priest, who commented: "The great black lion is fleeing." To which the king replied: "If my wish [of regaining my kingdom] is fulfilled, I will build a temple here."

Which he did, 14 years later after defeating the Tamils and driving them out of Sri Lanka – an act that was to become symbolic of Sinhalese nationalism, although the Tamils were of course to return to the north. For good measure, King Vattagamani Abhaya built his stupa right on top of where the outspoken priest's hermitage had once stood. "Abhaya" means "have no fear" in Buddhist mantra, so the king was living up to his name.

My tourist group returned from souvenir buying and I was called over to visit the grounds of the former monastery, led by a guide named Lal as enormous in human proportions as the stupa. His yellow shirt was like a tent and he wore a heavy gold watch that looked as though extra links had been added to fit his giant proportions. Lal had got the measure of our group: we were not, he had rightly garnered, experts on local history.

"I would like to tell you the history of Sri Lanka in a nutshell," he said. And so he did, starting with basics: "This island is 270 miles long and 140 miles wide. For 1,400 years from 377 BC the Anuradhapura kingdom thrived. This was where it all happened, an important place: 249 kings were buried here. Then, in 1197, the kingdom fell." Lal looked at us in hope rather than expectation that any of this was sinking in. "Then came the kingdom of Polonnaruwa. Then the kingdom of Kandy. Then, in 1505, the Portuguese. Then, in 1640, the Dutch.

Then, in 1815, the British, until 1948." Lal took a deep breath, slapped shut his folder of facts and regarded us once more. Beads of sweat had gathered on his forehead. It was a humid, overcast day. He chuckled to himself. History had been covered swiftly and to the point – our group seemed more than satisfied.

"Come," he said, and led us to a slab of stone laid in a courtyard beside the stupa known as a "moonstone", shaped in a semicircle like a half-moon and traditionally placed at the foot of entrances. Elephants, lions, bulls, horses and ducks had been carved into the rim of the stone as though moving in a procession from one side to the other. This, Lal told us, represented the cycle of life, or the *samsara*, a process of life, death and rebirth that one day leads to *nirvana*, the state of higher happiness when the chain of *samsara* is eventually broken.

You do not learn such matters during the tea break at Lord's.

The group went on in search of more souvenirs and I returned to the game in the park.

Cut shots sliced into the undergrowth. Hooks flew into the trees. Yells of success rang out. So did cries of despair. Amid the ancient temples, pilgrims in white robes and tourists gawping at the stupas, a heated contest was in full swing.

Park life went on, *samsara* amid the stupas, with some very good shots thrown in.

Home of the Little Tin Gods
Rani Jhansi Park, Shimla, India

Astride a rearing horse, arm thrust aloft wielding a sabre and her young son clinging to her back for dear life, the nineteenth-century freedom fighter Rani Lakshmibai of Jhansi cuts a swashbuckling figure in her statue, towering above a plinth on the terrace of the park named after her in Shimla.

Beyond a turreted wall, the foothills of the Himalayas rise on the hazy horizon, clouds gathering in milky pools in the valley below.

A chaotic clutter of abodes with corrugated roofs clings to the steep mountainside beneath Rani Jhansi Park's railing, beside which benches face the magnificent panorama, usually occupied by chatterers. Shimla is a sociable city and during the day Rani Jhansi Park is a magnet for family gatherings as well as old friends on perambulations. The best spots are much sought after and to nab one requires a degree of cunning. Lurkers are usually about, ready to move swiftly on vacated seats.

The thin mountain air smells of pine needles and forest herbs, with just a faint whiff of diesel. Despite being so remote, Shimla (population 170,000) is almost always all go. When horns do not blast somewhere close by, sirens wail. When sirens fail to wail, car alarms blare. This pattern repeats itself with the odd pause and variation well into the evening. Shimla is a hill station city 2,300 metres up on a mountain ridge criss-crossed with many narrow roads and passages. Rani Jhansi Park is sandwiched on a slender, vertiginous slope – everywhere in Shimla is vertiginous – with roads above and roads below and roads all around, just about wherever the ground is level enough to allow one.

Yet the park, no more than a 300 metres long and perhaps 70 metres wide, is a peaceful place despite all that, the cacophony quickly dissipating in the rarefied atmosphere. This is one of the few corners of green close to the Ridge, a paved area at the heart of the old town of the capital of the state of Himachal Pradesh. Plenty of forest may surround Shimla's centre, but Rani Jhansi is its main – if rather tiny – park.

The nearby Ridge seems almost to define Shimla. This was where the British built a Victorian Gothic church, a mock Tudor library and a Gaiety Theatre after "discovering" Shimla in the early nineteenth century and deciding that the site of what was then a tiny village would make a perfect hideaway from the ravishing heat of the Indian summer in Kolkata, then known as Calcutta and the capital of the Raj.

In came a grand Elizabethan-style mansion for the viceroy of India and from 1865 to 1939 Shimla transformed into the summer capital of British rule, complete with members' clubs, ornate hotels, a cricket pitch, a station for a winding narrow-gauge railway, porters (or coolies) to carry bags, rickshaws and visits from Rudyard Kipling, who christened one part of the Ridge "Scandal Point" after an elopement between a woman from the viceroy's mansion and a dashing Patiala prince. Officers seeking rest and relaxation flocked to the cool hill station, as did many women from Britain seeking officers enjoying their rest and relaxation. These women were referred to, a little cruelly, as the "fishing fleet", with those sailing back without an engagement ring known, definitely cruelly, as "returned empties".

For those who stayed and the wives and daughters of officers already living in Shimla, a "Ladies' Mile" running off the Ridge was established for women to go horse riding, as was, later on during the Raj in 1937, a guarded "Ladies' Park" for women and children to enjoy in seclusion (to the exclusion of men). Former outbuildings belonging to the Royal Hotel, which had burned down leaving the vacant space for the park, were co-opted by the All India Women's Conference, a group lobbying for women's rights and organizing educational classes. Flowers and trees were planted. Lawns laid.

Shimla had a new park, which remained Ladies' Park until 2012 when the latest name was introduced and the striking statue of Rani Lakshmibai unveiled, open to all; at some point in the twentieth century (I'm not sure when) the ban on males had been lifted.

There is, of course, heavy irony that a park once renowned for the fragrant other halves of the military elite of the British Raj was to be renamed after the most famous female freedom fighter of the Indian Rebellion of 1857.

Lakshmibai was a formidable character. She had assumed control of the princely state of Jhansi in northern India (about 500 miles south of Shimla) after the death of her husband, the maharaja, in 1852. So began her first confrontation with the British forces in India, then run by the East India Company. On her husband's passing, the governor general of India, Lord Dalhousie, had claimed the territory of Jhansi for the British, refusing to recognize Lakshmibai's right to preside given that her son, a toddler, was adopted. This, Lord Dalhousie declared, ruled him out as a legitimate eventual heir to the throne and meant that running the state was now entirely British business. As a wife of a deceased maharaja without a legitimate male heir to take over on maturity, she was deemed unfit to rule.

Lakshmibai was furious and ignored the British, declaring "I shall not surrender my Jhansi" on hearing the verdict, although she did cede some powers temporarily. Then came the rebellion across India during which Jhansi witnessed a massacre of as many as 60 European officers in 1857.

Lakshmibai's part in this is not entirely clear. Whatever the truth of that tragedy, it was a prelude to the capture of Jhansi Fort by the East India Company during full-blown conflict the following year. This was when Lakshmibai fled on horseback with her son, as depicted in the statue in the park named after her in Shimla.

She joined rebel forces and bravely fought on, commanding troops who had rallied round her charismatic leadership. The fight against the British led north from Jhansi to the state of Gwalior where 5,000 Indian soldiers were slaughtered and Lakshmibai was shot dead in the heat of battle. She was aged 32.

She died a national hero. There are now many statues of the freedom fighter across India.

Rani Jhansi Park, like so many parks, has a story, although it is not without its current-day controversy.

When Lakshmibai's statue was unveiled in 2012 the grounds were spruced up with a children's playground added and new landscaping, but at the same time the All India Women's Conference and another local women's group were moved to dingy premises outside the city centre.

Some locals regretted that what had once been a sanctuary for many underprivileged women, whom both organizations supported in a "safe" part of the city, had gone. Those involved in this work have expressed fond memories of the days of the Ladies' Park when a guard stood at the main gate to keep out men and boys. Now, they say, the park has become a "dating playfield" where "all kinds of objectional behaviour takes place". Drug addicts and alcoholics also frequent the park, it is said (although I did not witness any of this activity myself).

Rani Jhansi Park is simply a fine place to relax after tramping around Shimla's old colonial sights and up the hill to the temple of Jakhu, dedicated to the Hindu deity Hanuman, on the hilltop directly above the park. This tangerine-coloured temple, with its incense, figurines and quiet, is a place of great peacefulness with views of snow-capped Himalayan peaks, some rising to more than 6,000 metres.

It is also, however, home to a troop of monkeys, who slightly ruin all of this.

These creatures terrorize tourists by pinching any food or drink (straight away) and also sometimes grabbing cameras or pairs of glasses (a more thoughtfully considered theft). This is not merely to be naughty. It is part of a clever plan. The monkeys hold stolen possessions as hostages until nuts are purchased from a kiosk run by a tiny elderly woman in possession of a large stick and a pile of rocks used as defence against any monkey stupid enough to attempt to raid her supplies (she has pinpoint accuracy with her swipes and throws). Once the nuts have been given to the monkey-thief, the camera or glasses or whatever it may be is tossed casually to one side, perhaps slightly broken, perhaps not. Deal done. The monkeys of Jakhu do not go hungry.

All the more reason to enjoy the calm of Rani Jhansi Park, where the monkeys rarely venture (thanks to municipal street patrols to clear them away).

Yet you cannot visit this park without letting your mind wander and reflect on what its heroic namesake stood for and the far-from-calm events of back then.

If anywhere in India is suitable to dwell on Britain's money-grab meddling during colonial days, this is it. Shimla, after all, was the epicentre of the British elite, where the great and the good of the empire lived in finery while governing the lives of one fifth of the world's population and turning a tidy profit. Even among those running the Raj,

Shimla was elitist, nicknamed by minions in the ranks as the "Home of the Little Tin Gods" and "Mount Olympus".

Rani Lakshmibai had more than played her part in their eventual downfall. The rebellion of 1857–8 laid the foundation stones for independence in 1948. When Lakshmibai said "I will not surrender my Jhansi", she meant it. She fought bravely to her death against the odds.

Ladies' Park may be no more, but a heroine has arrived, sabre raised and her stallion facing Little England on the Ridge – looking ready to charge again.

City escape
Chitwan National Park, Nepal

On arrival at the Jungle Villa Resort within Chitwan National Park, the receptionist issued some instructions: "Do not go down to the river's edge. Crocodiles. Do not go to the area behind your room. Rhinos and things like that. Just use the pebble path, but watch out. Scorpions and snakes. Do not wear bright colours. Monkeys. Tigers. Here is your key. Have a nice stay."

OK, so this one is a cheat as far as the definition "urban park" goes… but let me explain.

Chitwan National Park is obviously *not* an urban park, it is Nepal's most visited wildlife park: 367 square miles of jungle, home to one-horned rhinos, Bengal tigers, elephants, leopards and sloth bears, among much else. However, a visit to Kathmandu, Nepal's capital, about 90 miles to the north-east, had drawn an almost complete blank in terms of "green". None seemed to be available.

When visiting the medieval temples of Durbar Square, "Freak Street" (where the hippies hung out in the 1960s), the great white Buddhist stupa at Boudhanath and the backpacker district of bars, cheap hotels and souvenir shops, the city seemed to crowd around in a never-ending chaos of concrete apartment blocks and tumbledown shops connected by a web of electricity wires that sagged precariously above as though on the point of collapse.

Then there was the smog. Kathmandu was shrouded in a haze so thick Beijing seemed like a fresh mountain glade. Before beginning tours, guides dished out face masks, warning you to wear them at all times (even if you did, by the end of the day your lungs ached and your throat was dry and itchy). The pollution was so dreadful it seemed to fly off the scale of anything the World Health Organization deemed possible. As mentioned earlier in the section on China, WHO's recommended air quality target is less than 10 micrograms per cubic metre of PM2.5, the most harmful small air particles. In Beijing, this had risen to what seemed an unbeatable 156 micrograms, yet in Kathmandu the figure was *834 micrograms* in one neighbourhood. No wonder lungs were sore and eyes stung, too. Yes, a handful of small central parks existed – I visited Ratna Park, a dusty place behind a fence next to some noisy roads – but after coughing around with red-rimmed eyes the impulse was: *get inside as soon as you can.*

Old vehicles, backstreet industries such as brick-kilns, and wood-burning fires in homes were to blame, as was the natural amphitheatre of Kathmandu Valley with mountains blocking winds to clear away fumes. The result was you simply did not really feel like hanging around outside (at least I didn't). Maybe I was just extremely unlucky, visiting during a particularly polluted time (in 2017). Maybe I simply did not pound the streets enough in search of park life. Perhaps, quite possibly, I am to blame for having failed to hunt down perfect oases of urban green tucked away somewhere in the city: I put my hands up to all such charges! Yet the long and the short of it was: Kathmandu had me defeated park-wise.

The lure of Chitwan was strong. The chance to see one-horned rhinos and Bengal tigers, just a few hours' drive away, was too good to turn down. To visit a park for a blast of fresh air and an escape from inner-city life in Kathmandu seemed, when I went, to require leaving the city altogether.

Hence Chitwan National Park. Hence this description of my visit, which I could not resist, dear urban-park-only lovers (should such people exist), if simply for the contrast. Hence a little detour beyond the city limits to a major national park and a view from the terrace by the reception of the Jungle Villa Resort of a lovely lazy bend of the River Rapti, with smoke rising from a controlled grass fire on the opposite bank forming a wispy haze even in the wilds. Jungle with an impenetrable-looking tangle of trees lay beyond the flickering orange flames, while directly below, the murky river hardly seemed to flow at all and down in the shallows, although this would appear suicidal after the crocodile warning, local boys were wading through the water carrying shopping bags. Presumably, they knew what they were doing.

This terrace proved a first-rate vantage point, offering a front-row seat to events that were utterly unimaginable (of course) in any urban park. As if my eyes were playing tricks on me, after no more than a few minutes a one-horned rhino lumbered into view looking as though it had somehow stepped out of prehistoric times and decided to join the twenty-first century for the day. It was spellbinding, and it was also rare. There are only 3,700 such Indian rhinos, each weighing up to 2.7 tonnes, and there was one of them, enjoying a soak in the afternoon sun as well as a munch on the riverbank grass.

What a captivating sight and not one to be taken for granted. At the beginning of the twentieth century the Indian rhino population had dropped to 200 due to hunting, although this had not stopped George V and his party killing eight of the wonderful creatures as well as 37 tigers on a trip in 1911. Edward, the Prince of Wales, matched that rhino count along with 18 tigers in 1921.

This, however, was child's play compared with the maharaja of Nepal, who between 1933 and 1940 was responsible for 53 rhino and 433 tiger deaths. Back then, there was a strong chance the Indian rhino was doomed to extinction. By the beginning of the 1970s, the rhino population stood at 95. Then came a backlash against the cruel and cowardly hobby of big-game hunting thanks to raised awareness brought about by the World Wildlife Fund and other groups. The tide was turned and the current count of 3,700 is considered a success story even if the creature is still on the vulnerable species list.

Matters that are all, as I have said, obviously quite a departure from usual urban park-life concerns. Step away from the city and parks naturally take on more important meaning in terms of conservation of creatures.

Jungle life went on everywhere you looked. It was intriguing to watch a *mahout* (elephant keeper) riding the back of an elephant down in the river. With a verbal instruction, he ordered the elephant to turn on its side, perched on the elephant's ribcage, watched the animal wash and then began rubbing the elephant's ears like a mother making sure a child is cleaned at bath time.

Kingfishers flashed in streaks of copper and blue. Herons stepped carefully amid riverbank reeds, stopping with bent necks to observe aquatic matters with almost unnerving stillness. Butterflies with crimson wings danced in the bougainvillea. Dragonflies flitted in reeds. Skittish spotted deer gathered for a drink, looking alert for leopards and Bengal tigers.

All this felt a million miles from the oppressive fug of Kathmandu, yet Chitwan National Park, Nepal's first such park dating from 1973, seemed under siege. Two thirds of the surrounding jungle had been destroyed since the 1960s and a sense of encroachment of urban settlements stretching out beyond the limits of nearby towns was palpable. The city, if you like, was heading for the park! Meanwhile, poaching was, and still is, another problem, with rhino horns sawn off and sold for their "aphrodisiacal" qualities, mainly in China.

Going on a bush drive is the highlight of Chitwan. To do so you join one of a fleet of army-green Tata four-wheel drives and head off at dawn into deep jungle beyond a checkpoint manned by soldiers.

Images, so far removed from the choking city of Kathmandu and developments on the outskirts of the park, soon accumulate in rapid succession.

A flicker of red in the treetops: a greater flameback woodpecker. A swoop of speckled brown with beady yellow eyes: a shikra hawk darting from a strangler vine. A glimmer of electric blue in a cotton tree: a peacock surveying its territory. A glimpse of a white nose and bushy black ears in the undergrowth: an extremely shy sloth bear. Grunts and a flurry of fur: a wild boar making haste. Wide wings and showy grey feathers gliding above: a crested serpent eagle. A pink-nosed, long-tailed creature scurrying by a bog.

"Ohhh, we are lucky," said the ranger. "A crab-eating mongoose. Very rare!"

The setting sun burned orange, reflecting in a lily-strewn creek. No sign of the "biggie": the Bengal tiger, of which a mere 235 survive. We drove back to the checkpoint to return to the Jungle Villa Resort.

Then it happened; "it" being a Bengal tiger padding across a clearing near the soldiers. The orange-and-black-striped cat stepped stealthily on wide paws with leg muscles bulging, turning our way with a whiskery look of: *I had not expected you.* Neither had we. The ranger, who had given up spotting anything, was in a fluster. "Oh! Oh! There! There!" And almost as soon as his words were issued, the king of the jungle turned and slipped away. Who could blame the creature? Humans do not have the best of associations. Yet we had laid eyes on the elusive beast (about a 1 in 20 chance of doing so).

More than 130,000 tourists visit Chitwan National Park each year. Most are on two-day packages, escaping Kathmandu. To many, the park almost feels like an adjunct of the smog-struck capital. Yes, yes, I know it is not an *urban park*. Yes, yes, I know I have just broken a "park life" rule I set myself. Yes, yes, I know all that. But what are rules if not to be broken, just this once? And goodness Kathmandu: what a non-starter of a city for parks. Or so, at least it had seemed to me: the fumes, the face masks, the honking traffic, the stinging eyes.

To see a Bengal tiger in the wild, though… well, that made up for all of that.

CHAPTER NINE

ISRAEL, EGYPT, LIBYA, TUNISIA: SHISHA PIPES, CARGO SHIPS AND DICTATORS

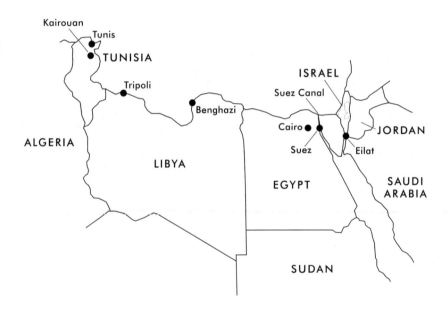

Urban parks have different places in different cultures, naturally, yet it is remarkable how similar they are really, just about everywhere. Sure, the prevalent western tradition, as I have mentioned, was to provide pockets of relaxation, originally away from the grime of industrialization of the nineteenth century. Then, when old-fashioned factories went away, these parks remained, proving key to city life as populations boomed alongside older parks in major cities that were once just for royals (such as Richmond Park) or for the ruling classes (such as the park that became the Royal Botanic Garden in Sydney) or for commemorating historical events (such as West Potomac Park in Washington DC).

Over the centuries, these urban park types, with their roots in European cities, turned up just about everywhere, oftentimes with colonialists in charge of planning, but not always. As cities grew, the requirement of space away from the clutter and clogged streets of "progress" was simply obvious, satisfying a deep-seated craving for a patch of grass with a few trees in which to relax and while away some time.

Human beings need space *whatever the culture*. Which is why just about everywhere parks exist to varying degrees; Kathmandu perhaps being at one end of the spectrum of park love thanks to seemingly chaotic city planning and unbelievable pollution (and much the worse for it).

With my "park thoughts" a little more settled after their outburst of enthusiasm heading into the Indian subcontinent – and with the mass production of vaccines having been approved in "real life", offering light at the end of the lockdown tunnel – it was time to move on.

From the mighty mountains and jungles of the Himalayas, this park quest would continue to Israel. From there, it would proceed westward across the top of Africa calling at a triumvirate of nations that have been through great upheavals of late. Urban parks watching quietly on as conflicts raged, regimes changed and bloody dictators fell. Park life with a little bit of politics, and a few more memories of colonial days, thrown in.

Last of the clay huts
Umm Rashrash, Eilat, Israel

From the edge of Umm Rashrash park in the middle of the Israeli Red Sea beach resort of Eilat, four countries can be seen. The one you are standing in, of course. To the right or south-west: Egypt. To the left or east: Jordan. And south-east, straight across the calm, misty water: Saudi Arabia.

Look at a map of the Middle East and this point would appear to be of crucial strategic importance, where the Gulf of Aqaba draws to a halt having split from the main body of the Red Sea, which in turn flows into the Gulf of Aden, eventually joining the Indian Ocean. To the north, in a slightly crooked line, are Jerusalem in Israel, Amman (Jordan's capital), Damascus (Syria's capital) and Beirut (Lebanon's capital); the direct distance from Eilat to Beirut being about 400 miles.

So you might expect a thriving, centuries-old port at Eilat, but there is none. When Israel Defense Forces arrived in March 1949 to secure the land for the newly founded Jewish state they discovered precisely: five clay huts, an old flagpole and no people.

These huts were formerly a British police post dating from the earlier period of Mandatory Palestine, an interim arrangement after the collapse of the Ottoman Empire following the First World War; Britain was overseeing local affairs "until such a time as they are able to stand alone". By 1949 this time had well and truly come and in Umm Rashrash park it is fascinating to discover one of these crumbly huts remains, locked with shuttered windows and a chain surrounding the structure. As fascinating as an old clay hut can be, that is.

When the Israeli soldiers arrived – taking Eilat, then known as Umm Al Rashrash, without firing a shot – they were jubilant at having secured the southernmost outpost of the new nation. To celebrate and mark ownership, the troops decided to raise the Israeli flag on the empty flagpole. The only trouble was, they had no flag. They had forgotten to bring one. So a piece of material was found and the flag was drawn on using pens with the Star of David at the centre. One of the officers then shimmied up the precarious pole, supported from below by his colleagues and hoisted the "ink flag", as it has become known, establishing Eilat as Israeli territory.

At Umm Rashrash, a statue of this moment has been erected, based on a black-and-white picture taken at the time. It is a dramatic photograph, echoed in the statue, with the symbolic importance captured as the soldiers look up anxiously as the flag is secured.

This picture is also interesting for another reason. In the background is a long curve of empty pebbly-looking beach, waves lazily breaking in streaks of foam and mountains forming far beyond in what was (and still is) Jordan. Moody leaden clouds rise above the peaks as though disapproving of the scene, the raising of the Israeli flag. As, of course, the leaders of the neighbouring country did.

Yet along the beach in the photograph, nothing is there. Nothing but windswept shore. Fast forward to today, however, and a popular resort has risen beside the pebbly beach. More than 52,000 people live in the city, where a port has been installed (the reason there was not one before was because shipping business in the bay was conducted across the way at the ancient port of Aqaba in Jordan).

The resort now attracts more than double its population in tourists each (normal) year. There are hulking hotels with step-shaped balconies that look like inflated Aztec temples. There are beach bars offering Heineken and lurid cocktails of the Sex-on-the-Beach and Dirty-Martini variety. There are cafes with low-slung sofas and carpets with throw cushions and waiters who bring shisha water-pipes lit with watermelon- and apple-flavoured tobacco. There are shopping malls with every international brand under the sun. There are duty-free outlets with all the booze in the world. There are fast-food joints galore. In the plot next door to Umm Rashrash a McDonald's is to be found next to a mobile phone shop, a confectionery and a late-night pizzeria.

The park itself is paved and palm trees are planted in rows in gaps. Shrubs have been added near the statue of the soldiers as well as along the borders of the small plot of the park, which forms a narrow break in Eilat's run of gaudy attractions. Were it not for the historical importance (Umm Rashrash was declared an official national site in 1994), another hotel, Burger King or a beach bar would no doubt be in place of the last of the clay huts.

Foliage from tall evergreen trees blocks out the worst of the Aztec-temple hotels. But they are still there, looming in the background. Meanwhile, traffic buzzes by on a roundabout. This little corner of history feels hemmed in. Tranquillity is, however, to be had closer to the shore, partly because so few holidaymakers come to see the statue and the hut. Guidebook writers sometimes describe Eilat as "brash" and "ugly", and this is true. It is shockingly in-your-face. Yet Umm Rashrash offers a refuge of sorts, a place to mull things over.

Including the park's name. Umm Rashrash is made up of the Arabic word "umm", meaning "mother", and the Arabic word "rash", meaning "strew". Legend has it that an elderly woman who suffered from painful feet once lived by the beach at Eilat. She had concocted a powder that she would "strew" on her feet to alleviate the pain. When pilgrims heading many hundreds of miles to Mecca came by with sore feet and heard of her miracle cure, they would stop to ask for treatment. So the story goes.

What is certain is that after the soldiers came and put up the ink flag in 1949 a debate was had as to what to call the new spot by the sea. Umm Rashrash would not do as Arabic names were being replaced to stamp nationhood on the new territory. An official names committee was formed and some members favoured "Eilat"; the reason being that an Eilat in these parts is mentioned in the Bible during the Exodus from Egypt, and it was also where King Solomon built ships. But other committee members said that this would be inaccurate as Eilat's true location was over the border in Jordan and that to name Umm Rashrash "Eilat" would be to create a false Eilat. In the end, after getting a bit tied up over the matter, "Eilat" came out on top, with Umm Rashrash remaining for the tiny park. And that was that.

Yet it was a highly charged discussion. Being at the far south of the Negev Desert, the new place on the map represented a target for the expansion of Israeli settlement. David Ben-Gurion, Israel's first prime minster, paid a visit to Eilat three months after the ink flag was raised in Umm Rashrash park. To give an indication of the location's importance, the evening before heading off by plane, he wrote in his diaries: "Tomorrow morning I leave for Eilat. On my first trip, more than 15 years ago, the sight of the Negev desert totally changed my Zionist perception. That trip played a major part in my decision to conquer the Negev this year." He added: "We have to settle it, make its desolate lands bloom, and utilize its economic resources."

To many, Eilat is a tourist resort with good times guaranteed and excellent scuba diving on magnificent coral reefs. Yes, it is all of that, but it means a lot more too.

It is also quite beautiful, never mind the Aztec hotels.

The beauty comes from the location: four countries facing one another across the bay, silently getting on despite so many differences. The beauty comes from the placid sea, lulling gently beyond the shore. The beauty comes from the warmth in the late afternoon as birds twitter in the palm trees by the promenade, the heat of the day dropping away. The beauty comes from the kaleidoscope of colours in the sky and the feeling of peace at dusk.

Ben-Gurion wrote of his visit to Eilat in June 1949: "The sun set beyond the mountains of Israel, but opposite us, the mountains of Jordan were bathed in the golden light of the sunset."

There is no better spot to take it all in than Umm Rashrash park.

After sunset you may wish to sample a shisha pipe at the cafe next door, where you may or may not, amid the bubbling smoke and laughter, meet a former Israeli soldier named Yuval, who served in Eilat in the 1960s. "There were only a few buildings then," he said, puffing his pipe. "We would take positions near the beach and watch the Jordanian border. There was so little here that people used to be sent as punishment: it was either gaol in Tel Aviv or life in Eilat."

So what changed? "The peace that came after the 1967 Six Day War, that's what," he said. "By the mid-1970s many hotels were built. The first charter plane arrived in 1975, then more came, more and more – people didn't want to go to Spain back then because of Franco."

Yuval and I discussed this and that, lazily amid puffs, as you do at a shisha cafe.

Eilat is a peculiar place, like so many tourist resorts. Drop by its little park and a whole new perspective opens up.

Cargo ship spotter
French Garden, Suez, Egypt

On the canal a cargo ship the length of three football pitches slid by, piled so high with containers the wheelhouse was almost buried. The ship, the CMA CGM *Balzac*, was travelling south towards the opening of the Suez Canal into the Gulf of Suez, which would soon meet the Gulf of Aqaba on its way to the ocean. Between Suez and Eilat lay the arid bulk of the Sinai Peninsula.

Seen from the French Garden in the seaport city of Suez, the cargo containers had a patchwork-quilt quality. Some were rust-red, others steely grey, navy, pistachio or tangerine-brown. The combined effect, set above the solid-blue hull with its solid-red stripe, was strangely artistic, like the work of some avant-garde painter experimenting in the juxtaposition of colours. Or maybe I was getting carried away. There was, however, something about the ship that caught the eye.

As did so many of the others that slowly came and went. The mountainous islands of commerce glided along the old canal one by one with the names of transportation companies printed on the containers: Maersk, P&O, China Shipping, Evergreen. Movement was imperceptible yet move they evidently did as after a few minutes of silently marvelling that such vessels existed, the mountain would be gone. Then another would slip into view and there was pleasure to be taken, I have to admit, in establishing via the internet where each was registered, their last recorded location, speed and course.

Yes, after an afternoon in Suez, I seemed to have become a cargo ship spotter.

The edge of the French Garden, overlooking a tiny sand beach next to a yachting club and a pair of shuttered social clubs, was a restful place to indulge in a little such spotting. The small park was square with wiggly paths between parched lawns. These were dotted with old camphor and mulberry trees, providing plenty of much needed shade in the desert setting. Mynah birds like the ones back in St Helena made a racket. From time to time a muezzin in a mosque launched into a long, mournful call to prayer.

The park's name comes from the nationality of many captains who lived in this neighbourhood during the heyday of French involvement with the Suez Canal, before the Suez Canal Company was nationalized by Egypt's President Gamal Abdel Nasser in 1956. Before then, it was a place of picnics and perambulations, a perfect spot to take a stroll after dinner at one of the half-forgotten social clubs by the beach.

Afterward, the canal was at the centre of such intense international power games that the French Garden never did quite regain its *joie de vivre*. Then, long after these troubles had been and gone, the park was briefly renamed Mubarak Park, after the controversial President Hosni Mubarak, before being renamed once again, this time Martyrs' Park of the Third Field Army (although for how long precisely is hard to establish). By the time of my visit, President Mubarak having been toppled in the Arab Spring revolution of 2011, the name had reverted to the French Garden. Which seemed likely to stick.

It was filthy when I went in 2012, litter strewn all about: plastic bags, rusting cans, old fast-food wrappers, flyers for political candidates wearing suits and ties (perhaps promising to clear up the mess). The outcome of the Arab Spring, who would take charge in the long run, was then unclear and uncertainty meant that Egypt was in limbo. During this period, which stretched until 2014 and the arrival, sadly, of a new authoritarian leader, many of the garden's trees were felled for timber and firewood.

Yet the French Garden holds a special place in the canal's history. And its Gallic connection goes back to the very beginning of the Suez Canal, which was to transform world trade on its opening in 1869, finishing off the Cape of Good Hope route for shipping (along with St Helena's usefulness, of course).

It was a Frenchman who got it all started. Ferdinand de Lesseps was a French diplomat born in Versailles, with a bushy moustache and a friendship with the Egyptian ruler Said Pasha. This connection paved the way for an official thumbs-up to deLesseps' plans to form a company to construct a canal linking the Red Sea with the Mediterranean.

Previously, Napoleon's engineers had considered the feasibility of a canal but deemed such a scheme impossible as they had calculated a 10-metre difference between the two waters. They had been wrong, as deLesseps had discovered, and the British – with their fingers in pies across the world and major concerns about the passage of trade from India – were furious at the audacity of deLesseps' move. Lord Palmerston, the prime minister at the time, dismissively said: "It cannot be made, it shall not be made; but if it were made there would be a war between England and France for the possession of Egypt."

Lesseps made it anyway, with financial backing from Said Pasha and his successor, Ismail, who saw the huge potential for returns. Unfortunately, Ismail ran out of cash and was ashamedly forced to sell his shares. Britain snapped them up, under the new leadership of Prime Minister Benjamin Disraeli, who had secured a loan for the purpose from the wealthy Rothschild family over dinner one evening; the way of the world back then (and, who knows, maybe still now). This allowed for British majority control of the Suez Canal Company, a lot of power in global trade and an excellent income. On completion of the deal, Disraeli is reported to have drily (and smugly) told Queen Victoria: "You have it, Madam."

Things went swimmingly for the British and French, who decided not to go to war against one another after all; the French also had a substantial share of the bountiful profits. Then came the 1952 nationalist revolution in Egypt against the ongoing British presence, followed by Nasser's 1956 audacious nationalization of the canal.

So began the Suez Crisis with America strongly against retaliation and restoration of Suez Canal Company control, although Britain, France and Israel had already become allies and begun military action to secure the canal. Pressure from Washington DC on Britain ensued (a threat to sell US-backed sterling bonds causing great potential financial difficulties) combined with Soviet Union aggression (a threat of rocket attack on Britain, France and Israel).

The result? The infamous humiliating backdown and a change in the world order. Britain could no longer throw its weight around on the world stage. In one fell swoop the pretence of empire was over and hanging on to colonies suddenly seemed anachronistic. Hence the historic push for independence in the likes of Sudan, Zanzibar, the Seychelles and Barbados.

All thanks to the canal at the end of the French Garden in Suez.

Troubles rumbled on after the 1956 showdown in the form of Egyptian-Israeli ill feeling. This boiled over in the 1967 Six Day War to which Yuval had alluded back in Eilat. A dreadful stalemate followed with the closure to traffic of the 100-mile canal for eight years; 15 ships unlucky enough to be transiting the canal were stranded for the entire period.

At my hotel by the French Garden, Adir, the reception manager, remembered the beginning of the conflict when he was 13 years old: "We moved from here into the valley. Almost everything was destroyed: about 80 per cent of the city. The Israeli army was on the other side of the canal. It was very dangerous. Every person moved to the valley. It was only the army that was left."

There were no French captains picnicking in the French Garden then. Everything had been put on hold and life never quite returned to normal. "Before 1967 it was much quieter and nicer and cleaner here," he said.

The French Garden has a ghostly feeling of an era that has been and gone and is never coming back.

Another park with a sense of history, just like Umm Rashrash back in Eilat and so many of the others, too. No other tourists were about when I went. All the other guests at the Red Sea Hotel were security staff soon to fly to Sri Lanka to join cargo ships travelling back through the treacherous Gulf of Aden. Yet the incredible engineering achievement of the Suez Canal and the sheer spectacle of the gigantic vessels seemed worthy of holidaymakers with a historical bent. Not just those interested in modern times. The quest to link the Red Sea with the Mediterranean dates from the pharaohs. In the third century BC a waterway linking the Red Sea to the Nile, long lost now, is believed to have been dug.

Probably, though, most visitors would agree with the assessment of the narrator of Joseph Conrad's novel *An Outcast of the Islands*, who describes the Suez Canal as "a dismal but profitable ditch".

Yes, it might be dismal to some, and it is certainly profitable to many, to the tune of £4 billion a year.

But let your mind wander in its little French Garden, indulge in a spell of cargo ship spotting – watching the ships roll in from the Gulf or the Mediterranean, depending on the time of day – and the canal and this special setting somehow come alive. This may have been a scraggly, dusty and litter-strewn park that was never going to challenge the National Botanical Gardens in the Seychelles or Ueno Park back in Tokyo for beauty. But for its intriguing setting, in an often-forgotten corner of the Middle East as important to world trade today as it was when the canal opened all that time ago, it was second to none.

King of the mad dogs
Green Square/Martyrs' Square, Tripoli, Libya

There is nothing much green about most of Green Square. Just a few palm trees by an ornate fountain carved with galloping horses (known colloquially as the Seahorse Fountain). This is a famous meeting point in

Tripoli, Libya's capital. Except when I went it was not working, just like so much else in the troubled country.

The very name "Green Square" seemed uncertain. Before my visit, Green Square had been hastily renamed Martyrs' Square to remember those who had died during the 2011 Arab Spring uprising against Colonel Gaddafi, the dictator who had ruled Libya since taking control in a coup in 1969. Meanwhile, before Gaddafi, during the reign of King Idris, the area had been known as Independence Square. Before King Idris, who had assumed control after a period when Allied Forces had been in charge (1943–51), the square had been referred to as Piazza Italia, a name left over from when the Italians colonized Libya for 30 years up to the arrival of the Allies. What it was called before the Italians, when the Ottomans ruled the roost, I do not know.

Add to this the current division of some maps into Martyrs' Square, a paved section with the fountain beside Al-Saraya al-Hamra (the seventh-century Tripoli Castle), and a wider zone with patchy lawns and another, larger fountain still referred to as Green Square, and there is an element of confusion about what exactly constitutes the square.

For the sake of keeping things simple, best to call the whole lot "the square", which is slap in the middle of the old town.

It is an eerie place. Close to the fountain, opposite Tripoli Castle, lemon-coloured Italianate buildings rise with arched colonnades beneath which juice kiosks and coffee shops lurk in the shade; no bars in Libya, which is 97 per cent Muslim. The Italian architectural influence in Tripoli remains strong. Looking out from the flamboyant fountain (itself the work of an Italian) towards the sea, a wide expanse of concrete marked with yellow criss-crossing lines spreads out. These were painted to organize parades during Gaddafi's time, while all around are football-stadium-style floodlights to illuminate evening celebrations in honour of the achievements of the "Brother Leader", as Gaddafi liked to be known, along with "King of the Kings of Africa". He was a leader with many nicknames. President Ronald Reagan's preference back in the 1980s was not quite so sycophantic: "Mad Dog of the Middle East", which seemed slightly closer to the truth.

This open space leads to two tall Italian-era pillars facing the sea, one topped with a rider on a horse raising a sword in the manner of Rani Lakshmibai back in Shimla, the other with a ship bearing billowing sails. From there, the square widens to incorporate the patchy grass and the other fountain. For those in need of a stroll, this is the place to go: the "park" bit.

On my visit four months after Gaddafi had been captured and killed, having been hunted down to a drainage pipe in his hometown of Sirte, the square was almost empty. A few characters in leather jackets smoked cigarettes by the Seahorse Fountain. Women in hijabs clutching bags scurried to an alley leading to a narrow bazaar. There, I already knew, stalls sold robes embellished with jewel-like beads, silk negligees, knock-off Manchester United and Chelsea shirts and jeans that looked exactly like Levi's (although on closer inspection the labels read "Live's"). Great tubs of olives, nuts and chillies were also to be had, along with every spice under the sun.

Near the entrance to the bazaar was something bizarre: a skinny gazelle-like creature, utterly adorable-looking with wide doe eyes, attached to a chain connected to a white chaise longue. Purple drapes hung from a frame behind the chaise longue and the idea was that romantic couples or whoever had sufficient Libyan dinars could sit and have their photograph taken with the cute little gazelle. An attendant eyed me initially with some hope; he was probably looking at the only "tourist" in the country. No one else seemed foolish enough to go so soon after the unrest of the revolution. On realizing he did not have a customer, he shrugged and continued smoking his cigarette. Almost all men in Libya seemed to smoke, and who could blame them after years of Gaddafi's terrifying regime followed by a recently conducted uprising that was about to spin into a long-running bloody civil war.

The square here was Gaddafi's favourite spot for long, rambling speeches delivered from the fortifications of Tripoli Castle. He was famous for them, with his subjects crowded below waving the then green flag of Libya. Gaddafi approved of the colour green and had got rid of the national flag's old red, white and black stripes after writing a tome about his political philosophy entitled *The Green Book*. In this he lays out his thoughts on "traditional democracy", arguing that "the institution of parliament is a misrepresentation of the people... a legal barrier between people and their right to exercise authority". Political parties are "a contemporary form of dictatorship". The media should be run by a People's Committee (overseen by him). And, in general: "In reality the strong always rule: that is to say those who are strongest in society hold the reins of power."

Other ideas expressed in *The Green Book* and delivered from the fortifications above were wide ranging. Spectator sport, he believed, should be abolished as sports were private. After all, "it would be foolish for a crowd to enter a restaurant to watch one or more persons eating" (the truth was he was fearful football clubs in the east of Libya would become hotbeds of resistance to his rule). He regarded tribes as superior to families as "an individual may sometimes behave in a dishonourable manner that a family will not condone... in contrast, individuals as members of a tribe cannot be free of its watchful eyes" (i.e., much better to have tribes acting as Big Brother to maintain his control). Meanwhile, men and women have "assigned roles in life", with women required to perform "the duties of motherhood", although, he concedes, "women, like men, are human beings".

Colonel Gaddafi was not, you might say, especially woke.

It was around the time of *The Green Book*'s publication in 1975 that land was reclaimed from the sea to expand the size of what Gaddafi was then dubbing "Green Square". "Greenery" in Libya has a multi-layered meaning.

Looking up at the battlements on the walls of the castle, it was hard to imagine Gaddafi up there just a year before. Most of his speeches during the revolution had been made from the security of a bunker deep beneath his Bab Al-Azizia barracks, about a mile from Green Square, including an infamous rant attacking "drug addicts, jihadis and rats" who were leading the revolution against him. He had promised to "cleanse Libya inch by inch, house by house, home by home, alleyway by alleyway, person by person, until the country is cleansed of dirt and scum". Unfortunately, this speech had backfired as revolutionaries took the phrase "alleyway by alleyway" (or *zenga zenga* in Arabic) as a rousing motto for the lengths to which *they* would go to clear Gaddafi from Libya.

Three days after his bunker address, the careworn dictator took to the ramparts again on 25 February 2011, shaking his fists and blowing kisses to the crowds of green flag-waving supporters down by the Seahorse Fountain. He was hunched in a winter coat and wearing a hunter's cap with woolly ear flaps. Already the east of the country around the city of Benghazi had fallen, although he disputed versions of events.

"I have a reply to the liars, a reply to the mass media," he roared. "The media of lies. The mass media. The mass lies… We will defeat any foreign aggression just as we defeated the former Italian imperialists." He was referring here to NATO's air attacks to support the revolutionaries. "Life without dignity is worthless. Life without green banners hoisted is useless… you the youth, be comfortable in the streets and squares. Dance and sing, stay up all night and live a life of dignity with high morals… dance and sing, rejoice!"

These were not Gadaffi's final words to a rally at his beloved Green Square, he was to give a longer speech to a much larger crowd in July just three months before his death, only on that occasion it was made by phone over speakers: a strange event. A few weeks after this address a giant poster bearing the Brother Leader's image was unveiled on the square; yet another propaganda stunt to suggest all was well when all was clearly not.

On his 25 February appearance there is almost a poignancy to the scene as the elderly man shakes both fists above his head and blows more kisses to his remaining loyal subjects before turning to go. A flicker of doubt crosses his expression as he does so, as though he knew his game was probably up.

Standing by the Seahorse Fountain looking out over the criss-cross markings of the parade yard to the park's palm trees by the sea, almost exactly one year after Gaddafi's "dance and sing" parting, the sense of *what next* for Libya was strong.

In a holy city
The Aghlabid Basins, Kairouan, Tunisia

After Mecca, Medina and Jerusalem, the ancient city of Kairouan in central-eastern Tunisia is home to the fourth most holy site in Islam. It is said seven visits to its Great Mosque are equivalent in terms of devotion to a single pilgrimage to Mecca. It is also extremely hot in the summer and out of the way, surrounded by miles of arid olive groves. A correspondent of *The Times* passing through in 1939 hit the nail on the head when he said: "What a Hell of a place to put a Holy City."

The centre of Kairouan does not have much by way of green spaces other than a small children's play park. Its labyrinthine streets and alleys are tightly packed, confined within the eighth-century walls of the medina. Losing yourself in this spaghetti-land of whitewashed houses (most requiring a bit more wash and a little less grime) is not difficult. Turquoise shutters and front doors provide a consistency of colour, although rotting frames and peeling paint suggest Kairouan has seen better times.

Mangy ginger cats prowl by, stepping carefully between scattered sweet wrappers and old cigarette packets. Battered vehicles with panels bearing evidence of a thousand scrapes along the passages creep by. Most are making deliveries: decrepit Renault 4s with loaves piled in the back and wonky roof racks heaped with sacks.

Archways lead to residential alleys where you cannot help but feel a complete outsider. Which of course you are. This is a secretive holy city. In bygone years infidels (such as me) could not walk freely through its gates. Special permits were required, issued by the ruling Bey, the name given to Tunisian monarchs from 1705 to 1957.

On his visit in 1835, the Victorian adventurer Sir Grenville Temple, wrote in his travelogue *Excursions in the Mediterranean*: "More than one walk in the town we were not allowed to take; as I was told, that if we were known to be Christians, whilst walking about, we might probably be torn to pieces by the infuriated populace."

It is possible Sir Grenville may have been over-egging it, given his predilection for disquieting tales. A few pages earlier, he recounts the Kairouan legend of a local ruler who, upon hearing that a baker was overcharging for bread – the price being strictly set – visited the bakery and smashed the scales to discover quicksilver affecting the balance: "The baker's oven happened at that moment to be properly heated, and the Kaeed [ruler], ordered the culprit to be immediately thrown into it." When a member of his court remonstrated that this was harsh, the Kaeed is said to have replied: "I have done great good – bakers will in future deem it preferable to heat their ovens for bread of a proper weight, than to bake themselves, of whatever weight they may chance to be."

A story that makes you think twice when eating your toast at breakfast in Kairouan.

It was only with the arrival of French colonialists in 1881, who had fooled the ruling Bey that their 36,000-strong army was on a mission in neighbouring Algeria rather than invading Tunisia (which was what they were really doing), that Bey permits were abolished and anyone could enter the holy city of Kairouan.

With free passage, infidel tourists soon arrived. The mystique of the story of the establishment of Kairouan in 670, when the Arab general Oqba Ibn Nafi discovered a golden cup he believed he had lost in Mecca in the empty, dusty landscape, had an allure. This stroke of fortune had been compounded by the uncovering of a well that was said to draw the same water as found in Mecca. These two signs were enough to establish the holiness of the land. Soon a thriving conurbation with a Great Mosque at its heart emerged from the desert.

To understand this mysterious city properly, a trip to its best bit of green, up on a hill on the northern edge of the medina, is the way to go.

This is where you will find the Aghlabid Basins, a series of four man-made pools dating from the ninth century that were dug to collect water, fed by an aqueduct stretching more than 20 miles to the west. Around these pools is a parkland of dried-out lawns, clumps of shrubs, teetering palms and rows of hardy-looking eucalyptus trees that is a favourite place for locals on sunset strolls as golden light bathes the domes and minarets of the sleepy, secretive desert city.

The basins themselves are extraordinary, the largest with a circumference of 128 metres and the remains of a stone pavilion at its centre. This was where rulers of old could relax in comfort and safety during hot summers. The pools had a dual purpose of supplying water to the city and providing a bathing spot to cool off; ancient leisure centres of sorts. Unfortunately, they had a third unexpected outcome. They also attracted malaria-bearing mosquitos, putting the basins out of use for long stretches.

From the roof of a small building with a cafe, the great sweep of Kairouan spreads out before you in all its glory. Muezzins let out long warbling calls to prayer, voices combining in a collective murmur of holiness across the sacred cityscape. While beyond the outskirts, olive groves taper to the horizon in long stripes following the contours of the orange-soiled land. Ibrahim ibn al-Aghlab and his dynasty, after whom the basins are named, ruled these parts from 800 to 909, the golden age of Kairouan when so many of its mosques, palaces and schools were built and the countryside cultivated. He left a fine legacy.

It was while admiring his city that a tourist guide in his 60s named Guizani sidled up to me on the rooftop.

He was wearing a ski jacket and a scarf (it was early February and cold). He had a thin brush moustache. His eyes glistened as though enjoying the scenery for the first time, though he had come to the Aghlabid Basins almost every day for decades. He had wizened eyes and a calm, almost philosophical manner.

Somehow, we fell into conversation, almost as though picking up on a previous discussion and, without formal agreement, Guizani became my guide for the Aghlabid Basins.

"It was sixty years ago," he said. "I swam here as a boy. But then two children drowned: the water is five metres deep. Swimming was banned. Very sad." He paused for a while as though remembering both the joy of splashing about in the Aghlabid Basins as a child as well as the tragedy of the drownings.

"In this one," he continued, pointing to the largest basin, "the governor used to sit on that stone in the middle. He would go across on a boat. People would make promenades around the pool."

He pointed to a smaller basin. "This one is a polygon. It has 48 edges. The only other one like it is in Mecca," he said, losing me a bit. I think he was referring to the number of buttresses breaking up the circular shape of the basin. I was, perhaps, beginning to learn more than was strictly necessary about the Aghlabid Basins of Kairouan.

Guizani seemed to sense that. "Forgive me," he said, and we switched the subject to current affairs. It was hard not to. Tunisia was in the midst of great upheaval. As in Egypt and Libya, Tunisia had just witnessed the fall of a dictator during the Arab Spring: President Ben Ali, who controlled Tunisia from 1987 to January 2011, overseeing widespread corruption much of which benefited his extended family. He had fled by private jet to Saudi Arabia, never to return.

Before visiting Kairouan, I had stopped at the remote town of Sidi Bouzid, south of Kairouan, to visit the grave of Mohamed Bouazizi, a street vendor who had set fire to himself outside the main police station as a protest against harassment at the hands of corrupt police a few months earlier. He had died, but his dreadful demise, captured by a mobile phone's camera, went viral across Tunisia, sparking widespread protests that not only led to the fall of President Ben Ali, but also had a domino effect across North Africa, with protesters recognizing the strength of the internet to organize resistance. The result was the toppling of President Mubarak in Egypt and then Colonel Gaddafi in Libya.

"For the first time in my life," Guizani said, "I am very happy for democracy. Very happy! I lived with the French. They left when I was ten years old. There were good French and there were bad French…" his voice trailed off as though lost in memories once again.

Guizani talked about President Bourguiba, who had taken charge after the French left in 1956, introducing secularist policies including family planning, very much against the wishes of local Islamic hardliners in Kairouan. "He was not good for religion," he said, "but he was good for schools and for the liberty of women."

We discussed President Ben Ali and corruption for a while. Then Guizani, cutting to the chase as far as he was concerned, exclaimed: "Now we have democracy! But it is very bad for tourism! The worst for forty-two years!"

We had a long talk on the rooftop that continued over coffees in the cafe below – what would happen to Tunisia now that President Ben Ali was gone? Guizani did not seem sure. What mattered most was the bottom line. If coachloads of holidaymakers from Gatwick, Manchester and Munich turned up tomorrow and kept on coming, well then – and only then – could the Arab Spring be deemed a success. It seemed as good a way as any to judge the outcome. We shook hands and parted, and I went for a stroll around the unusual Aghlabid Basins, staring out across the city's 300 mosques.

Park life can come in all shapes and forms, and that is one of the joys of it.

Chance encounters. Stories on windswept rooftops. Old hillside basins in holy cities where rulers once came to cool down amid kingdoms in mighty deserts. A hell of a place perhaps, as *The Times* reporter had said, but somehow Kairouan had risen from the sands.

CHAPTER TEN

GREECE, CROATIA, ITALY, AUSTRIA, GERMANY:
WAYS OF ESCAPE

As these "park dreams" continued and it became increasingly obvious that travel beyond local parks was going to take a long time to return, it was interesting to see how we were all handling not being able to go anywhere.

The answer to this was, frankly: not very well. Before the lockdowns, a great many of us had been happily hopping about on budget flights to the Continent in the manner our parents and grandparents (especially) might have considered catching a train or driving to the seaside or the West Country, Scotland, Wales or the Lakes. Deprived of these no-frills airlines – these cheap passages to the sun and interesting city breaks to which we had become hooked yet loved to grumble about on account of their "cattle class" approach – it seemed that we had all become slightly holiday obsessed. That is if conversations with friends, family and colleagues were anything to go by, as well as the many, many headlines in the British press.

Early on during the lockdowns, newspapers had begun to play a seemingly never-ending game of speculation: *when would travel be possible once again?* Front page headlines screamed of "SUMMER HOLIDAYS ON!" or the opposite, depending on the latest off-the-cuff remark on the subject by government ministers. Such mutterings were poured over and analyzed, the slightest comment seized upon. At times it felt as though Britain's newspapers had taken to reading tea leaves in the hope of gleaning *what next for holidays?*

Meanwhile, travel sections of papers were having a torrid time. How, after all, do you write about travel if no one can go anywhere? When it is *illegal* to travel? Watching how Fleet Street's travel editors tackled this conundrum at the height of the pandemic was a lesson in survival.

Some put up graphics beside travel articles with messages such as "When we can travel again", "When things are back to normal" or "Plan now!". Others opted for constant reminders that travel was banned and that readers should consult the Foreign, Commonwealth and Development Office's website to learn more. A few began armchair traveller-style columns, focusing on latest travel books, films and television shows.

Others still set aside space for articles of the "Dreaming of…" or "A perfect Sunday morning in…" variety. These I devoured with interest: fellow dreamers were out there! If not dreaming specifically about parks.

It was not, you might say, exactly a golden age of getting about.

Of all the travel frustrations, however, one stood out for the British: not being able to hop across to Europe.

This, however, was not bothering me. Not a jot. I had been doing a great deal of "travelling" on a round-the-world "voyage" of a lifetime and Europe (enticingly) awaited, along with many happy park memories. With a feeling of beginning to return home after a very long trip, I was about to head north-eastward to Greece, across the Adriatic Sea and into the heart of Europe everyone seemed to miss so dearly (despite having recently voted to Leave it).*

Monkey business
National Garden, Athens, Greece

The ancient temples of the Acropolis may crawl with tourists ogling the magnificent remains of the Parthenon and the Erechtheum. The archaeological museums may be chock-a-block with visitors fresh off €20 EasyJet flights. The souvenir shops and restaurants may be overrun with tourists wielding selfie sticks.

Yet one little corner of this cradle of western civilization to which so many holidaymakers flock offers a quiet haven.

The National Garden comprises 38 acres of tranquil parkland that lie in the busy heart of the Greek capital yet somehow feel completely removed from the hullabaloo.

To the north is the grand sand-coloured facade of the Hellenic Parliament, formerly the Royal Palace. To the east are the Prime Minister's Residence and the Presidential Palace. To the west is the busy tourist

---

* But that's another matter entirely.

hotspot district of Plaka below the Acropolis. To the south-west are the colossal Corinthian columns of the Temple of Zeus. To the south-east, the marble magnificence of the Panathenaic Stadium, where the first modern Olympics were held in 1896.

Dotted in all directions – north, south, east and west – are museums of Cycladic art, arches in honour of Emperor Hadrian, Roman baths, monuments, Byzantine churches and archaeological sites galore. Rich pickings! The National Garden is in the centre of the action.

Yet you soon forget all of that wandering along the garden's meandering paths beside blooming oleander trees, towering eucalyptus trees and carob trees hung with long brown pods. Date palms from the Canary Islands shoot up. Australian pines and cypress trees, too. Tangled shrubs form a warren of undergrowth. In all there are said to be 7,000 trees and 40,000 bushes covering more than 500 species in the National Garden. The buzz of traffic, the rush of a busy city and the manic "holidaymaking" of Athens are soon behind you upon entering this haven of green. You have become enveloped in foliage in what feels like a secret hideaway. The temperature seems a degree or two cooler than the rest of the usually baking city. You have escaped the madding crowds.

To make the most of this contrast, one of the best ways to arrive is from the heat and cacophony of Syntagma Square (Constitution Square) beside the Hellenic Parliament. This is where the changing of the guards takes place each day by the Tomb of the Unknown Soldier, quite a spectacle as guards are dressed in extraordinary garbs of red berets hung with tassels, elaborate embroidered cloaks, mini skirt-style kilts, woollen stockings, garters and strange slipper-style shoes. During the changeover they goose-step about with rifles slung over shoulders while saluting one another with extremely serious expressions, looking like something out of a Monty Python sketch.

After this entrance, well worth the detour, you are in a garden with an intriguing history.

There would be no National Garden had not the Royal Palace been completed in 1843 on the orders of King Otto, a Bavarian prince.

King Otto had been selected to rule Greece after the Convention of London of 1832 where Britain, France and Russia met to discuss and pronounce upon the country's future. These world powers had supported the Greeks as they broke free of the Ottoman Empire during the Greek War of Independence. Having played this role, the British, French and Russians took it upon themselves to decide the country's future, believing that stability in Greece would be most likely under a king from the outside, thus preventing resentment between local factions should a head of state be chosen from one faction and not another.

The result was that King Otto soon after arrived blinking in the sunshine and heat with his wife, Queen Amalia, who promptly announced it was rather too arid for her liking in their adopted city. She would prefer some greenery beside their new palace. So, in came the very best French and German horticulturalists and designers, who set about laying paths in fashionable French baroque patterns around duck ponds and small lakes while importing trees and plants from across the globe; many of which were unable to cope with the hot conditions in Athens.

However, enough could and Queen Amalia took a great interest in the project, spending many hours each day tending to the garden. The main corridor of palms, now more than 25 metres high, was her handiwork. Although the official name back then was the Royal Garden, unofficially it became known as the Garden of Amalia. Her name may have been similar to Princess Amelia's back in Richmond Park in the 1750s, but she was made of different stuff.

That said, despite Queen Amalia's green-fingered down-to-earth tendencies, many Athenians were shocked and outraged by all the expenditure on the fancy horticulturalists and plants, which became a symbol of the outsiders' royal excesses. Queen Amalia had on occasion, a little cheekily, ordered the few ships in the possession of the Greek navy to make collections of her beloved plants from Genoa. To be fair, they had not had much else to do at the time. Nevertheless, these gardening missions did raise eyebrows.

Yet it was not all simply for the Queen's pleasure. Parts of the park were opened to the public at certain times of day, quickly becoming popular places to take perambulations. Later, with the temporary abolition of the monarchy in 1924, the gardens in their entirety opened and the name of National Garden was adopted. This stuck despite the return of the royals in 1935 until the monarchy was abolished for a second, final time in 1973.

That is how the park came to be. But there is another royal connection – an unusual one – involving a monkey.

Before the first abolition of the monarchy in 1924, King Alexander had been taking a stroll around the Royal Garden with his German shepherd, minding his own business one day. Suddenly however, his dog ran off in pursuit of a Barbary macaque monkey that is said to have belonged to one of the gardeners. It caught the monkey and they proceeded to have a fight that was soon joined by another of the gardener's pet monkeys. At this point, the king intervened, breaking up the melee while suffering a monkey bite for his efforts. He did not dwell on the matter – it was just a scratch – but he developed sepsis and died three days later, aged 27.

This had wide-reaching consequences. On King Alexander's death, his controversial father, King Constantine, returned. Constantine had been reluctant to align with the Allies during the First World War, partly, it is said, because his wife was German. This had led to him being deposed and Alexander given the crown.

In Constantine's absence, Alexander had had grand plans, known as the Great Idea, to expand Greek borders into Asia Minor, securing lands that had historical connections to Greece within Turkey. Conflict with the Turks had already begun in 1919. However, Constantine's bullish approach on taking up his son's Great Idea lacked military strategy and he ill-advisedly pushed on towards Istanbul. This ended in a devastating defeat at Smyrna in Turkey, where an enormous fire broke out in the part of the city in which locals with Greek ancestry lived, resulting in thousands of deaths and a mass exodus of refugees.

Winston Churchill's take on the whole affair was: "It is perhaps no exaggeration to remark that a quarter of a million persons died of this monkey's bite."

What a tragic park tale.

Aside from simply sitting in the shade and letting an hour slip lazily by – perhaps thinking back to the park's eventful royal days – one of the highlights of the National Garden in Athens is to visit the Roman mosaic that was uncovered during gardening work in the nineteenth century.

Queen Amalia's fancy garden designers had struck historic gold when they unearthed the floor of a Roman villa. The mosaic may not be in the best of conditions, but its faded tangerines, yellows and greys offer a tantalizing glimpse into life way before King Otto and Princess Amalia in a quiet corner of the National Garden. Other ancient ruins, fragments of columns and walls, are to be found throughout the park.

A tour of the National Garden's 38 acres delivers all sorts of riches. Just south of the official boundary of the National Garden is an imposing neoclassical building, the Zappeion, flanked by Corinthian columns and a splendid statue of Lord Byron. The poet died in 1824 when fighting on behalf of the Greeks in the Greek War of Independence aged 36 and is considered a national hero. The Zappeion was home to the fencing hall during the first modern Olympics and was also where the athletes stayed: the first "Olympic Village".

Across the road from the Zappeion is the Temple of Zeus: beyond the park's boundaries (and usually overrun with tourists). Across another road, also just outside the National Garden but so close it feels within, is the white marble horseshoe of the Panathenaic Stadium.

Such an evocative place and strangely empty of EasyJet hordes when I went. Races have been held at this site since the sixth century BC with a stadium since the fourth century BC (when athletes competed while naked), followed by the days of gladiators and wild beasts during Roman rule, and then the resounding success of the 1896 Games when 60,000 spectators watched as athletics moved into a new era and the Greek runner Spyros Louis won the first marathon to great national acclaim.

Sitting in the stands today is the perfect way to appreciate the National Garden: the fine jungle of green ahead in the middle of all this antiquity. In 1939, the writer Henry Miller wrote: "It remains in my memory like no other park I have known. It is the quintessence of a park, the thing one feels sometimes in looking at a canvas or dreaming of a place one would like to be in and never finds."

Stop by if you ever find yourself in the Greek capital: tranquillity and a corner of cool shade await.

Just try not to think too much about all the trouble that monkey caused.

The only way is up
Mount Srd, Dubrovnik, Croatia

Long-standing local concerns about "overtourism" – the term coined to describe too many tourists at some of the world's most popular sights – seemed almost anachronistic as I "moved on" to Croatia.

Overtourism? There were no tourists! At least there had been very few indeed of late during the pandemic.

However, chances were that the floodgates of mass tourism would reopen soon enough and swarms of tourists would return to the world's best-loved cities. Yes, Athens is enormously popular and the Acropolis can be unpleasantly hectic. But Dubrovnik is on another level altogether. The "pearl of the Adriatic", Lord Byron's description (the poet did get about), seems to have an almost irresistible allure… plus some fine greenery a few strides from all the crowds, if you know where to look.

Dubrovnik's problems with overtourism are largely due to the old city and the main "attractions" being squeezed within medieval walls that once enclosed the former Republic of Ragusa. This republic lasted for many centuries from around 1270 until Napoleonic troops arrived in 1806 bringing an end to the independent state, and those plucky days of independence remain at the heart of Dubrovnik's mysterious appeal.

Behind the high stone walls teetering on craggy rocks above the crystalline waters of the Adriatic lies the epicentre of what was once a stubbornly self-reliant and progressive city-empire with fleets of merchant ships, bejewelled churches, thriving monasteries and opulent mansions, as well as hospitals, pharmacies, almshouses, orphanages, aqueducts and public fountains. Some of the wealthiest traders anywhere outside of Venice lived in the extremely well-organized citadel.

Through its great gates, tourists find themselves being funnelled along narrow flagstone passages leading between terracotta-roofed structures little changed since those glory days. Fortifications remain and visitors can walk the battlements, which run for 2,000 metres, giving an indication both of the size of the old town centre (tiny, really) and the sheer audacity of the days of Ragusa. Such a little place standing proudly alone for so many centuries as great conflicts swirled around the Mediterranean.

Above the gate of the formidable fortress of Lovrijenac, an important former defence just outside the walls on the western edge of the old town, a motto in Latin, the official language in Dubrovnik until 1472, reads: *Non bene pro toto libertas venditur auro* (All the gold in the world cannot buy freedom). The flag flown by the merchant ships of the Republic of Ragusa was embroidered with *libertas* (freedom). This message not only encapsulated the enlightened free spirit of the republic, which abolished slave trading in the early fifteenth century well ahead of other European nations, but also allowed for less problematic passage on the high seas; aided and abetted by a plentiful supply of cannons and cannon balls. Excellent weapon-making also had something to do with the republic's longevity.

With its turrets, bell towers, battlements and great walls rising from the rocks below, forward-thinking Dubrovnik has all the trappings of a medieval dream. No wonder the *Game of Thrones* fantasy television series set so many scenes here.

No wonder also that its old streets get so overrun by tourists, especially when cruise ships arrive at the nearby port, sometimes as many as four at a time. More than 10,000 visitors bought tickets to walk the city walls one day in August 2016, prompting UNESCO to threaten to cancel Dubrovnik's prestigious World Heritage Site status unless something was done to limit the influx. While 606,000 tourists had come in 2011, almost a million arrived in 2016.

In response, the city's mayor, Mato Frankovic, set a daily limit of two cruise ships with a maximum of 4,000 tourists. Not only that, with earlier headlines screaming "The death of Dubrovnik? Crowds and cruise ships have ruined the city, say locals", the mayor had gone into overdrive issuing a 17-page document entitled "Respect the City"laying out many other ways to develop sustainable and better tourism, such as clearing the streets of unregistered guides hawking cheap tours, closing pop-up restaurants with tables spilling out into narrow lanes and improving official ticketing to attractions. The rather wonderful, if not totally catchy motto of the campaign was: "If you have a bitter, 'angry', orange: make a marmalade."

This was the background to any visit to Dubrovnik, where annual tourist numbers *rose* in 2019 to 1.4 million despite the new cruise limit. This was also why, even with a mere 4,000 cruise passengers each day, your instinct at times may be to escape, no matter how spectacular and awe-inspiring the city undoubtedly is.

And this is why, like me, you may wish to climb the mountain.

Mount Srd rises to 412 metres directly behind Dubrovnik. A cable car can whisk you up, but the best way to go is to walk along the zig-zagging path ascending a hillside of designated parkland a few minutes from the old town's jostle of tourists wearing gaudy wristbands and lanyards (so tour guides will not lose their flock). Just as in Cape Town back in South Africa, going up soon transports you to another world.

This time I was not in the company of hungover Barmy Army cricket fans. This time I was alone on a drizzly day, exiting the city's north gate, passing a pizzeria and a kiosk selling octopus burgers, before ascending alleys between quaint houses with green shutters, and crossing a highway to reach a brown sign marked *Krizni Put* (Walking Trail).

Following this trail, you soon find yourself deep in woodland, tramping steeply upwards. The rocky, red-mud track climbs into a tunnel of umbrella pine and cypress trees; traffic sounds blocked out as you rise and the wall of green behind thickens. A sense of splendid isolation on the hill strikes you straight away. You are almost certainly the only person on the path; very few tourists bother to hike up because of the cable car. You are also probably sweating a bit, even on a damp day. The route, after a long traverse to the right at the start, quickly turns into a series of sharp switchbacks.

Pine resin and the scent of sage fill the air as the track twists upward amid patches of gorse with bright lemon-yellow flowers. Tall spiky bushes with blooms of lilac rise here and there, combining with the yellow of the gorse as though nature is putting on a show just for you. After a while, the frequency of cypress trees increases and then abruptly, when you are about halfway up, all trees disappear. As they do, the view opens out and the sublime walled city emerges below.

In the past, this vista would not have been possible until you reached the very top as the entire hillside was once covered in oaks – or *dubrava* – hence Dubrovnik's name. Over the years, however, these have been chopped down for the building of ships and the city itself.

On my misty day, the shape of the city walls down below, with the pool of tumbling terracotta roofs within, was both exhilarating and timeless. There was a view that cannot have altered much over the centuries. There before you lies the Republic of Ragusa in all its splendour looking as ready as ever – minus tall ships in the harbour – to set forth into the Med to strike deals under the banner of *libertas*.

At the top of Mount Srd, about an hour's hike, you are met by a pile of stones surrounded by thistles and topped by a makeshift cross comprising two old planks purloined from a half-collapsed military bunker. A short walk from here, you arrive at an old Napoleonic stronghold, Fort Imperial. Part of the fort has been transformed into the Homeland War Museum, documenting the conflict begun in 1991 during the break-up of former Yugoslavia. Croatian forces crucially held this position, protecting the city below from an even worse pounding than it received from Serbia and Montenegro, when seven out of ten buildings were damaged by shelling. The fort has become a proud symbol of Dubrovnik's resistance and displays inside recount events blow by blow.

Next to the fort is the Panorama Restaurant and Bar, attached to a structure housing the stop for the cable car. There is not much else at the top of Mount Srd.

The Panorama Restaurant and Bar, however, makes a pleasing target for an ascent. After trudging up the rocky trail between the gorse bushes, white tablecloths, jazz and high windows await with "the view" (Dubrovnik) filling the frames. Grilled beefsteak, "chicken rustica" and "king prawns panorama" are on the menu, as are an assortment of cocktails laid on for the cruise passenger day trippers: banana daiquiris, mojitos, frozen piña coladas and Caribbean dreams of rum, vodka, grenadine and pineapple. The overall feel is of having entered the captain's dining lounge: quite enjoyable really, if a little cheesy.

From the Panorama Restaurant and Bar, the journey down to Dubrovnik is 4 minutes in the cable car while listening to tinny pop music as the old Republic of Ragusa draws closer and closer.

And somehow, after your hike up Mount Srd, you feel you know Dubrovnik a whole lot better than just a couple of hours before.

#EnjoyRespectVenezia
Giardini Papadopoli, Venice, Italy

Look at a map of Venice and there is almost no green. The Grand Canal curls in its lazy backward "S" surrounded by ancient palazzos, churches, hotels and townhouses. Land seems too precious for parkland in *La Serenissima* (the most serene). Seen with a map laid out on a table, the city is – like Dubrovnik – all terracotta tiles, other than that sliver of blue winding through.

Yet look a little closer, squint and search a second time, and one small patch of green stands out.

Giardini Papadopoli faces the Grand Canal at the north-western tip of the backward "S", close to Piazzale Roma with its bus terminal and Venice's big bridge over the lagoon to the mainland. There it is tucked away just south of the canal across from Venezia Santa Lucia Station, the city's railway terminus. Easy to overlook when pacing your way onward to the big sights at St Mark's Square, the Bridge of Sighs and the Rialto Bridge.

It is tiny: about 1.5 acres. A red brick wall runs along its perimeter by the Grand Canal, where a gateway is flanked by classical statues of a man and a woman posing in flowing robes (and looking rather pleased with themselves). This wall curves round beside a small canal known as Rio Novo and cuts inland, becoming a cast-iron fence and arriving at the entrance of Hotel Papadopoli Venezia, a surprisingly modern building with sliding glass doors, a purple-marble reception and a hundred rooms pitched as "retaining the spirit of the Venetian Age of Enlightenment but equipped with the latest twenty-first-century amenities".

The park has another entrance next to the hotel. This leads into what feels like an almost completely overlooked corner of the city surrounded by elms, magnolias, horse chestnuts and lime trees. Lawns are planted around flowerbeds that bloom with tulips in the spring, close to a statue of a famous nineteenth-century Italian engineer, Pietro Paleòcapa, responsible for much Venetian canal work (as well as drafts of the plan for the Suez Canal, oddly enough). Wooden benches are scattered all about; the pick being beside a small circular pond.

The great thing is that the park's design somehow seems to block out the city beyond its boundaries: the buses, the arrivals with rolling cases from the station, the crowds following guides, the general commotion of what is probably the world's number one "tourist city". Problems with overtourism in Athens and Dubrovnik are like spilt milk compared with the difficulties arising from the daily deluge of visitors to Venice, in usual times.

Giardini Papadopoli has long been a place for quiet and repose. In the sixth century it was chosen by Benedictine monks for their Monastery of Santa Croce. After that, the monastery switched to a nunnery aligned to the Order of Saint Clare. And religious days continued without disturbance on this patch of Venice for more than 1,000 years, only coming to an end when Napoleonic troops arrived and destroyed the old church to make way for a space for training and organizing regiments. When they were gone, however, peace returned later in the nineteenth century when a family with Greek ancestry, the Papadopolis, built a house with a large private garden that was eventually turned into a park.

After this, another threat to the quietude of this little corner of Venice was to come in the form of the fascist leader Benito Mussolini, who ordered the construction of the bridge across the lagoon, originally named Ponte Littorio when opened in 1933 but changed to Ponte della Libertà after his downfall. Luckily, even though a third of the park's land was purloined to expand Piazzale Roma to allow a better flow of traffic at the time of the bridge's opening, Rio Novo was dug, too. This acted as a barrier to all the revving traffic. So Giardini Papadopoli's calm was maintained. By then, though, all traces of the old monastery/nunnery were long gone, save for a pillar said to be from those times that can be found by Santa Croce bridge.

There you have Giardini Papadopoli's "back story", although when I was about to enter for the first time, all was not quiet near the back gate.

This was because a classic Venetian scene was being played out by the Rio Novo.

Two young women were sitting by the canal enjoying a snack and chatting in the sunshine when two suave middle-aged men wearing peaked sailor caps and designer clothes – plenty of Gucci by the looks of it – stopped their shiny varnished speedboat before the pair. A proposal was being made to the young women: would they like to join the middle-aged men in sailor caps and designer Gucci clothes for a ride?

The suave middle-aged men were quite shameless and persistent about this, not seeming to mind what anyone passing might think. The young women responded in the negative and the middle-aged men doffed their peaked sailor caps, bowed flamboyantly, blew kisses and went on their way. All part of *la dolce vita*, I suppose. Not speed dating: speedboat dating.

I crossed into Giardini Papadopoli and made my way to one of the benches by the pond.

There, I closed my eyes and listened to the buzz and hum of boats on the canals. For a few minutes I rested, feeling totally at ease with the world. To be in the heart of my favourite city in such a peaceful spot seemed almost miraculous.

Upon opening my eyes, I found I was being regarded by a pair of elderly women dressed in black, loaves poking out of shopping baskets by their sides. They were discussing something or other with great intent that clearly had nothing to do with me, but as I was in their line of vision, this was where their eyes had fallen. I smiled and one of the two smiled faintly back. Then they glanced at one another for a moment before switching their focus to somewhere in the direction of Rio Novo. It was as though they needed a shared point of attention. Their gossip galloped on.

Other characters on the benches by the pond included a cross-legged bearded man with a distinguished visage and disconcertingly bright-blue eyes. His hair had maintained much of its jet-black colour, greying in patches at the temples, and had been swept raffishly to one side. His clothing was crumpled and too warm for the weather, yet well-worn looking rather than scruffy.

Every little while, with a nonchalance combined with a faraway expression, he reached into the pocket of his jacket and fetched a small bottle from which he took a couple of sips. Then he carefully re-screwed the cap, placed the bottle back in his pocket, readjusted his gait and continued his thoughts, which seemed wide-ranging given his little occasional murmurs that appeared to provide verbal assent to a conclusion he had just that very moment drawn.

All his movements were cautiously calibrated; keeping up appearances was clearly an important consideration. He was either down on his luck – a permanent resident of Giardini Papadopoli, bedding down behind the shrubs beneath the elms – or a member of a noble Venetian family dropping by from his palazzo for some air. It was difficult to tell which.

Aside from the elderly women and the man of indeterminate circumstances, the benches were occupied by pie-eyed office or shop workers on breaks, although a pair of backpackers on the far side of the fountain laughed and canoodled contentedly, oblivious to all around. Perhaps they were students on a summer break. Seeing them so happily in a world of their own made the whole park seem carefree and somehow auspicious. The benches by the fountain that afternoon offered a quietly joyful corner of Giardini Papadopoli.

Overtourism felt a long way away. Yet overtourism is, of course, the modern Venetian curse.

The mayor of Venice, like his counterpart in Dubrovnik, has already stepped in, with latest measures including a ban on cruise ships of more than 100,000 tonnes, turnstiles to restrict movement to most popular sites and entrance fees for day trippers to the city centre (£10).

An official campaign under the banner of #EnjoyRespectVenezia recommends that visitors book qualified tourist guides, buy locally produced souvenirs and explore "hidden treasures to appreciate Venice's exceptional beauty". Although some believe this is not going far enough. An activist group named Gruppo 25 Aprile has been formed to urge city officials not to turn Venice into a "kind of theme park". Members believe that entrance fees are not the answer, only a strict quota will do, given more than 36 million tourists arrive each year with as many as 32,000 daily cruise ship passengers on top of 465,100 day trippers.

This influx has been driving out locals and destroying the community. Since 1970, those living in the city have fallen by about 100,000 to 53,000. Meanwhile, many of those most recently leaving have added their homes to rental properties offered by Airbnb, encouraging even more outsiders to come. Marco Gasparinetti, one of the leading activists of Gruppo 25

Aprile, says: "We need to create conditions for people to stay." Living in a theme park is not conducive to a properly functioning community, he says. Waiting jobs and working "selling tourist stuff at a kiosk" are not strong enough incentives to keep bright youngsters from moving out.

Crammed onto its little islands in the lagoon, Venice is so full of tourists that a feeling of suffocation can sometimes set in.

So Giardini Papadopoli is both wonderful and somehow sad, too: a lonely blob of green on that pink-roofed map. A place in which to sit quietly and soak up this ethereal city on the water. A place to savour some solitude away from the madding crowds. A place to close your eyes and dream, dream, dream.

Park heaven
Prater, Vienna, Austria

Now to a very old park in a city with plenty of green – and character.

According to the City of Vienna government's Parks and Gardens Municipal Department Number 42, about half of the 200 square kilometres that make up Vienna can be classed as "green area open to public use".

So you have Donaupark built on an island on the Danube in the 1960s that was previously the site of a rubbish dump, a squatters' camp and a notorious Nazi parade ground where executions were held. Now it is home to rose gardens, a petting zoo and the 250-metre Danube Tower, an "attraction" with a viewing platform and a restaurant serving schnitzels. Then there is Setagayapark, a Japanese garden in a northern suburb complete with a teahouse and pagoda. Then you have Stadtpark by the banks of the River Wien with meadows, art nouveau bridges and a famous sculpture of the composer Johann Strauss. Then there are the picturesque ponds and undulating hills of Türkenschanzpark, so named as trenches dug by the Turks during the Siege of Vienna in 1529 were discovered ahead of its opening in 1888 by Emperor Franz Joseph I.

Throw in the fruit trees and lilac gardens of Herderpark; the playgrounds and fields of Kongresspark; the wide-open landscape and thermal spring at Kurpark Oberlaa; and the much-loved Rathauspark, near city hall and renowned for its Christmas market and skating rink. Rathauspark was another of Franz Joseph I's creations, dating from the 1860s. The emperor, whose declaration of war on Serbia triggered the First World War, was evidently a park fan.

Put them all together and you have *a lot* of parks.

Vienna is an extremely green city indeed, way ahead of the game with its 50 per cent of green; London, after all, only aspires to such greenery by 2050. There are many, many fine parks. Yet one park in Austria's capital that has been around for a long time, since 1766, has pride of place among all these lovely open public spaces.

Prater is a large park (3,200 acres) on a long, misshapen island formed by the Danube Canal and the River Danube in the east of the city in the district of Leopoldstadt; referred to simply as "Prater" rather than Prater Park. You can get there on the metro, stopping at Praterstern Station and crossing a busy road. Up ahead a funfair of swings, carousels and ghost trains rises with one of the symbols of Vienna looming above: a 65-metre tall nineteenth-century Ferris wheel adorned with cherry-red gondolas that look from a distance as though little public buses have been stripped of their wheels and attached to the solid metal framework. When visiting the park for the first time, something about the Ferris wheel seems to draw you in its direction.

Beyond the Ferris wheel, to which I will return, a 3-mile tree-lined avenue, the Hauptallee, shoots south-eastward in a straight line ending at a roundabout beside a golf course. When Joseph II donated this royal hunting ground to the public back in the eighteenth century, he made a lot of friends owing to the Hauptallee, which quickly became an established part of the social scene.

Stepping back in time to those magical, almost legendary, early days is a way of unlocking some of what makes Prater so singular.

Because ghosts of the past seem to haunt Prater Park as they tend to in so many parks if you cast your mind back, especially along the Hauptallee.

Luckily, the memoirs of a well-connected, exuberant Irish opera singer who visited not long after the opening shed light on Vienna's best park during its glamorous golden age.

When Michael Kelly visited Prater in the 1780s, the talented tenor was much taken by the lively social scene. Kelly had befriended Mozart, sometimes dining with him or playing billiards (usually losing) and had taken on the part of Don Curzio in the premiere of *The Marriage of Figaro* in 1786. He had also become pally with the influential composer Antonio Salieri, whose students over the years included Beethoven, Schubert, Liszt and Mozart (with whom, it is said, Salieri formed a fierce rivalry, as depicted in the multi-Oscar-winning 1984 film Amadeus).

In his memoir *Reminiscences* Kelly describes Salieri as: "A little man, with an expressive countenance, and his eyes were full of genius." And on occasion, the singer would enjoy trips to the park in the composer's company.

His account of one such jaunt is captivating:

> The Prater… I consider the finest public promenade in Europe, far surpassing in variety our own beautiful Hyde Park. It is about four miles in length; on each side of the road are fine chestnut trees, and a number of avenues and retired drives. These roads, on spring and summer evenings, are thronged with carriages. On all sides, as in our Hyde Park and Bushy Park, deer are seen quietly grazing, and gazing at the passing crowds. At the end of the principal avenue is an excellent tavern, besides which, in many other parts of this enchanting spot, there are innumerable cabarets, frequented by all ranks in the evening, who *immediately after dinner* [his italics] proceed thither to regale themselves with their favourite dish, fried chickens, cold ham, and sausages; white beer, and Hofner wines, by way of dessert; and stay there until a late hour: dancing, music and every description of merriment

prevail; and every evening, when not professionally engaged, I was sure to be in the midst of it.

Kelly appears to have had a blast. "The women, generally speaking, are beautiful," he adds with un-woke eighteenth-century candour. "They have fine complexions, and symmetrical figures, the lower orders particularly. All the servant-maids are anxious to shew their feet, which are universally handsome, and are very ambitious of having neat shoes and stockings." He and Salieri go for a drink by the banks of the Danube where they are interrupted, with Salieri in mid song, by a large wild boar coming their way. They flee leaving "a flagon of excellent Rhenish wine behind us, which was to me a greater bore than the bristly animal".

Prater seems to have been made for frolics. During the nineteenth century, a tradition of *Praterfahrt* (promenading in Prater) had become well-established on Sundays, with all finery on display as carriages rattled up and down the Hauptallee. As the years went by the park became a magnet for events. World Trade Fairs were held at Prater, attracting millions of visitors. May Day parades of socialist workers marched by each year, to the consternation of the ruling classes.

The funfair, known as the Volkprater, got bigger and bigger with more and more rides, including the Ferris wheel in 1897 and a narrow-gauge steam train in 1928, travelling in a 2.5-mile loop. By the twentieth century, a warren-like world of little pubs, coffee shops and restaurants had sprung up; perfect for carousing an afternoon away à la Kelly/Salieri.

This funfair, with its echoes of raucous days gone by, is my favourite part of Prater.

And a ride on its Ferris wheel is a treat.

Up the cherry-red gondolas creak, Vienna unfurling below and Prater sweeping alongside the muddy brown Danube. As the ride rises, the many parks of Vienna can be seen here, there and everywhere, their broccoli-like trees breaking up the buildings of the old town, where the spire of St Stephen's Cathedral pokes up proudly as forest-clad mountains rise in the distance. Everything looks so neat, so well organized, so civilized and also *so very green*. City of Vienna's Parks and Gardens Municipal Department Number 42, take a bow! This may be a major European capital, home to almost 2 million people, but with so many open spaces you sense it is easily living with that number.

Which it is, generally speaking (to borrow a phrase from Kelly). This is not just my gut feeling simply because I like parks a lot. Each year, Mercer, an international consulting firm, releases a worldwide Quality of Living City Survey. For the past ten years, as I write, Vienna has ranked number one on this list based on personal freedom, healthcare, political stability, crime, housing, education, public transport and recreational facilities of 231 cities. Good parks playing a big part in all of this.

Juddering around the Ferris wheel, the old-fashioned gondolas stopping regularly as passengers are dropped off and picked up, there is plenty of time to admire the greenery of this ten-times-number one city from above. And as you do so, a tune may drift into your brain, especially if you are one of the legion of fans of Graham Greene's writing, which you may have gathered by now includes me among their number.

The tune is the chilling theme music from the film adaption of Graham Greene's novella *The Third Man*, about life in Vienna in the immediate post-Second World War period when the city was divided under the control of the Russians, Americans, British and the French. The vivid, brilliantly moody black-and-white film stars Orson Welles, who plays the lead character, Harry Lime, a seedy amoral man running a watered-down penicillin racket causing many deaths (based on real goings-on at the time). It is filmed in Vienna and the eerie music is played on a zither, a distinctively twangy stringed instrument.

It is as he takes a trip on Prater's Ferris wheel that Lime attempts to justify his illegal trade in what is the film's most famous scene. As he does so, Lime points at the "dots" of people in the funfair down below: "Would you really feel any pity if one of those dots stopped moving – for ever? If I said you could have £20,000 for every dot that stops, would you really, old man, tell me to keep my money – without hesitation?"

It is, for me, one of the most gripping scenes in any film ever (as relevant today as ever). The zither twangs. The "dots" move between the carousels and the *wurst* stall. And a sickly feeling of moral ambiguity imbues the flickering black-and-white screen; the claustrophobia enhanced by the setting with nowhere to escape up in the gondola.

Squint your eyes and you are in the film, looking down on Prater park just as Harry Lime once did.

Open them wide and one of the best cities for parks on the planet rolls forth in all its splendour.

Lustgartens and beer halls
Tiergarten, Berlin, Germany

Down by the River Spree a duck was making a racket. Having waddled with great urgency from a tangle of vegetation by the water's edge, followed by six little ducklings, the creature had plunged into the river and was quacking, squawking and flapping its wings for all it was worth. Could this be the noisiest duck in the history of ducks, I wondered, admittedly slightly hungover from a beer hall the night before? Were all Berlin ducks like this? Or had this one simply lost its mind?

On the riverbank, the answer padded into view, turning its long brown nose towards the mad duck and her bemused ducklings. The bushy brown fox, a fine specimen, regarded her with an expression of irritation and disdain before scurrying into the undergrowth. The duck let off an indignant parting volley of quacks. Peace descended on central Berlin.

Welcome to the heart of the capital city of the economic powerhouse of Europe, a short distance from its legislature, president's residence and main train station: impromptu nature shows all part of the entertainment on Sunday mornings by its most famous park.

Tiergarten is another big one: 494 acres of prime land that was once a royal hunting ground before being turned into gardens open to the public in the 1740s by Frederick II, also known as Frederick the Great.

Keen to improve the landscape but not a keen hunter – he was more of a culture vulture – the Prussian king was soon overseeing the removal of fences, previously erected to keep in game, as well as the installation of a formal baroque-style *Lustgarten* (pleasure garden) with mazes and fountains and elaborate geometrically shaped flower beds and lawns. All of this was quite a to-do. It was, after all, still a quarter of a century before Prater park in Vienna.

So began Berlin's finest park, a great slab of greenery in a metro area that now boasts more than 2,500 parks covering 16,000 acres according to the Senate Department for Urban Development and the Environment's Public Parks Green and Recreational Spaces division (I do love these extraordinary city park department names). At least 30 per cent of the urban area of Berlin is now parkland and woodland. So, just like Vienna, Berlin is a green city, if not quite matching Viennese levels of supreme greenery.

Tiergarten was for Berlin the start, park-wise. And much has happened in it over the years.

For a while, things went peacefully enough. Frederick the Great's park evolved into a landscaped, natural style that became fashionable in the early nineteenth century. To achieve this end, the star garden architect Peter Joseph Lenné, born in Bonn, had been called in to replace the flamboyant "Louis-XIV look" with the new "English" style of landscape architecture. Lenné had even been over to Britain for three months to learn the latest techniques used at parks designed by the prolific William Kent, responsible for the gardens at Stowe House in Buckinghamshire. He was a quick learner. On his return, lakes, meadows and forests were blended at Tiergarten to create perfect "compositions" of the three. Marshy areas were drained and a network of paths added. A zoo also opened (in 1844) on the southern edge.

Thus Tiergarten slowly went about matters over the years, pootling along with refinements introduced every now and then at the hands of experts who were au fait with all the latest garden trends from across the globe and careful to do everything just so. Lenné himself had been acquainted with the soon-to-be-legendary Frederick Olmsted of Central Park fame back in New York City.

Then came the Nazis. On Hitler's orders, the main avenue across the park from Brandenburg Gate in the east toward Charlottenburg Palace in the west was doubled in width to more than 50 metres while being renamed the East-West Axis. Great military parades were held through Tiergarten on this expanded passage, making a bold statement of Nazi power in the capital at a time when the cult of Hitler was at its height in the late 1930s. The Victory Column, built to commemorate triumph in a Prussian and Austrian war against Denmark in 1864, was moved from outside the Reichstag to a prominent roundabout on the avenue, with space added for proclamations of future expected glorious German victories.

Further plans for Tiergarten were rapidly drawn: an extravagant archway to cross the East-West Axis; a huge North-South Axis road for yet more military parades; and a mammoth domed *Volkshalle* (people's hall) designed by Hitler himself to rise by the River Spree on the northeast edge of the park.

Tiergarten had suddenly found itself at the epicentre of Hitler's dreams for the capital of a new world order – to be named Germania. On the Fuhrer's fiftieth birthday on 20 April 1939 more than 2 million adoring subjects lined the newly completed East-West Axis waving swastikas while being held back by SS men and stormtroopers from the birthday motorcade along the 4.5-mile route from Brandenburg Gate.

On this day, at the far western end of the avenue near the Technical High School, Hitler had left his Mercedes and relocated to a plush red chair on a raised dais surrounded by swastika banners and a giant gilded eagle as 50,000 troops goose-stepped past followed by a trail of tanks. Up above, a thunderous fly-by of Messerschmitt fighters was to follow. William Shirer, an American correspondent, who witnessed the scene, said: "I've never seen so many flags, standards, golden eagles and floodlit pylons in my life. Nor so many glittering uniforms, or soldiers, or guns. Nor so many people at a birthday party."

Fortunately, shortages of resources during the war meant that the archway, North-South Axis and *Volkhalle* never came to be. Instead, under the Nazis Tiergarten soon fell on hard times. During the conflict and in the tough years directly afterward, trees were felled for fuel and land dug for allotments to alleviate widespread hunger. Bombing during the 1945 Battle of Britain resulted in much of the park being destroyed. Of 200,000 trees, only 700 survived the war.

During the Cold War, however, a period of rejuvenation began from 1949–59, during which thousands of trees were replanted in the park. Slowly, the greenery returned and West Berliners were soon cherishing their precious park, especially when the Berlin Wall went up in 1961. A trip to Tiergarten after then was effectively a "trip to the countryside" for city folk surrounded by concrete, barbed wire, checkpoints and watchtowers.

So, there is plenty to contemplate on a stroll in Tiergarten.

After my wildlife encounter, I followed a path that curved southward toward the Victory Column on the roundabout on what was the East-West Axis.

This path is now renamed Strasse des 17 Juni, a date that commemorates an uprising of workers against long hours and poor living conditions in East Germany in 1953. Before the Nazis and then after the war up to 1953, the avenue had been known as Charlottenburger Chaussee after the royal palace in the west; the whole point of the street originally had been to ease the movement of monarchs between palaces.

From the plinth of the Victory Column, you get a sense of the enormity of the avenue, which seems somehow to be the defining feature of this park. The road, after all, completely (quite brutally) cuts Tiergarten in two. In the final days of its incarnation as the East-West Axis, the avenue was used as a runway for Nazis fleeing Berlin as airports by then had been damaged. On a visit it is, frankly, hard not to think of those last planes buzzing off, or the scenes of sheer hysteria on Hitler's 50th.

From the Victory Column, it is either a straight walk west along the avenue or a meandering one if you cut into the shaded woodland if you are going in the direction of Charlottenburg Palace (which I was). This is when Tiergarten comes into its own with lakes covered with water lilies, willows, streams, fountains and little hidden glades, plus plenty of joggers. Tiergarten always seems full of joggers, just like so many of the best city parks.

Because that is what Tiergarten is, despite its giant avenue: another "green lung" in the heart of an important metropolis. Once you are away from the great boulevard you are soon peacefully ensconced in nature.

At the end of one of the long twisty paths, you come to a flea market on the far western edge of Tiergarten (if visiting on a weekend, as I was).

This is a joy and full of all sorts of junk. Yet there are many "finds" too along its two long passages of stalls run by enthusiasts, many of whom have specialities. So, you have the brass candlestick, brass door fittings and brass hooks specialist. Then there is the retro 1970s beige, orange and brown felt material clothing aficionado. Close by might be the paintings-of-old-ships connoisseur. Or the romantic-landscape-painting expert, the pewter-mug specialist, the flowery-porcelain-table sets pro, or the railway-paraphernalia go-to man.

The stallholders are not pushy, but they are proud of their wares and the area of expertize they have cornered; ready to talk at some length about old railway signs from Dresden and Leipzig given the opportunity. They are also willing to knock off a euro or two. My brass candlestick cost the same as my lunch: a Turkish flatbread known as *gözleme* filled with spicy minced meat. Snack kiosks and cafes break up the run of stalls.

What a great "park flea market"!

Brass candlestick in pocket – feeling like a character from the board game Cluedo – I went on another long meandering walk to see the fine old Charlottenburg Palace before returning to Tiergarten, winding along more twisty paths and getting thoroughly lost before finding myself near the zoo at a beer hall named Schleusenkrug.

What a great "park beer hall"!

Half covered in vines with unusual French chateau-style crystal chandeliers above the ordering counter and a cluster of picnic tables in a secluded garden, this is even – I would go as far as to say – *an excellent park beer hall,* with cheery service and extremely large tankards of bubbly pilsner delivered to your table. There you are in a green hideaway in the middle of this economic powerhouse of Europe, happily drinking an extremely large tankard of bubbly pilsner. Could I think of a better park beer hall *anywhere* in *any* park? No. Schleusenkrug was the very perfect gem of a very perfect German park beer hall.

Was the beer going to my head? Perhaps.

Yet Tiergarten is one of my favourite parks not just because of its Schleusenkrug pub, or impromptu nature shows by the River Spree, or its long twisty paths through its "English" style gardens, or its curious flea market, or its many hidden corners of green. It is also because I could not help thinking *thank goodness the troubles of the twentieth century are no more.*

Even if so many others seem to have taken their place.

CHAPTER ELEVEN

UKRAINE, BELARUS, POLAND, FINLAND, SWEDEN: UP, UP AND AWAY (IN PARKS)

One of the great things about parks is that no two experiences are quite the same. One person's memories are necessarily quite different from another's. You may walk through a park one day and everyone smiles and says "good morning". The next you may find yourself among a succession of misery guts.

The sun may shine, or it may rain. Wildlife may gambol about, or all the creatures may be shy that day. Flowers may be in full bloom, or you may have missed their best. You may be feeling positive and "up", or in the dumps and "down". You may have time to kill, you may be in a rush. You may be heading for a "sight" or on business, or just passing the time of day. You may be listening to music. You may be dreaming. Your mind may be a million miles away.

Parks mutate. You mutate. Happenchance plays its part: in parks as in everywhere. You may revisit a park and think: *This is not how I remember it at all, why did I ever imagine I liked this place so much?* You may revisit a park and think: *Wow, I'll always love it here.*

In short, parks can have on and off days, just like us. A thousand or more considerations, I was realizing, may colour a visit. Sitting in my study, observed by my Ecuadorian fox as my girlfriend participated in a live-streamed online oriental dancing class in the front room (as you do during a lockdown), I was having more than enough time to chew over park-related matters.

Bearing these thoughts in mind – and after another good look at my globe – I was about to "move" south-east from Germany then up, up, up into the Nordic countries, with good days, bad days and everything in between.

Drunken sailors
Shevchenko Park, Odessa, Ukraine

Do not enter Shevchenko Park in Odessa just before sunset and take one of the paths down toward the beach past a group of Ukrainian sailors who seem to have been drinking all day and, when one of them pulls a face at you, pull a face back because you do not like people pulling faces at you.

This is, potentially, not particularly good for your health.

It was my own fault really, on several counts. From some way off it was clear to see that the individuals ahead were in a raucous mood, cavorting and yelling, laughing and wobbling, grabbing on to each other in comradeship and, quite possibly, to stay upright. The rattle of a can being kicked emanated from the gloom of the shaded area of trees in which they lurked. This part of Taras Shevchenko Park of Culture and Recreation, to give the park its full name, clearly "belonged" to them for the time being.

The pathway passed them although there was another way to go to the beach; the group could be easily avoided. Curiosity, however, got the better of me. What do drunken Ukrainian sailors, almost certainly in the Ukrainian navy judging by their buzzcuts, get up to on their time on shore? Being on the edge of the Black Sea in a port city not far from a conflict zone in the east of the country, tipsy sailors seemed to be part of this particular park's "attractions". Pleasant avenues of lime and elm trees? Tick. Well-tended flower beds blooming in delightful cornucopias of colours? Tick. August monuments to famous Ukrainian poets and writers? Tick (the park is named after Taras Shevchenko, a nineteenth-century scribe considered by some to be the founder of modern Ukrainian literature). Sports fields? Tick (there is even a football stadium in one corner, home to FC Chornomorets Odessa). Viewpoints by the sea? Ancient archways? War memorials? Tick, tick, tick.

Earlier, officers in white uniforms with peaked caps and gold epaulettes had strolled arm in arm with their belles near the granite obelisk and eternal flame by the Monument to the Unknown Sailor. The elegance and poise of these couples was such that it was hard not to stare; they looked as though they had stepped out of a film or been transported from another age. Sweethearts holding each other tight while trouble brewed on the front: it was just 100 miles across the Black

Sea to the disputed territory of Crimea, occupied by the Russians in 2014 although Ukraine considers the peninsula an integral part of its nation. Skirmishes resulting from pro-Russian insurgency in other parts of the east rumbled on.

How did the lower-deck hands amuse themselves? I was soon to find out.

My feet kept going towards the shaded area of trees. As they did, one of the group – so inebriated his eyes looked like bloodshot pickled eggs – spun round, staggered forwards and glowered theatrically, a bottle dangling in one of his hands, the other fist clenched as he muttered something in Ukrainian that was possibly not: "Good afternoon dear visitor to this city." From body language (aggressive) and tone of voice (sneering), it was more like: "And who the bloody hell are you?" Or probably worse. Intimidating tourists seemed to be how this lower-deck hand got his kicks. What do you do in such a situation? Without thinking about the possible consequences, my knee-jerk response was possibly a little ill judged: to glower back, add a smirk and a mutter of my own for good measure and continue down the path.

The effect on the incredibly drunk Ukrainian sailor was initially dumbfounded incomprehension. Then he gathered his thoughts, turning to his friends as though seeking acknowledgement that he had witnessed such bare-faced effrontery from a tourist. After which came a volley of slurred Ukrainian abuse and the sound of rushing footsteps. A quick glance back ascertained that the crew of Ukrainian frigate seemed to be coming to get me. I had 20 metres on them already – and I began to run, turning again after a few paces to check how I was doing. The Ukrainian sailors had stopped and were jeering and gesticulating at me: they had only meant to give me a scare. This had more than worked. I slipped down the path to Langeron Beach without needing to call upon my travel insurance medical cover (or break into another undignified sprint).

Parks can have their moments, as I have mentioned, just like all of us.

Shevchenko Park covers 155 acres on an escarpment that was once an old fort facing the Cape of Langeron, named after a former count who served for the Russian Empire. The park itself was previously named Alexander Park, after Alexander II, the emperor of Russia, and the tsar had been the official guest of honour at the park's official opening in 1875 when he planted the park's first tree (an oak); Odessa was the Black Sea playground of the great and the good of the empire back then. On Alexander's death six years later, a monument was subsequently erected in his honour on the hill overlooking the football stadium and this is still there, a rather bleak black-stone column above a well-maintained lawn that is promoted as one of the city highlights in tourist brochures.

All slightly odd given that Russia is now the avowed enemy across the sea in Crimea, but understandable perhaps due to the strong ethnic Russian population in Odessa; about one in five people in the country have Russian ethnicity. The politics of Ukraine since independence from Soviet influence in 1990 have been far from straightforward.

The name Shevchenko Park was adopted in the 1950s and it was not without controversy. Taras Shevchenko, born in Ukraine in 1814, was a firm believer in Ukrainian independence from Russia and had caused great offence in a damning nationalistic poem, "Dream", that referred to dreadful living conditions under serfdom, unfair incarcerations of political prisoners and, in unflattering terms, Nicholas I himself as well as Nicholas' wife. This particularly insulting section was what raised the tsar's ire resulting in Shevchenko being exiled first to the Ural Mountains, where writing materials were withheld, and then to a remote penal settlement in Kazakhstan. Hardly surprising, perhaps, given the tsar's ability to do just this and his fury at lines written about his wife, Alexandra Feodorovna:

Here comes himself, the tsar,
To stretch his legs; and at his side
His empress struts and preens,
All wrinkled like a dried-up prune,

And like a beanpole lean,
While every time she steps, her head
Goes jiggling on her neck.
Is this the beauty rare they praise?!
Poor thing, you are a wreck!

So the poem continues in similar vein attacking the tsar's entourage, who are described as dripping in gold and silver clothing with bellies bulging from feasts on well-fed hogs. At a time when so many serfs were suffering this was calculated to cause embarrassment in the court and feed discontent in the countryside. Shevchenko really went for it. And he also really got it in return. Yet for this bravery and his cutting poetry he remains a Ukrainian national hero. A statue of the rather fierce-looking poet stands on the western edge of the park facing the city centre.

Just as in Tiergarten back in Berlin – and so many other parks – politics and public spaces devoted to greenery seem so often to overlap.

Having paid my respects at the Monument to the Unknown Sailor and having avoided single-handedly taking on the drunken crew of a ship, I reached the beach.

The sun had only just dropped away, leaving the horizon bathed in soft peach light above the wide calm water. The Black Sea here feels like the edge of the world and it is indeed an edge: out there beyond the water, Europe turns into Asia, the "Stans" of Kazakhstan, Turkmenistan and Uzbekistan rising way off in the hazy distance.

The sea is not black. The water is jade-green, a lovely inviting jade-green, translucent and warm to the touch. A few bathers splashed around, some on proper early-evening swims. Lights on distant ships flickered at sea as the peach horizon turned slowly caramel, mixing with the soft grey haze lifting from the sea. A luminous soup of gentle pastel colours lit up the sky. What a fine place to end up after a walk in the park.

Restaurants and bars are at one end of Langeron Beach: one with a veranda where the clientele was enjoying the last of the light with wine glasses the size of small bird baths. Shevchenko Park is not just for daytime strolls, at night the bars and nightclubs by the beaches that stretch southward are the place to go, especially in the summer. A club is even to be found within the park's official boundary: the purple neon Nice Club by the football stadium, complete with champagne booths, sushi canapes, bouncers with bow ties and karaoke. Perhaps my friends from the ship were going to drop by later, though somehow I doubted it.

Odessa has another fine, smaller park, Istanbul Park, just north of Shevchenko, home to the famous Potemkin Stairs that featured in the dramatic bloody scene in the 1925 silent film *Battleship Potemkin*, when Cossack soldiers fire on civilians on steps leading to the shore. One of the classic, and most tragic, moments in cinema history.

There is something tough and raw about the city's parks, yet captivating too.

Just remember to smile at the drunken sailors – even if they do seem to want to have a fight.

Park strife
Victory Park, Minsk, Belarus

On the day Victory Park was due to open in Minsk on 22 June 1941, Belarus did not live up to the park's (eventual) name. Nazi Germany launched Operation Barbarossa, attacking the Soviet Union, which included this Eastern European country, and going on to conquer and control Belarus until 1944.

During this awful period, the war on the eastern front and extermination camps resulted in approximately one in five Belarusians dying, possibly more. It is believed 90 per cent of the Jewish population was murdered, more than 800,000 people. The historian Timothy Snyder of Yale University estimates that half of the population of Soviet Belarus was either killed or forcibly displaced during the war and that "nothing of the kind can be said of any other European country". The overall figure for those who died is put at more than 2.2 million by some; this is higher in percentage terms than any other nation in the war. Belarus was devastated. It took until 1971 for the population to regain its pre-war level.

So, this park's name has bittersweet connotations.

Yes, the Nazis were eventually defeated, but at horrific human cost.

Sadly, many of the members of the youth groups who had spent a year and a half helping to landscape Victory Park were to perish during the Second World War, some after joining the partisan movement in Belarus, which numbered as many as 400,000 people. This is said to have been the largest of its kind in Europe, contributing to the eventual defeat of the Nazis in the east. Belarusians are rightly proud of this resistance, which did indeed help bring the victory of Victory Park.

The park finally opened in 1945, straddling around 500 acres of land by a stretch of the River Svislach dammed to form a lake. Despite many communist-era apartments and ugly hotels in the vicinity, built to replace the buildings flattened during the war, it offers a wonderful open space with paths leading off through woodlands of ash and birch trees and along quiet riverbanks populated by ducks and wading birds.

However, when I went, Belarus had been living through yet more troubled times and all was not well in the capital (or the country).

My visit occurred three years before the 2020 protests over the rule of President Alexander Lukashenko, dubbed by many "Europe's last dictator" on account of his repeated disputed victories in elections believed to have been rigged. Tension, it was clear even after just a few days in the country, was on the rise. Lukashenko had run Belarus with an iron rod since 1994, almost the entire period since the country's independence from the Soviet Union in 1991. Many regarded him (and still do) as a puppet reliant on Russian backing. The discontent that was obvious back then was soon to bubble over and the violent clampdown on peaceful protests of 2020 – continuing as I write – shone a harsh light on the regime's brutality. Countries across the globe backed the pro-democracy protesters and called for fair elections.

Quite understandably, few tourists visit. I was on an obscure cycling holiday and I am, as you have probably detected by now, drawn to off-the-beaten-track places. I was staying in one of the grim tower-block hotels facing Victory Park, which may sound dreadful and dreary.

Yet the grim tower-block hotels of Minsk can be interesting in their own special ways, as I was soon to find. They can also help with "park orientation".

For a start and most obviously: being in a multistorey tower most rooms have excellent views. Mine looked out across the Svislach as the river meandered in tight little S-shapes through Victory Park. Concrete apartments rose in clusters immediately beyond the park. In the distance cooling stacks protruded, looking like giant totem poles belonging to some far-off tribe. And all about, enormous, almost traffic-free boulevards cut great swathes through the city. Not quite as big as Berlin's avenue in Tiergarten or the ones in Pyongyang... but not far off.

As far as comforts went, there was a low-level bed with a mattress almost as stiff as a plank and a small wooden chair. Decoration was in Soviet-era shades of brown mixed with tangerine and aquamarine stripes (charming in a way that was hard to pin down). The bathroom was the size of an old-fashioned telephone box: shower, sink and toilet squeezed within. But never mind all of that! Out of the window I could enjoy the cityscape and the wide green expanse of Victory Park.

I could also "enjoy" – maybe not quite the right word – the decidedly edgy, if not downright dodgy, gangster-ish atmosphere in hotel public areas. Characters in shades lounged in leather armchairs in reception. Bouncers at a glitzy casino demanded to see dollars up front (no dollars, no entry). Saturday night "exotic dancing shows" in the bar were advertized.

Edgy, dodgy, gangster-ish and seedy, too: perhaps not suited to family weekend breaks, but an intriguing insight into how things went in the last dictatorship in Europe.

From the front door, I crossed a giant, empty boulevard and entered Victory Park, following a trail beside the giant, empty boulevard for a mile before arriving at the park's big attractions: the Minsk Hero City obelisk and the Belarusian Great Patriotic War Museum.

Belarus has gone to town celebrating victory in Victory Park. The Minsk Hero City Obelisk towered way above, a long, thin slab of concrete guarded by a bronze of a winged female figurine clasping a bugle. From a distance, though, this musical instrument had looked distinctly like an automatic weapon and as I was walking up to the Victory goddess it was hard not to wonder: *Is that really a sub-machine gun?* Anything seemed possible under the rule of President Lukashenko. But no, on closer inspection, the Minsk Hero City Obelisk was not defended by a Belarusian Hells Angel, though it had certainly appeared that way. My eyes seemed to be playing tricks on me; perhaps Belarus' edginess was infecting me.

The Belarusian Great Patriotic War Museum is in a mirrored-glass building full of old tanks and planes, many captured from the Nazis or donated by the Red Army. Mock-ups of battleground scenes are recreated with burning villages and towns depicted on wall murals (the Nazis torched many homes in vicious reprisals). A great deal of barbed wire, fake mud, mocked-up versions of bomb craters, trenches, sandbags and sentry boxes are scattered about. In one room, a battered old Nazi train carriage is displayed. Horrific stories of the death camps are told, as are tales of resistance including the assassination in Minsk of the vehemently antisemitic Wilhelm Kube, the Generalkommissar for Reissruthenien (in charge of Belarus), on 22 September 1943. A time bomb hidden by partisans in his mattress had killed him, although this act was to lead to a vicious spell of Nazi revenge-deaths.

By the entrance, beneath a glass dome, vases of fresh roses were placed by a moving stained-glass memorial to the hundreds of thousands who died in Belarus from 22 June 1941 to 28 July 1944. The sheer scale of the death toll in the country is extraordinary: the museum puts the ratio of deaths of citizens at one in three and the number of dead at more than 3 million (800,000 more than figures used by some academics). This compares with Britain's total of 384,000 British soldiers and 70,000 civilians during the Second World War, which works out at about one in a hundred people. It is spine-chilling to consider the sacrifices Belarus made and almost impossible for an outsider to understand the psychological impact this must have had on the war-ravaged nation.

If a good museum is supposed to make you reflect on the past, perhaps seeing events in a new, clearer light, Victory Park's Belarusian Great Patriotic War Museum certainly achieves that.

Walking around the park beneath an oyster grey sky on a weekday, down an avenue of ash trees to a birdlife sanctuary on a little island, there was plenty of food for thought. Not many people were about, just the odd jogger. Yet even though the park itself was calm and quiet, blissful if you "lived in the moment", there was something menacing about Minsk.

At first this was hard to put a finger on, but then – looking up – it became clear.

It was the tower blocks. The apartments ringing the waterfront beyond the park's boundaries had an unnerving effect. All those people living in all those rectangles of concrete. All those people penned in. All those people (possibly) looking out. All those people accounted for and monitored, living under Lukashenko's regime.

The calm of the ash trees, the shrubs, the flowers, the birdsong and the light playing on the rippling lake seemed to be sucked away by the silent anonymity of the buildings. Yes, some apartments by the lake looked well-to-do with big windows and balconies – almost penthouse-style (no doubt occupied by bigwigs). But they were still dull and utterly characterless: units within institutional-like buildings that might pass for government offices.

The whispered words of a local I had met the day before, who had asked not to be named for fear of upsetting authorities, came back to me. "For many years young people have been afraid to talk out, although that is slowly changing," he had said, speaking quietly so other diners in our restaurant could not hear. "The media in Belarus has just about been killed off. Turn on the TV and every two or three hours the president will be on making an announcement. It's the same as in Russia. Surveillance happens. Not like in North Korea, but it happens. People in powerful places, they all have good jobs. Why do they have good jobs? They are connected. Why are they connected? Through family. Through saying the right things. Through not getting in trouble."

No matter how well-landscaped, peaceful and picturesque Victory Park may have been. No matter how impressive its monuments were. No matter how moving its museum was. This park left me cold.

Visiting the last dictatorship in Europe can do that to you.

A polonaise in the park
Łazienki Park, Warsaw, Poland

Now for a park that is a little more joyful, one of my favourite parks anywhere. All down to a wonderful tradition that has been running since 1959.

This is how it goes.

From around about 11.15 a.m. every Sunday from mid-May to the end of September, come rain or shine, groups of music lovers begin to congregate by a little oval pond with an unusual statue at Łazienki Park in Warsaw.

The early birds – the real addicts for what is to come – nab the benches facing the pond, though some prefer to spread blankets or place little fold-down chairs on an amphitheatre of lawns beside the water, selecting the very best spots facing the statue, having got there ahead of the game. The first benches are usually commandeered by elderly "regulars" who come without fail each weekend, many of whom sit at the same bench out of habit and are soon gossiping to one another.

These regulars are in no danger, however, of standing. Great respect is shown to seniority among attendees of Łazienki Park. Should anyone of a certain age not be able to find space on a bench, younger parkgoers will make way as a matter of course, moving to the grassy mound. This respect for elders is touching to witness.

In this manner, over a 45-minute period running up to the stroke of noon on summer Sundays, just about every conceivable vantage point around the oval pond with the unusual statue in Łazienki Park is taken. Late arrivals hoping to find a spare patch of lawn, or a curb by a path, or even a standing spot will find their task exceedingly tricky. By 5 minutes to noon: forget it, everywhere is gone! It would be wonderful to see a sped-up film of this settling-in process as an enormous amount of fidgeting, fussing, switching of places and of people generally making themselves more comfortable, or fetching and consuming cups of tea and coffee from a kiosk, or sipping from flasks or eating homemade snacks goes on.

Then at noon precisely, all murmur, chatter, laughter and movement come to an abrupt halt. Silence descends and everyone is dead still with eyes on the tiny stage to the right of the statue.

On to the stage comes a compere, oftentimes a woman dressed to the nines in an evening frock and high heels as though about to attend a classical music performance at a grand concert hall. The first part of this at least is right. The compere clicks on the microphone and proceeds to announce in Polish the compositions by the composer and national hero Frédéric Chopin that are about to be performed on a grand piano on the stage by the statue. On the completion of this swiftly delivered information, as well as an introduction to the invariably elegantly dressed guest pianist, polite applause ripples before the compere repeats the announcement in similar fashion, speaking English. A typical hour-long performance might cover ten sonatas, polonaises, nocturnes, waltzes and other forms that Chopin mastered.

With a crackle, the compere's microphone is clicked off. The compere then disappears with swishes of her evening dress behind the statue. And the pianist takes a deep breath and plays the first delicious notes.

At this moment on a warm summer's day, with a soft breeze in the chestnut trees around this corner of Łazienki Park, there is no place

I would rather be. As heavenly music descends across the oval pond, the effect is electric. Across the rapt audience, dreamy looks come across faces. Some close their eyes. Some lay back on the lawn, staring at the sky. The concentration on the perfection and precision of Chopin's work is absolute, the enjoyment all-encompassing. Several hundred Varsovians (the name for locals) and tourists become as one: transfixed in stillness, silence and a deep contentment that is all the stronger for being shared.

When somewhere out in the city, beyond the fences of Łazienki Park, a police or ambulance siren happens to blare – maybe once or twice per performance if you are unlucky, or not at all on some occasions – the spell is temporarily broken. Then the siren fades and the magical notes cascade onward, drifting and rising, playfully dancing, one moment tenderly loving or gently meditative, then lifting to a crescendo or rumbling like thunder or slipping into a melancholy before tiptoeing across the keys with a sense of hopefulness and joy.

These concerts are subsidized by the City of Warsaw and provided free of charge; there is a later afternoon hour-long performance, too. They are magnificent occasions. Sometimes Chopin's music seems almost hypnotizing, as though it was made to be played at this very pond in this very park beside the River Vistula.

The unusual statue, of course, is of the maestro himself. Chopin was Varsovian by birth and died in 1849 at the tragically young age of 39 in Paris (of a rare tuberculosis-related illness), having made his name during his lifetime as a celebrity musician whose talents had been recognized from his days as a child prodigy onward. Such was his genius and such was the high regard among fellow Poles that on his death his heart – removed from his body to be taken to Poland at his request before his burial in Paris – was encased in a stone pillar in pride of place at Holy Cross Church in the centre of Warsaw.

What is remarkable about the statue is that Chopin is shown with his eyes closed as though transported by music, his wavy hair looking windswept while his right hand is held aloft with fingers ready to play and above him a strange wave-like object, half willow tree, half eagle (the

Polish symbol), arises. It is brilliantly odd and so visually striking that on first sight it takes a little working out.

It also hides a story. This is not the original statue. That was blown up in 1940 by the pond where the new version stands. The Nazis regarded Chopin's music as so powerfully stirring that it was banned; the invaders of 1939, cropping up yet again in parks in this part of Europe, wanted to wipe out Polish national heritage. By drawing on Polish folk music as inspiration, Chopin had imbued his compositions with a deeply ingrained "Polishness" that was deemed a threat to Nazi control. Luckily, the cast of the 1907 sculpture had been kept and the replica was erected in 1958.

Little wonder the Sunday concerts are so popular. In Poland, Chopin means a lot.

There is more, however, to Łazienki Park than the Chopin pond.

The former royal park, once a hunting ground of kings, covers 188 acres and is excellent for long walks with trails leading between ash trees, sycamores, silver poplars, oaks, horse chestnuts, beech trees, spruces and many varieties of fruit trees: pears, plums, apples. Much of Łazienki is woodland and one of the great delights is to watch the nippy red squirrels dashing about: foxy little flashes darting here and there. These are quite unexpected at first and you find yourself picking up on them from the corner of an eye and wondering for a split second: *What on earth was that?* Then you remember: *Oh yes, another red squirrel.* This process is repeated many times, no matter how used to them you feel you have become. Some of these squirrels have turned extremely tame after being fed by parkgoers, and you cannot also help wondering: *Why can't some people simply let wild animals be wild?* (Visions of tourists taking pictures of deer and sometimes feeding them back home in Richmond Park, despite this being prohibited with a rule to keep 50 metres away, spring to mind).

The park's crowning glory, Chopin aside, is the Palace on the Isle, which is exactly that, a late-eighteenth-century palace built by the last Polish king, Stanislaus II Augustus, on a little island in a lake to act as a bathing house and a rural getaway, complete with a ballroom and a portrait gallery. It has been much worked upon over the centuries but retains an unusual baroque/neoclassical combination of architecture that some refer to as "Stanislaus-style". This style extended to creating a Theatre on the Isle in the image of an ancient Roman amphitheatre deliberately built to look "ruined". Other such baroque/neoclassical "temple buildings" or follies are dotted around the park including an Egyptian Temple and a Hermitage in which Stanislaus is said to have consulted his official court fortune teller. Rarely do you walk far in Łazienki Park without stumbling upon some Stanislaus-style folly or other.

More recently a Chinese Garden with a pagoda and a lane of lanterns has been added. This is close to the Trou Madame Café, a coffee house in a former guardhouse where waiters in ties and waitresses with frilly white aprons serve excellent cappuccinos, icecream sundaes, *piwo* (beer) and shots of vodka (this is Poland). This is a perfect place to rest with a tipple beneath one of the chestnut trees and hope that the legend of a note left on the plinth where the Nazis destroyed the first Chopin statue is true.

That note, written for the local Nazi officers to discover the day after the demolition job, is said to have read: "I don't know who destroyed me, but I know why: so that I won't play the funeral march for your leader."

Is there another park where a musician feels so part of the landscape, their spirit seeming to roam in the woods? I can't think of one.

Sunny side up
Tokoinranta, Helsinki, Finland

During the winter in northern Finland the word "night" becomes confusing. Due to the curvature of the planet, darkness descends for 24 hours a day from late November. This annual "sunset" can last as long as 50 days, with daylight returning in mid-January. This is just the way it is; northern Finns are accustomed to the arrangements, even if most do not like them that much.

In the south of the Nordic country – never call Finland "Scandinavian" as there is a touchiness about the term to which I will return – a mere 5 hours of winter light illuminates the capital, Helsinki, over the same period. At least this is *something*, usually from about 10 a.m. to 3 p.m., but the truth is that overcast conditions often mean locals do not see sunshine or blue skies for weeks on end. Little wonder that the peak period for overseas trips to sunny climes is January and February when most Finns are thinking: *Enough is enough!* Little wonder also that some Finns descend into dark funks during winters, barely speaking to neighbours or friends, almost hibernating from the world. The phenomenon of seasonal affective disorder, a mental health disorder associated with depression induced by lack of sunlight, afflicts many.

Then just to add to the topsy-turviness of Finnish existence, during the summer, light bathes northern Finland for up to 24 hours a day for several weeks at a time. In the south it is the same, just a bit gloomier in the early hours. During this period, some Finns suffer from anxiety and weight-gain problems.

The result is that the Finnish have a complex relationship with seasons and when the sun does come out properly and it is warm enough to sunbathe, boy do they go for it.

At Tokoinranta park in Helsinki, just north of the central train station overlooking Eläintarhanlahti Bay, a channel connected to the Gulf of Finland, it is possible to witness Finnish summer sun-worship in action.

What this means in practice is a very large number of people filling almost every space along the waterfront, the most sought-after spots snapped up early. This is quite unexpected for first-time visitors. After crossing Pitkäsilta Bridge, coming from the train station, you turn left and there they are: the sun worshippers of Tokoinranta park. Lots of them, lying out like seals.

The contrast is startling. From the taxi ranks, Burger Kings, odd shifty characters and bustle of passengers, some having disembarked from trains from Moscow, you are suddenly amid a colony of sunbathers with a great deal of pale Nordic skin on display that has almost certainly not seen the sun for many a month. Most hardly move a muscle in their dedication to soak up as many precious rays as possible during this narrow annual window of warmth. Like plants absorbing sunlight for photosynthesis, the people of Helsinki lie out soaking up vitamin D. There is a sense of blissful contentment about the scene. No need to jet off to the south in search of sunshine; euros reserved for annual holidays were blown back in the winter, anyway. When the sun comes out in Helsinki, so do the Helsinkians.

Tokoinranta park is small, tucked away by the bay between the bridge and the railway line; one of the park's simple pleasures is to watch shiny red trains sliding along the lines on their way to Russia and Estonia. Helsinki has a sense of being a frontier city of sorts, on the very northern tip of mainland Europe. The city is, at latitude 60.17 degrees, the second most northerly capital on Earth after Reykjavik in Iceland (64.13 degrees) and just beating Oslo in Norway (59.95 degrees). You are a long way up.

Tokoinranta is not the most famous park in the Finnish capital: that honour probably goes to Kaisaniemi Park, Helsinki's oldest park (founded in 1812), beside the train station and complete with a botanical garden featuring glasshouses with lilies and palms. It is not the prettiest: that prize is claimed by Haagan Alppiruusupuisto Park, which comes alive when azaleas and rhododendrons bloom each June. Nor is it the most culturally important park: Sibelius Park, with its abstract monument in memory of Finland's greatest composer, Jean Sibelius, has the edge on that count (perhaps the spirit of Sibelius is just as strong there as Chopin's in Łazienki Park back in Warsaw, I never did visit). Nor is it the most diverse: Central Park covering a splendid 6-mile strip of spruce-tree forest, home to Siberian flying squirrels, wins hands down for its flora and fauna. But Tokoinranta Park is a much-loved local park: a curve of green in one of the most interesting neighbourhoods in the city.

When you cross the channel into the northern shore of Eläintarhanlahti Bay to reach Tokoinranta, you enter the Kallio district of Helsinki, known by some as Helsinki's Notting Hill. At least that was how my extremely charming, tiny, extremely talkative guide, Maria, put it.

She was employed by Visit Finland and had joined me for a tour that was starting in Kallio as that was where my hotel was. Before checking out the bohemian cafes, vinyl-record shops, markets, noodle bars and soul-food joints of Helsinki's hipster-central neighbourhood though, we took a turn in Tokoinranta as Maria explained Kallio's place in the city. When I say: "extremely talkative", read "motormouth". Maria could represent Finland in international chatterbox championships.

"You see, Tom, you went over Pitkasilita Bridge to get here, Tom," she began, at speed. "Pitkasilita translates as 'long bridge' but we call it 'short bridge' or 'the longest short bridge' or 'the longest bridge in the world'. That was because it separates the bourgeoisie from the working class, Tom. Well, it used to, Tom. Definitely a hundred years ago, still a little bit. It's been gentrified, Tom, but it's still not as expensive as on the other side, Tom."

Maria was referring to the southern side of the (in reality, short) bridge towards the station, where many plush houses and apartments could be found. She was on a roll.

"It's a bit like the Notting Hill of Helsinki round here. The Notting Hill, not the Chelsea. Or you could say the Queens of New York, not the Manhattan." Maria paused. "Helsinki you see, Tom, was only the capital of Finland during Russian times, from 1812 onwards, Tom. Then Kallio grew. It was where the working class predominantly lived. Then, during the civil war in 1918, Tom, there were the Reds and the Whites. They bombarded each other at the bridge. The working class were the Reds, Tom, and the bourgeoisie the Whites. The Reds wanted to return to the motherland. They were supported by the Bolsheviks in Russia, Tom. The Whites were supported by the Germans, Tom. The Whites won. History is written by the winner, Tom. There are still cannon marks on the bridge. They've been kept to remember what happened, Tom."

I asked Maria about the sunbathers.

"All of the Nordic countries are the same, Tom," she replied. "When the sun comes out, the people go out and they are absorbing the sun rays. They don't know how many days of sun there will be. If it is sunny,

Tom, we go outside: we drink coffee on our balconies, we go to the park or go to our summer cottages in the countryside, usually by lakes, if we have one. This park [Tokoinranta] it is not the best park in Helsinki. But you see: on a sunny day, every bit of square grass everywhere, they cover. Picnics, sunbathing, Tom."

Maria paused, a rare event, and looked deep in thought for a while, before telling me at some length about her trips to Tenerife each winter to get a blast of heat: "It is so cold and unsocial in the winter – which is why of course, alcohol can help. Finns are different people in the summer. Yes, sometimes in winter you can feel a bit down, Tom. But if I go to Tenerife, Tom, in just one week, Tom, I feel fantastic."

With that, Maria grabbed me by the arm and said: "Come on, let's get cracking!" And off we went for a whirlwind (highly entertaining) tour of Finland's capital, leaving the sunbathing seals of Tokoinranta.

Helsinki is blessed with many parks: it is estimated that 40 per cent of the land comprises parks and gardens. Finland's capital is an extremely green city, and the intention is to be carbon neutral by 2030. It was recently awarded European Capital of Smart Tourism status by the European Commission for its sustainable tourism. It regularly makes the shortlist for the Commission's European Green Capital award, being praised for its sustainable transport habits: three quarters of all journeys made by Helsinkians involve walking, cycling, public transport or using electric cars. Hundreds of charging stations for vehicles are dotted about the streets and hundreds more are planned. It is, you might say, super green.

Yet you also might argue that having such a small population (630,000) in a nation with an overall population of 5.5 million and a national population density of 18 inhabitants per square kilometre (even less than Laos), makes it is easier to be that colour in Helsinki (city population density 2,986) than elsewhere. And you would probably be correct. But that does not take anything away from the capital of Finland's many "green" achievements.

Oh yes, so why do Finns get touchy about being called Scandinavian?

The answer, depending on whom you ask, is that the language and ethnicity of Finland are quite distinct from the countries traditionally referred to as Scandinavian: Denmark, Norway and Sweden. However, "Nordic", or northern countries, are part of a wider category merely defined by geographical location, including Denmark, Norway and Sweden as well as Finland and also Iceland, Greenland and the Faroe Islands, too. Maria's take? "People get this wrong the whole time, even Finns get it wrong: we are Nordic, not Scandinavian, Tom!"

On that note, I'm moving on from Helsinki's Notting Hill and its little sun worshippers' park to one country that quite definitely counts as "Scandi".

Super trouper
Djurgården, Stockholm, Sweden

When the AV Stockholms Spårvägar class B19 double-axis bidirectional narrow-gauge tram – painted fetching sky blue and built in the 1920s – rattles across the old metal-framed bridge to Djurgården on a sunny Swedish day, there is a feeling of arriving at Stockholm's number one park in style.

The clickety clack of the carriages along the line is somehow soothing and delightfully old-fashioned as the bespectacled conductor with a peaked cap checks your ticket and mumbles: *"Ja, ja. Ha en bra resor"* (Yes, yes. Have a good journey). Up ahead woodlands rise, while all around the glistening waters flowing from Lake Mälaren to the Baltic Sea are alive with activity, tiny pleasure boats bobbing all about.

Not many parks have their own retro tramlines. But Djurgården, one of a dozen or so main islands that form Sweden's capital, does.

Depending on your luck, you may find yourself in a one of a handful of lovingly restored Café Trams, which run once or twice an hour with tables with lamps, natty blue-green booths, lace curtains and waiter service: the best way to go. This is a Stockholms Spårvägar class B31C four-axis unidirectional carriage painted in gold and royal blue dating from 1949, so says an extremely informative pamphlet.

People may poke fun at rail enthusiasts – they are, of course, easy game – but when they create these wonderful little heritage lines, as back in Prater park in Vienna, they do us all a grand service. It must have taken a huge amount of effort and know-how to procure the old carriages, find the parts, fix, polish and reupholster everything before obtaining relevant licences and rooting out drivers and engineers. And when we see such lovely old contraptions clattering along, most of us involuntarily think: *Oh, isn't that lovely*. And if we ever go on one: *Oh, what a laugh*. Yet when it comes to rail enthusiasts our knee-jerk reaction tends to be: *What a bunch of oddballs*. Which is completely unfair. The Djurgården Line covers about 2 miles from Norrmalmstorg in the city to the middle of Djurgården and was opened in 1991. It is wonderful and exceedingly well run; popular not just with tourists but also with the community of wealthy locals living on the island who take the tram to go shopping at the "Swedish Harrods", Nordiska Kompaniet (some Stockholmers jokingly refer to the service as the "NK Express").

Anyway, thank you, Swedish Tramway Society.

Sometimes the unsung heroes of parks need a bit of recognition – especially when there is so much else going on at Stockholm's most popular park.

Kungliga Djurgården, to give the island its full official name, translates as "Royal Game Park". It is about 2.5 miles long and 1 mile wide; the total territory is around 700 acres. It is also slightly complicated to explain. Rather than comprising one area of park, the island has many pockets of green linked by paths and is also home to a large number of museums and attractions as well as some well-to-do residential zones: about 800 people live on Djurgården. The island is not really a traditional "park" as most parks are usually understood. Yet Stockholmers consider the entire island to be "parkland", especially the wildest part on the east side where the kings used to go hunting for deer and elk.

It is a very good one and a sign of great civic foresight on behalf of Stockholmers from the late eighteenth century onward that the land should be set aside for recreational purposes. First came open-air theatres, then a "rural palace", Rosendal Palace, now open to the public for tours (a little like Stanislaus II Augustus' Palace on the Isle back in Warsaw). But the main burst of development of the island as a place for pleasure-seeking that did not merely involve taking perambulations in the woods came in the late nineteenth century, when Gröna Lund, an amusement park with carousels and other rides, opened and remains open to this day, occasionally staging concerts (Bob Marley played to an audience of 32,000 in 1980). A few years after Gröna Land in 1891, another attraction named Skansen started up: an open-air museum with examples of traditional housing and displays explaining ancient craftwork and folklore, plus a zoo that is home to indigenous creatures including bison, reindeer, wolves and bears.

The creation of this nineteenth-century "pleasure island" culminated in Stockholm's hosting of a World Fair in 1897, with a fantastical building with minarets installed (since dismantled) as well as an almost eccentrically extravagant neo-Renaissance castle complete with spiky copper-tipped towers. Since 1907 this has housed the Nordic Museum and no fewer than 1.5 million exhibits associated with old Nordic traditions from folk art, ancient clothing and common household arrangements – it is possible to learn all about sixteenth-century Swedish table settings, if that is your thing (Swedish home living expertize dates from a long time before Ikea). There are also, somewhere within the large building, 6 million photographs covering Swedish life taken since 1840.

An obelisk by the entrance is inscribed with the words: "The day may dawn when not even all our gold is enough to form a picture of a bygone era."

Not if you are interested in how ancient Swedish people used to live – and visit the Nordic Museum.

You may be thinking, *There's a lot going on at Djurgården*. But all this is merely the tip of the iceberg. Add in a museum dedicated to the pop group Abba, an art gallery containing one of the world's finest collections of works by Edvard Munch (the Thiel Gallery), a museum for children highlighting the Pippi Longstocking books of Astrid Lindgren (Junibacken), a Biological Museum, an Aquaria Water Museum, a well-kept rose garden, lakes teeming with birdlife and various mansions belonging to old princes – and you have enough to keep you going for a Swedish summer. Is this the world's most action-packed park? Possibly.

But there is one museum on Djurgården that stands out above all others: the Vasamuseet.

To reach this museum, the most popular in Scandinavia, you disembark your vintage tram at the first stop after the bridge. From there it is a short stroll to what looks like a large ramshackle farmer's barn with one noticeable difference: the masts of a seventeenth-century tall ship sticking out of the roof.

The story of the *Vasa* is tragic. In 1628, the state-of-the-art warship, the pride of the Swedish navy, set sail on its maiden voyage before large crowds only to sink after 1,300 metres at the cost of 50 lives. The catastrophe was a huge embarrassment and a long inquest was held into who was responsible. Nobody, it was declared, was to blame, especially as the king, Gustav II Adolf, had approved the ship's designs, the designer had died before the disaster – and it would be unwise to single out the king. The cannons were salvaged and the ship forgotten; that is, until the mid-1950s when a fuel engineer in the Swedish navy and amateur archaeologist named Anders Franzen discovered a fragment of the ship while dragging the waters of Stockholm, 100 metres off the southern tip of Djurgården. It was a piece of the mighty *Vasa*. A painstaking recovery and conservation programme was launched and in 1990 Vasamuseet opened.

The result is captivating, a ghost ship risen from the deep. So many hundreds of carvings intact: ancient, bearded warriors in armoured plating clutching shields and swords, roaring lions, royal crests. The oak timber is blackened with age and sea, the gun ports are held open, 64 of them in all, revealing glimpses of cavernous chambers within. Each of the guns for the *Vasa* had weighed 1,200 kilograms and it is this bulk on an insufficiently broad ship – not enough "belly" was the expression at the time – that is believed to have caused the sinking.

One matter regarding the desperate affair stands out. About a month before the ship set sail, the captain had arranged for a vice admiral to come to the quay to witness 30 men running back and forth on the top deck. The effect was to create such swaying that the ship almost sank there and then. The king was away at the time and the vice admiral was overheard to say: "If only His Majesty were at home!" However, pressure was on to get the *Vasa* launched in time and the king in absentia wanted swift progress. So launched it was.

Vasamuseet is as much about human folly as the ship itself, as magnificent as the vessel may be. It is also about the dogged persistence of Franzen and the many others who brought the ghost ship from the depths.

Djurgården is a strange park. There is a danger when you go of trying to cram too much in, filling your head with a thousand images of ancient Swedish ways: from princely palaces to rustic abodes to table place-setting protocols from centuries gone by to pop music divas and the intricacies of folk art.

Best (on first visit) to stick to the *Vasa*. Then take a long walk; out beyond the looping roller-coasters of Gröna Lund, the stately palaces, the mansions of the great and the good, the clusters of bohemian houses, home to actors and artists, and the galleries with their Edvard Munches; out to where the channels widen to the east and the Viking Line ferries with their scarlet funnels churn towards Helsinki and St Petersburg beyond the archipelago of islands of the Baltic Sea; out to where there is a rawness to the seascape even on a tranquil summer's day.

You are in a major capital city. You do not feel for a moment that you are in one.

This is when a city park has done its job.

Afterward, you may wind back through the old royal hunting ground, hop on a ferry or catch the rattling old Tram Café – if you feel like a cup of tea.

CHAPTER TWELVE

THE NETHERLANDS, SWITZERLAND, FRANCE, SPAIN: IN SEARCH OF A PERFECT PARK

THE
NETHERLANDS

Amsterdam

GERMANY

The English Channel

BELGIUM

FRANCE

SWITZERLAND

Dijon

Zurich

ITALY

SPAIN

Barcelona

Mediterranean
Sea

Valencia

The more I was thinking about urban parks – as this world tour of them began to move into the finishing straight on the way back to Britain – the more I tried to nail down what it was that was so appealing about them.

One of their biggest plus sides, I was realizing as I looked back on so many, was not just their ability to transport you "out" of the city for a while, away from the noise of traffic and the general cacophony and bustle of daily life amid millions of citizens, but also their invisibility. Or rather: their ability to make you, the urban parkgoer, invisible.

You are in a big city where life hurtles forth madly seeking whatever big cities seek: money of course; "progress" perhaps; the organization of large numbers of people in the best possible way (when they are well run). Whatever this "purpose", the underlying reality is cities move fast. To keep the spinning plates of city life upright, speed is of the essence. Is that report in yet? Have you made that delivery/ finished that job? Have you checked with so and so? Have you seen your emails? Did you look in junk? Can I have that ASAP (ay-sap)? Can I have that end of play?

The rush does not stop. Addictions to social media make us twitchy, not helping matters. The world is in our pockets, connected to 4G or 5G and anything and everything seems possible, fast, fast, fast. We are available. Communication with, and knowledge of, others is available. We are on call. We are all on call. We are visible – like never before.

When you consider this, as I was, city parks play a vital role: a step away from it all. They are places to go "off duty": breathe deep, zone out, turn off the phone (even, shock horror, leave it at home), enjoy nature, blend in. Perfectly possible no matter who you may be (former presidents of the United States and the like aside).

The only question is: do you dare switch off? Even for an hour?

Vowing to leave my phone behind on the next venture into Richmond Park, I took stock of the "route" ahead: the final stretch laid out in front of me.

From Scandinavia, I would meander south through low countries, high countries and to the south-west of Europe through some very busy cities with some very lovely (quiet) parks.

"Can you hear the birdsong?"
Oosterpark, Amsterdam, the Netherlands

Friday night at the octagonal bandstand in Oosterpark in the east (*ooster*) of the biggest city in the Netherlands and a huddle of Amsterdammers with yoga mats had gathered, looking chilly.

It was still early evening on a drizzly September day. The odd jogger was about, taking a turn around the long S-shaped pond. Cyclists whizzed by on the way home from work. Clouds had dropped so low they almost merged into the elms, poplars and plane trees. Looking across the park and squinting your eyes, two colours emerged in a blur: the olive-green of vegetation below and the great luminous white of the sky above. No city was visible at all. Not a single building beyond the trees. Just a mysterious abstract world of green and milky white.

Coming to the bandstand, curiosity got the better of me. The group had unfurled mats and was lying back, knees up, eyes half-closed in the drizzly park. Standing nearby beneath an umbrella, I paused to watch – and listen.

The instructor wore Lycra leggings and a purple hoodie. She spoke in a soft, soporific voice, gently issuing thoughts with the rhythm of a metronome set at slow. She spoke in English. This was, it appeared, a meditation group.

"There is a connection," the instructor was saying. "A connection. Can you feel it now, in the silence?" The instructor was silent for a while. Drips were slipping off the roof of the bandstand. The drizzle had turned to steady rain.

"There is no separation between how we feel and what we see and what we hear," she began once more. "I want you to connect to your senses, to connect to your real person." She paused as the group was given time to connect. "We have 90,000 thoughts a day." She paused again to let this thought sink in, pushing the daily count to 90,001 perhaps. "Ninety per cent of those thoughts are the same as yesterday's thoughts and the day before." Pause. "Try to connect, to listen to what is real. What sound do you hear?"

A plane was passing above. One of the people on the yoga mats mentioned this. "Good. OK, good." The instructor considered the comment for a few moments as though listening herself. "Yes, right now the furthest sound is a plane, but are not planes human made, and are not humans made of nature? Listen again. Breathe in. Breathe out. Eyes closed. Listen. Can you hear the rain on the leaves? Listen. Can you hear the birdsong?" Amid the sound of rainfall there was, surprisingly, birdsong, if you listened. I had not noticed it before. Was I falling into a trance?

The urge to lie flat out on my very own yoga mat and zone out under the spell of the instructor's dulcet tones was, admittedly, strong.

The group began to hum. So did I too for a while beneath my umbrella. There are worse ways to pass an early evening in Amsterdam.

Then I walked round Oosterpark in what had become, without my noticing, a downpour.

Oosterpark was opened in 1891 in the "English" style that seemed so popular in nineteenth-century mainland Europe; this one the handiwork of the eminent Dutch park maestro Leonard Anthony Springer. It was Amsterdam's first big municipal park, landscaped on what was previously a cemetery (which was moved to the city edge despite local protests). The park is in a district of Amsterdam known for its large Moroccan, Turkish, Surinamese and Eastern European population – and it is said to have a vibrant, culturally diverse atmosphere (possibly more evident when not visiting on pouring Friday evenings in September).

On the northern side of the park, with appropriateness or perhaps inappropriateness given the multicultural neighbourhood, is the Tropenmuseum with displays dedicated to Dutch colonialism and its many wrongdoings, focusing on Indonesia and the Pacific. This is housed within an imposing yellow-brick building with gables and minaret-shaped towers: a nod to the old colonial lands, it would seem. It is the only tourist attraction anywhere close by that merits mention in guidebooks.

Beyond the octagonal bandstand, walking clockwise into the green and milky-white world, curiosity defeated me again and I stopped to watch yet more Dutch parkgoers "in action".

A personal trainer dressed in a pakamac was leading a woman, also in a pakamac, through a rigorous routine of exercises. Both were dripping with rainwater. Circular plastic markers had been placed at intervals in a wooded area and the woman in the pakamac was sprinting in a rustle between them holding small dumb-bell weights. When she returned to her "PT", she dropped to the muddy grass and, using the weights to balance, performed an impressive number of push-ups. After these, a series of complicated manoeuvres involving a plastic step the PT had brought were conducted, followed by a flurry of jumping jacks. A moment's rest after the jumping jacks was taken, during which the exerciser drank from a bottle. Then she repeated the routine, still as agile as a gazelle despite all this exertion and being wrapped in a plastic bag. How long she was able keep this up I do not know; quite a long time by the looks of it. Extraordinary.

I continued my orbit of Oosterpark.

A bit further on, at the other side of the long S-shaped pond, a short man was balancing on one leg beneath an elm tree. This was the next "show".

The short man had cleverly positioned himself close enough to the elm to be sheltered from the rain. His arms were held at slightly different levels with his palms facing forward. Every now and then he shifted position, using both legs or moving to the other leg or subtly adjusting the direction of his torso or the configuration of his arms. At all times, his head held steady with his posture perfect. Yet his body seemed to flow, his movements like brushstrokes on a watercolour painting. It was a magnificent display of power and control, hidden away at the foot of the mighty elm.

Oosterpark seemed to be full of Amsterdammers doing curious things. More joggers had taken to the paths despite the rain; some better defined as "runners" as they were going pretty fast. Forget spliffs and red-light districts, a health kick seemed to be in full swing in the famous Dutch city; at least in Oosterpark. What was it like when the sun shined: an Olympic training village?

Though perhaps all of this should have come as little surprise. Looking at the map of Amsterdam's centre with its spider's web of canals, there is hardly any green (just as back in Venice and Dubrovnik). Amid the city's main hotspots with all the museums, galleries, flower markets, Smokey Joe coffee shops and other establishments where things go on that are not detailed on the tourist board website, it is easy to overlook that Amsterdam is not simply a theme park of cultural treasures mixed with risqué entertainment. Overtourism may swirl all around yet terraces on quieter stretches of canal are of course home to plenty of real Amsterdammers, not for-the-tourist Amsterdammers. These real Amsterdammers need somewhere to let off steam. On the eastern side of town, Oosterpark is one such place.

A running club sprinted by, re-emerging at intervals after completing (fast) park circuits. As it did so for a second time, I arrived at the National Slavery Monument.

The multicultural neighbourhood and the proximity to Tropenmuseum made Oosterpark a logical choice for the location of this monument unveiled by Queen Beatrix in 2002. The monument, by the Surinamese artist Erwin Jules de Vries, depicts chained prisoners approaching an arch through which a figure breaks free as though diving into a bright future. This site has not been without controversy as when Queen Beatrix did the honours at the opening a fence covered in black plastic had been installed surrounding the sculptures, supposedly for security reasons. This angered some ethnic groups who felt excluded, especially with the Netherlands' colonial history being a touchy subject. The country was among the last in Europe to abolish slavery in 1863 and many believe that regular public referrals to the Dutch "Golden Age" from the late sixteenth century to the 1670s in museums and in teaching at schools do not sufficiently cover historical crimes of the past – a neglect true of the period up to 1863 as well. Some feel that much more recognition of misdoings is required than a monument in a corner of Oosterpark.

Another public memorial close by highlights another tragic story. On 2 November 2004, the filmmaker, actor and author Theo Van Gogh was assassinated nearby by a Dutch-Moroccan who had objected to a short film Van Gogh (a distant cousin of the painter) had directed about the treatment of Islamic women, written by the Somali author Ayaan Hirsi Ali. The murder shocked the nation and resulted in violent racist acts of reprisal against Islamic schools and mosques. It had taken place as Van Gogh cycled to work one morning, about 300 metres from the striking memorial, which depicts a face turned upwards in agony as though crying out. The memorial is named *The Scream*.

I completed my lap of Oosterpark as light began to fade.

By the bandstand the meditators were rolling up their mats ready to leave and the runners had stopped to take a break.

My hotel was close by the bandstand, overlooking Oosterpark, where my room came with a ceiling-to-floor window facing the canopy of elms, poplars and planes – so close you could almost touch the branches.

A strange and strangely wonderful sensation. A strange and strangely wonderful park.

Lake democracy
Quaianlagen, Zurich, Switzerland

Down by the lakeside, water lapped on the shore and sunlight bathed the snowy peaks of the mountains above. It was a fine summer's morning in Zurich, Switzerland's financial capital where Porsches prowl the lanes, pampered pugs are pushed in prams and queues form at Gucci on Saturday before the doors open (when I went by, at least).

Down by the lakeside, though, money did not matter a jot.

The water was calm and warm. I swam towards a floating jetty as the scenery seemed to envelope me, like the lake, and cast its spell. The solemnity of the snow-tipped mountains. The sparkle of light on the gentle swell. The steadfast spires rising in the old town. The wide, watery expanse heading south. The lazy Alpine breeze. The inviting shade of the clusters of trees by the banks. The splendid mansions in the hills. The sky so perfect blue. The temperature rising. The delicious flow of water on your body. No particular hurry. Nothing to do that day. No meetings. No emails. No reason to check your phone. No worries, down by the lakeside.

There is something democratic about Quaianlagen, the promenade that runs for 2 miles around the lake at Zurich, connected by a series of mini parks. The lake is for everyone: the heavenly mountains; the thin, fresh air; the soothing eddies of the water. Who cares about bank balances? Rolex or Timex? Big deal. Gucci or Gap? Ditto. Some of Europe's richest people may reside nearby, but the Alps are for all... no one can take that away.

The story of how Quaianlagen came to be highlights how city planners back in the late nineteenth century realized just this. The problem in those days was that, although the mountaintops were criss-crossed with paths and hiking was attracting folk from all walks of life, the lake near Zurich was out of bounds. The reason? Mansions occupied the land by the water. There was no public right of way and – simply – no passage through. In 1881 a decision was made to build a quayside with a tree-shaded promenade curving round the lake on each side of the River Limmat. This river marks the centre of Zurich, where the eminent eleventh-century Fraumünster Church faces the equally eminent twelfth-century Grossmünster Cathedral, forming a kind of gateway of God into the heart of town.

Over the course of the following six years around 50 acres of land was reclaimed – or, I suppose more accurately, *created* as it was never there before. The promenade was opened in 1887 featuring thin strips of park with benches and trees, some sections deeper than others with more room for picnics, as well as a main, small park, named the Arboretum, on the southern side of the River Limmat. The late nineteenth century really was a boom time for parks across the globe: Oosterpark in Amsterdam had been four years later, while the headiest days of Stockholm's Djurgården came in the 1890s (just to mention the last two).

Quaianlagen was a huge hit, transforming Zurich from a medieval town of medium size by the lake into what was to become and still is the biggest city in Switzerland (almost 2 million people in the metropolitan area). Part of the reason for this turnaround was the opening of the railway station in Zurich in 1871 followed swiftly by the stock exchange in 1877; the wealth flowing into town on the back of both helping to finance Quaianlagen, which in turn allowed for expansion in the form of new housing along the lakeside in each direction. This is a park that is not just extremely pleasant to visit: its formation helped make Zurich the city it is today.

The secret to its success was that Quaianlagen allowed – and still allows – Zurich to breathe. A feeling of claustrophobia can set in amid the narrow medieval lanes, alleys and little courtyards of the old town, yet walk for a few minutes to the shore and the wide, charming promenade awaits with its trees, lawns and of course the lake, seeming to stretch forever through the valley between the dreamy mountains. Switzerland really is such a lucky country, when you think about it: the extraordinary abundance of natural beauty with such power to lift the spirits. A glance across the lake to the snow-capped peaks is all it takes (for me).

The Arboretum is one of the best places for this. It also possesses the best parkland, landscaped with rolling "hills", no more than mounds, about 3 metres in height. These, however, cleverly cut off the traffic and the city within, while an intriguing medley of magnolias, beeches, pines, cedars and elms add to the seclusion. Benches are positioned beside a peaceful lawn. More are by the shore, offering some of the finest lake views in the city. In a quiet spot on the northern side of the park, a statue with a bust of Arnold Bürkli, the chief engineer of Quaianlagen who died seven years after his marvellous creation opened, pokes out above beds of fuchsias. With his moustache, bow tie and faint smile, he looks quite content. As well he might.

Another park hero to add to what is becoming a long, distinguished list. Bravo Bürkli!

Bravo also to the Zurich tourism bods as there is *a lot* going on at, and very close to, Quaianlagen (if not quite as much as back in Djurgården).

For bird lovers: an aviary and bird sanctuary at the Arboretum, dating from 1897, with parrots, singing birds and other rescued winged creatures. For football fans: the FIFA World Football Museum, just around the corner, home to the World Cup Trophy, a great many old leather balls and a 1966 Wembley Stadium corner flag signed by Geoff Hurst. For plant aficionados: the glasshouses of a botanical garden, a short stroll to the south, packed full of succulents including an impressive array of cacti, the garden's speciality. For architect buffs: Pavillon Le Corbusier, on the northern shore, a multicoloured glass-and-steel house by the famous French architect (the last Le Corbusier was ever to build in 1967).

For absolutely everyone: glorious swims in the lake. This is one of the world's great parks for taking a dip.

Zurich, you see, has nailed the concept of lakeside bathing houses. These are dotted around the promenade on Quaianlagen, each subtly different. Settling on one I had spotted on the walk to Le Corbusier's house the day before, I returned at 9 a.m. to the Seebad Utoquai bathing house, wearing my trunks.

Already it was busy. For a handful of Swiss francs you have access to a 120-year-old floating bathing palace with wooden decks, changing chambers, showers, a small wood-panelled cafe and a little library of help-yourself discarded books. In the middle is a mixed deck, while to the left is a men-only section and to the right a women-only area, both with little separate pools of lake water and seating on raised decks where Moorish domes once rose. These were, sadly, removed to allow for more bathers in the twentieth century. Yet with all the balustrades, columns, passages and embellishments of curved wood by the entrance, the Moorish inspiration remains.

The established procedure at the Seebad Utoquai bathing house is to secure a piece of deck to call your own, pronto. This is why everyone arrives so early. There appears to be no shame in squeezing between others, just so long as a reasonable amount of space is free. That said, there is a certain territorial attitude among some, and you may attract a "Swiss look" or two. Judging where seems "reasonable" without traipsing gormlessly around the deck for a while with your towel and possessions, accumulating quite a few "Swiss looks", is not necessarily easy for the first timer (I shall admit). Eventually, however, somewhere will turn up and you may find yourself simply sitting or lying in the sun for a while thinking: *Thank goodness that is over.* The bathing houses have their regulars, who tend to be cool customers, often in Ray-Bans and extremely blasé (except if one of your flip-flops happens to touch a towel).

There is another factor to consider, as you look around. Some of the bathers may well be multimillion-Swiss franc stock exchange traders, others waiters or hotel receptionists on mornings off. That again is part of the democracy of Quaianlagen. The lake is, as I said, for all: most can afford the bathing houses.

The mixed deck is the place to be for easy access to the cafe, where you may wish to go, stepping exceedingly carefully, for a hot drink or a smoothie to reward yourself for having secured your spot. Then from the deck, the steps go straight to the lake and, as you drop in the water, float on your back and look up, the lake soothes all your worries away.

That is how a Zurich bathing house works. For a city park to have such places is simply brilliant and enough of a reason to visit Zurich in the summer if you happen to be a keen swimmer. If not, hire one of the delightful retro-style pedalos and observe Zurich and its Quaianlagen promenade-park afloat on the water. If not a retro-style pedalo fan, go for a long walk through the park and onward along the shore. Or just find a bench and admire the splendid Alpine views (no need to rush about).

Zurich may be rolling in Swiss francs, but down by the lakeside on Quaianlagen – with its many parts and little pockets of green tucked away here and there between the bathing houses and attractions – it is pretty rich in park life, too.

Monsieur Darcy
Jardin Darcy, Dijon, France

Oftentimes parks hide secrets, as we have found. Seldom, however, are they quite as concealed as the one at Jardin Darcy in Dijon.

Jardin Darcy is a pretty park close to Dijon's main railway station covering 2.5 acres. Its entrance is through a spiky green metal gate whereupon you are met by a prominent sculpture of a polar bear that is a copy of a renowned work by the famous French "animal sculptor" François Pompon found at the Musée d'Orsay in Paris. Many people have their photograph taken by this haughty-yet-cute polar bear (I did). Then they venture further into the park, ascend some steps and admire the fountain. This flows out of the mouth of a stone carving of an amphibian creature perched above a stone sculpture of a giant clam shell. On each side of this shell, eye-popping stone fish glare out at you. The fountain cascades down into a series of pools surrounded by stone balustrades. The water in the pools is surprisingly turquoise and this adds to the feeling of oasis-like tranquillity of Jardin Darcy.

After ascending a few more steps to a terrace above the fountain, you may wish to take another, wider picture of the park (I did) while admiring the trees that rise on each side – cedars, chestnuts and plane trees, which enclose Jardin Darcy in a curtain of foliage. Then you may decide to take a turn around the park, following a path behind the fountain that leads to a shadowy woodland opening into a circular courtyard. This courtyard, you will soon discover, is dominated by an octagonal monument topped by neoclassical columns within which a bust of Henri Darcy, a famous Dijon-born hydraulics engineer, stares down. Darcy, you may note, has an intelligent brow and impressively long fluffy sideburns.

At this point, given you may now be cutting it fine to catch a train for your day trip to the town of Beaune, Burgundy's wine capital (as I was), you may think: *Interesting up to a point, I'd better get to the station.* Your eyes may linger on an old green door within the plinth of the monument upon which Darcy's bust resides, without even really registering the doorway exists (as I did). Then you may go to Beaune and drink fine red wines and not consider Jardin Darcy much again, even though you have made a mental note of the park as a fine place to kill time if you ever happen to be waiting for a train in Dijon.

What a "park error" this would be (and was for me). For I later found, despite visiting the park once again to sit on a bench eating a snack before taking another train, that Jardin Darcy is an extraordinary park... if you poke around a bit.

First of all, there is the story of the park's namesake: Henri Darcy.

Monsieur Darcy was a down-to-earth hard grafter – rather than an aloof English Mr Darcy – who graduated with honours in civil engineering from the School of Bridges and Roads in Paris in 1826. After completing his studies, he returned to Dijon and soon rolled up his sleeves, setting to work on an ambitious engineering project involving transporting spring water via an 8-mile underwater aqueduct to a reservoir in his home town. The plan was to supply water to all main buildings, with extra connections for hospitals, via a network of 28,000 metres of pipes. A total of 128 public fountains, each spread 100 metres apart, were also to be installed.

By 1840, Darcy had achieved this incredible task, 20 years before Paris had anything of the sort – in one fell swoop providing Dijon with the best potable water supply of any European city apart from Rome. Having performed the seemingly impossible, he turned down a reward of 55,000 francs offered by city officials, instead accepting a gold medal and that his home be provided with a lifetime's supply of water.

After this, Darcy's career really took off. He was promptly appointed chief engineer for the *département* of Côte d'Or, whereupon he ensured that the city of Dijon was not bypassed by a main train line being built between Paris and Lyon. Instead, he proposed a (literally) groundbreaking 3-mile tunnel through mountains that were blocking off the city in other engineers' plans. This was accepted and Dijon, which had been in danger of becoming a backwater, thrived on the back of the new iron horses bringing trade into and out of town. Not long after, Darcy was awarded the Legion of Merit. Then, not long after that, he was appointed chief engineer of the Municipal Service in Paris. On taking up this new job, he accelerated much needed progress in sanitation in the French capital, before retiring early due to ill health. Then he returned to Dijon and, to cap off his marvellous engineering adventures, proceeded to crank out the formulations of not one, but two important rules of hydraulics that are used to this day: Darcy's Law, regarding the flow of compressible liquids though porous substances, and the Darcy-Weisbach Equation, concerning energy dissipation in pipes. Both are considered foundation stones of the study of hydraulics.

Darcy died in 1858 at the age of 54 and was so loved among his fellow citizens in Dijon that the main square, which faces Jardin Darcy, was named after him.

What an extraordinary life, and it just goes to show: ignore that dusty old monument in the corner of the park at your peril, a joyous story could be hiding in the shadows beneath those plane trees. Darcy's achievements did, after all, greatly improve the public health of the city, transforming lives and probably even saving a few thanks to reduced spread of disease.

A small plaque on the plinth touches on Darcy's achievements, mentioning his *désintéressement* at being financially rewarded. But there is little else to promote the local celebrity. Perhaps theories of energy dissipation do not exactly set the pulse racing and Dijon tourist chiefs, with plenty of other local attractions, knew better than to push its hydraulics genius too much.

But then there is the mysterious old green door next to the plaque at the front of the dusty old monument… and what lurks within.

This is the entrance to a spiral staircase that twists way down below Jardin Darcy opening into cavernous, vaulted chambers and tunnels that form one of two key reservoirs for Dijon built by Darcy to meet his 8-mile aqueduct from the spring. These big brick chambers were (and are) able to receive 7,000 litres of water every minute, having travelled for 3 hours along the aqueduct. This source has, however, long been cut off and now the reservoir is only used for spill-off water from surfaces on a nearby car park that would otherwise flood. The collected water is used by city street cleaners, for public fountains and plants.

Once a year, the reservoir is flushed out to allow those with an interest in public sanitation, underground reservoirs, hydraulics and theories of energy dissipation to visit on specially arranged tours to pay homage to Darcy, usually in late November. These tours are organized by the local water authority, the Suez Dijon Metropole agency, and must be booked three years in advance, such is the legend of Darcy in hydraulics circles.

Having not been down there myself – obviously – but having watched a YouTube film of a tour, I can agree with the no-nonsense description of the head of the Suez Dijon Metropole agency who was once asked by a reporter what the underground reservoir is like: "It is a beautiful work of art. As it is underground, it has a somewhat mysterious side." Which seems about right judging by the video: there *is* a beauty and eeriness down in the old chambers.

Yes, I do realize I have gone off on rather a long tangent about Henri Darcy. However, when you think that this great reservoir – a trailblazing system that influenced cities across Europe and, no doubt, the world – lies loitering beneath a little city park and you have no idea at all when you visit, then a long, slightly rambling (I'll admit) tangent is perhaps deserved.

Jardin Darcy was landscaped above the reservoir in obstinately French style rather than the fad for "English" that seems to have been all the rage just about everywhere else, opening in 1880, 22 years after the engineer died. Yet another late-nineteenth-century park to add to all the other recent ones. And none of this is mentioned in my guidebook to Dijon: not Darcy, not his park, certainly not his reservoir. When I visited the city for a chapter of a book about the high-speed train revolution then sweeping Europe, *Tales from the Fast Trains*, I had no idea about Darcy and his exploits, even though he had helped put the city on the rail map. I ignored him, too.

Shame on me: shame! Yes, Dijon has its mustard – the main mustard shops are just beyond Place Darcy, a 5-minute stroll from the park. Yes, it has its medieval dukes – their magnificently ornate tombs are further on past the mustard shops at the Palace of the Dukes. Yes, there are the masterpieces galore at the Musée des Beaux-Arts.

Yes, Dijon is a Busy Tourist Place. But there is also Jardin Darcy.

After Bürkli skulking amid the fuchsias in Zurich, now Darcy tucked quietly behind the fancy fountain. One day, pandemics permitting, I'll be back.

After the flood
Jardín del Turia, Valencia, Spain

On 14 October 1957 the River Turia flooded in Valencia, Spain's third-largest city, after Barcelona and Madrid. More than 80 people died as waters rose above bridges and swept into the city centre, rising to first-floor windows in some neighbourhoods and destroying many properties. It was dubbed the *Gran Riada de Valencia* (Great Flood of Valencia) and city officials decided, finally, to take action; over the centuries bursting banks had periodically brought devastation and the feeling was *suficiente es suficiente* (enough is enough). So, the river was diverted south to a man-made channel bypassing the city.

The project was completed in 1973. The result was twofold: firstly, a safe city centre at last, to everyone's great relief; secondly, 6 miles of new land snaking through Valencia, about 200 metres wide on average.

This is a lot of extra territory for a city to find unexpectedly in its possession and a forward-thinking local planning department, refusing to give in to lobbying to build a big new road, designated the space as parkland. This was duly named Jardín del Turia.

For a glimpse of how cities might be in an ideal future, park-wise, Valencia is the place to go.

Walking along the old riverbed it is hard to imagine you are in a city at all, and on a first-time visit Jardín del Turia takes a bit of getting used to. Tropical trees with drooping branches trailing Spanish moss grow in shadowy woodlands. Orange trees hang heavy with fruit in sunlit groves. Ferns unfurl in clusters in verges. Cypress trees shoot up in rows beside ponds. Emerald lawns spread out with grass so green you at first wonder: *How?* Are your eyes deceiving you? Is this thick lush pasture for real? No grass could possibly be this green so far south in Spain. But yes, it is for real: irrigation channels transporting enough river water for plants, connected to many pipes and sprinklers, mean Jardín del Turia has all the liquid refreshment a park could ever need.

Everything is very, very green. For an urban park lover, everything is also simply wonderful.

Palm trees tower above, leaning toward one another as though sharing secrets. Shrubs sprout glossy fronds. Crimson flowers bloom. Lilac bougainvillea tumbles from wherever it might possibly tumble. Vines and creepers, too. All is well maintained: squads of municipal gardeners make sure of that.

Lining Jardín del Turia, banks rise with balustrades and walls intact from the river days, water marks and old metal hoops for tying boats still to be seen. Being below and removed from the city streets, even on a hot summer's day, the air is refreshing, cooler and cleaner down on the old riverbed than up above. Cicadas screech. Butterflies flicker. Visiting this park is like entering an urban Arcadia of sorts: a controlled wilderness bursting with life. Leave it alone for a while, you fancy, and a jungle might soon climb out of the riverbed and begin to take over Spain's third-largest metropolis.

Bridges loop like great stone caterpillars crawling across this verdant "valley". There are 18 in all. Some are relics of centuries gone by with statues and columns. Look up and old-fashioned lamp posts with clusters of art nouveau lights stare down. Or marble renditions of the Virgin Mary. Or beatified Franciscan monks. Or fearsome creatures with fangs and wings: half-dragon, half-man. Meanwhile, long curving sweeps of pedestrian walkways seem to float miraculously above, supported by beams held by wires configured like harp strings. How do they stay up? It does not seem possible.

On the paths: so many bicycles. The River Turia continues to flow, but not with water from the mountainous interior. Commuters listening to earphones pedal steadily by. "Pros" in Lycra shorts and shirts of famous racing teams slip past, all sinewy calves and sweat. Children yell and race after one another. Tourists on brightly painted rental bikes stop to consult maps, point and take pictures. Valencia must have more bicycle hire shops than any city anywhere; around the cathedral just about every other premises offers bike-and-helmet-and-padlock deals.

Yet there is plenty of room for everyone: cyclists as well as walkers and joggers, who number many. Looking into the park from above at Puente del Mar, a sixteenth-century bridge with pointed arches and a patchwork of wobbly flagstones, bike lanes and walkways below may be busy but there is ample space. Were they ever to become overcrowded, simply add a few more! No problem! The riverbed has a surfeit of land going spare.

As if to prove just how much room Valencia has to play with, at Puente del Mar, on the north side, municipal gardeners have fashioned a giant version of Valencia's coat of arms out of plants: rows of yellow and red (well, purple-ish) hedges form the colours of the city's distinctive shield, while above the shield is a green hedge shaped like an enormous bat. Heraldry experts believe this unusual city symbol, which dates from medieval times, is either because a bat landed on the flag of King Jaume I just as he was about to retake the city from the Moors in the thirteenth century (which he considered a good omen), or simply because a great number of bats are to be found in Valencia. I prefer the first explanation.

Within Jardín del Turia are Ferris wheels, five-a-side football pitches, ponds, fountains, rose gardens, tennis courts, basketball courts, dog-walking zones, exercise stations, abstract sculptures, children's playgrounds, skateparks, baseball fields, rugby fields, espresso bars, barbecue zones, ping-pong tables, athletics tracks, fairgrounds, tapas bars, sandwich kiosks, restaurants, mini-golf courses, music venues and, at the far northern end, a wild animal reserve. Throw in the futuristic Ciudad de las Artes y Ciencias (City of Arts and Sciences), a theme park that attracts visitors from across Europe to the southern tip of the old riverbed, close to where the water once emptied into the Mediterranean Sea, and you have a whole lot going on.

Yet the vast majority of Jardín del Turia remains parkland, as marvellous as all these many activities and attractions may be.

I have, I realize, started gushing about Jardín del Turia. Who cares! It is the final foreign park on this world tour of parks, after all. A little gushing is permitted. But what, you may be wondering, makes this park so very special? *Come on, spit it out*, as an acerbic television interviewer might say. What is it about Jardín del Turia in a nutshell? What is the feeling you get when you walk through the dappled sunlight beneath the palm trees, a soft breeze sweeping down the old riverbed?

Well, the overarching sensation for me – the great thing about Jardín del Turia – is quite simply that nature, with the help of human beings, has "won".

Jardín del Turia feels almost post-apocalyptic – in a good way. When you imagine a "jungle" rising to take the city above, well this is just an extension of what has already happened to the riverbed below. Nature is in the ascendency. Here is a big, growing modern city, with a metropolitan area population of 1.5 million and 5,800 people living per square kilometre (not far off Hong Kong in that measurement). Here is a city that has boomed during the twentieth century, quadrupling in size. Here also is a great big, relatively new, park bang in the middle. Take a look at the map of Valencia and it is not all terracotta roofs as in Dubrovnik and Venice. Instead, a fine band of green slides around the old town, coming to an end by the Mar Mediterráneo, the port, the marina and the strip of sand at Playa de la Malvarrosa. The balance seems right. Nature – the park – and the city seem in the right proportions.

As with the much-heralded 1.5 miles of disused raised railroad that was classified parkland in New York City in 2005 (High Line park in west Manhattan) and the old airport-turned-park at Quito in Ecuador, space that otherwise might have been swallowed by city has been saved. Yes, in Valencia's instance the park may have been "natural" beforehand: i.e., river, but imagine a major road along the riverbed. Imagine hotels and offices alongside. Imagine apartment blocks. Imagine roundabouts. Imagine a whole different city.

When walking along the old riverbed, the feeling that Jardín del Turia represents how cities will one day have to become to embrace "greenery" is overwhelmingly strong. Not just lip service to targets that may be met piecemeal somehow by clever reclassifications of land – sleights of hand to extend city boundaries to take in swathes of countryside that are already green, as you half suspect some cities will have to do, and are already doing, to meet ambitious green targets. Big civic projects that shun quick money and have the long-term future in mind will be required if visions of truly "green" cities are really to come true.

When I visited Jardín del Turia, I scrawled in my notebook: *After the end of the modern world when everything has started again, too good to be true (?), weirdly perfect.* It is definitely the latter. All around Valencia looms: ancient fortifications, spires, beautiful nineteenth-century art nouveau buildings, ugly Franco-era apartment blocks. Yet there is the park, slicing through the middle, and the most wonderful thing of all? It is being used. Just about every time I asked a Valencian what they liked most about living in the city, within moments the park cropped up. The entire outlook of Valencia seems shaped by Jardín del Turia.

We know, instinctively, we need green. Valencia realized that a while back.

I walked a long way down the riverbed, in the company of so many others; just one member of the community, if you like, of Valencian park lovers that day. In Vancouver, back in Stanley Park, the attraction of a city so in tune with its natural surroundings made me think I could live there. The same was true of Valencia; all down to this magnificent park.

Sometimes great ideas are born out of adversity, such as the *Gran Riada de Valencia* of 1957, yet why wait for troubles to come? Get in there first! Cities need parks: lots of them.

Valencia's Jardín del Turia is a lesson to the world.

CHAPTER THIRTEEN

SCOTLAND, ENGLAND: HOMECOMING

OK, so there it was: around the world in parks and back to Britain, catapulting north across the Bay of Biscay from Spain to where this adventure began. I had watched the seasons change from spring through summer through autumn into winter while sitting at my study desk overlooking my suburban street and "travelling" an enormous distance.

By this stage, with vaccines about to be rolled out and a seeming end to the pandemic in sight, I had reached yet another level of park appreciation, superseding even the transcendental state of park zen I had been feeling in Europe: these park stories were becoming not just a celebration of green places in cities across the globe and all their secrets, quirks and pleasures. They were also, I dared to fancy, turning into a (gentle) call to action.

This was what several months locked down in a small room dreaming of urban parks could do to you: cabin fever had turned to park fever.

If we all loved urban parks so much – a point upon which I considered most of us could agree, having spent plenty of time in them of late – then maybe we should stop taking them for granted.

If seven in ten of us will live in cities by 2050, as the United Nations was predicting (compared with 5.5 of us now), then city life was about to become more intense than ever.

If we thought that cities were too crowded as they were, just wait to see what they could be like pretty soon. If we were sick of cramped commutes. If we were tired of pollution. If we thought that living in a big city could be dehumanizing and spirit-sapping. If we felt that the odds in cities were stacked against "normal life". If we thought all these sorts of thoughts and others like them, perhaps it was time also to start thinking, *It does not have to be this way.*

My "grand conclusion" was simple: the greener the city, the happier the city – true in Valencia, true in Vancouver, true in Vienna, true in Helsinki, true the world over. Perhaps it was time to reconsider "progress" in cities that almost inevitably saw skyscrapers shoot up. Perhaps it was time also to start thinking of urban areas in terms of parks and "green". Not just saying it… doing something about it.

So ended my Parks Political Broadcast.

With a feeling of having travelled full circle, before returning to the city in which this park quest began, one last journey north to Scotland lay ahead to another wonderful park. Then down south I would return, to the other side of London to Richmond Park and a Sunday morning visit, face mask packed, to the capital's oldest purpose-built public park.

On an old volcano
Holyrood Park, Edinburgh, Scotland

These tales of urban parks have involved a fair bit of "up". Mountainous South America, unsurprisingly, provided most altitude: Parque Metropolitano in Santiago, Chile; El Panecillo in Quito, Ecuador; and Montserrate in Bogotá, Colombia. Then there was Diamond Head State Monument Park in Hawaii, Table Mountain National Park back in Cape Town and Mount Srd above Dubrovnik. Now for Holyrood Park, like Diamond Head, the remains of an old volcano.

Its vital statistics – as well as those of Scotland's capital city over which Holyrood presides – provide an indication of the park's position in Edinburgh, both geographically on its eastern edge and, if you like, psychologically. The highest point of the hill around which the park is wrapped, named Arthur's Seat, rises to 251 metres (slightly higher than Honolulu's volcano) and the park covers 640 acres with a diameter of 5 miles and a terrain comprising crags, marshes, lochs, glens and moorland.

This diversity of landscape means you effectively have a microcosm of Scotland bang on the doorstep of Scotland's rulers both of now and centuries past: the gleaming geometric rooftops of the Scottish Parliament next to the eminent outline of the Palace of Holyroodhouse (the Queen's official Scottish residence) lie at the foot of Arthur's Seat.

There they are: the corridors of power, where all the big decisions have been made, looking like toy block buildings from above as the city of half a million stretches out into the hazy distance beyond Georgian townhouses and spires to the River Forth as it empties into the North Sea. Beyond the Forth, the county of Fife arises – and, somewhere up there in the north-west, are the famous lochs and the Highlands.

Arthur's Seat is a mysterious brooding bulk. The name is nothing to do with the legend of King Arthur. It is probably derived from the Gaelic *Ard-na-said* (height or arrows), which morphed into "Archer's Seat" and then into Arthur's Seat as years rolled by. The hill and the land around were for centuries royal hunting grounds. When in 1128 King David I was in pursuit of deer, the monarch was knocked from his horse and confronted by an enraged stag. Miraculously, at this very moment a cross appeared before him, thus warding off attack. As thanks for this divine intervention, the king founded the Abbey of the Holy Cross, Holyrood Abbey. Hence Holyrood Park, so the legend goes ("rood" being Old English for "cross" or "pole"). The park officially became "park" in 1541 under the rule of King James V, who built a stone wall around Arthur's Seat. What fantastic foresight, you might say, way, way ahead of the Valencians and Jardín del Turia.

To strike out from Lawnmarket on the Royal Mile, along cobbled streets past the jumble of woollen jumper, jewellery and whisky shops, the medieval grandeur of St Giles' Cathedral, the jolly pubs, the inviting coffee shops and the shiny, modern parliament to arrive at a wall of heathery green with crumbly cliffs sliding above on a ridge known as the Salisbury Crags is one of the greatest "park escapes" of any city on the planet. Quite different from Vancouver's switch from skyscrapers to wilderness at Stanley Park, but just as uplifting.

Edinburgh's volcano ceased erupting 340 million years ago, so you are OK on that front. From the city centre, going as directly and as sensibly as possible, you set off across a zebra crossing from the Holyrood Park Information Centre (this is a park so splendid it even has a visitors' centre), up steps and then along the "Radical Road". This old route was paved in 1822 by unemployed weavers from the west of Scotland who had failed in an uprising two years earlier over poor living conditions that had seen a national strike declared during what was dubbed the "Radical War". They were co-opted into the toil after King George IV visited Edinburgh and the novelist Sir Walter Scott helpfully suggested they were deployed to do so. How well this went down with the radical weavers of western Scotland is unclear.

It is a glorious way up with the cliffs of the Salisbury Crags towering above, although the path was recently closed and still is, as I write, after a major rockslide in 2018. There is a chance the route may be permanently shut, which would be a great shame, although there are plenty of other paths with equally magnificent views to the top.

My walk was a couple of years before the closure on a crisp, hopeful autumn day. As you rise, the gothic splendour of Edinburgh unveils below and your heart begins to lift at the sight of the fortifications of Edinburgh Castle at the end of the Royal Mile beyond Lawnmarket; the castle is perched on another much smaller hilly remnant of Edinburgh's old volcano. All around are spires, cupolas, domes, turrets, terraces and winding lanes. What a charming higgledy-piggledy capital. To be away from the traffic and up on a hillside so suddenly feels almost impossible and this sense of release from the throng of its busy ways, combined with the prospect of even greater rewards ahead in the form of even better views, spurs you on.

Halfway up, however, is a curious story that is nothing to do with King David I and his God-sent cross.

In June 1836, not long after Sir Walter and the King's visit, schoolboys hunting for rabbits on the old volcano entered a small cave on the hill's north-eastern side and discovered a stash of 17 little wooden "coffins" containing carvings of figures beneath a lid of loosely stacked slate. Boys being boys, they chucked the odd, 6-inch figurines about a bit, destroying a few of the more water-damaged relics. But word soon got out about the find and great conjecture followed as to their provenance. Were the figurines the handiwork of witches? Might they be good-luck icons placed for sailors on the hillside before they set out to sea? Or were they, possibly, something much more macabre?

Only eight years earlier the notorious Burke and Hare murders, committed by William Burke and William Hare, had involved precisely 17 victims, whose corpses were sold for dissection for medical research. The numerical coincidence got people talking. Were the wooden carvings somehow connected to these gruesome killings? No one is sure, but it is possible to see the intriguing remaining coffins for yourself at the National Museum of Scotland.

Their legend and Arthur's Seat have become entwined. When the crime novelist Ian Rankin visited the National Museum a few years ago to meet a French television crew for an interview, a museum assistant serendipitously suggested he took a look at the objects, which he had not seen before. He duly did so and his mind was set racing. The result was his crime thriller *The Falls*, with an eerie modern parallel plot running alongside the enigma of the little coffins. Some believe this to be the finest in his bestselling Inspector Rebus crime series.

So, there is a dark side to the craggy landscape as you ascend Arthur's Seat into Holyrood Park and the wind from the west picks up, especially when you consider former goings on in the Palace of Holyroodhouse down below. This was where Mary, Queen of Scots, when six months pregnant, witnessed the murder of her trusted secretary and supposed lover, David Rizzio, an Italian. Lord Darnley, her jealous husband, had authorized the attack, which involved no fewer than 56 stab wounds conducted by a bloody gang of 80 assassins.

Yet more not-so-pleasant thoughts on a crisp autumn day.

The novelist Robert Louis Stevenson's take on Arthur's Seat in his colourful *Edinburgh: Picturesque Notes* gets the hillside and Holyrood Park in one: "A hill for magnitude, a mountain in virtue of its bold design." And yes, it does, despite its modest dimensions, feel like a *mountain*. And yes, it does seem *bold*, an icon of Scottishness in its prime position in the city. Take away Arthur's Seat and Edinburgh would of course seem completely different: quite exposed, not nearly as splendid. And had building over the centuries been allowed in the lower reaches (restraint in the past showing great foresight given recent landslides) the hillside itself would not be quite so inspiringly mysterious: the crossover from old town to the escape into the greenery less immediate. Official park status saved Arthur's Seat from that.

Scampering up the slopes, the top from the visitor's centre can be reached in half an hour or so. When I got there, the wind was up. A few of us gathered on the bare rocky summit where a compass face etched into a metal panel showed the distance to various Scottish castles and peaks. The sea was silvery and the surrounding countryside around Edinburgh a deep green. The city looks so small from the top. No wonder some refer to Scotland's capital as being like a village.

One last curiosity from Arthur's Seat. Somewhere down below, near the Radical Road, the Scottish geologist James Hutton once studied the hillside's intriguing rock formations, his observations later published in his groundbreaking 1788 work, *Theory of the Earth*. This book was to transform the common understanding of the age of the planet. Now known as the "father of geology", Hutton concluded that the Earth was not at all young nor feasibly created in seven days, as in Christian tradition; the study of rocks on Arthur's Seat showed it must be far more ancient than any concept of the beginning of mankind then understood. A part of the Salisbury Crags where Hutton worked is now called the Hutton Section.

So, the age of the Earth was narrowed down in Holyrood Park, the long-held belief in the origin of the planet according to the Bible questioned! Not bad for a "park claim" (putting Darcy's discoveries regarding energy dissipation in pipes back in Dijon rather in the shade).

A lot, as I believe I may have mentioned before, has gone on in parks.

People's Park
Victoria Park, London, England

At 7.30 a.m. on a Sunday, all was action by Bonner Gate at Victoria Park in London's East End.

Teams of workers in fluorescent jackets were milling by Regent's Canal, where smoke drifted lazily from the chimneys of house barges. The workers were preparing to clear litter from bins. Meanwhile, a banner was being hoisted to advertize a weekly market to be held at 10 a.m. A supervisor stood behind a trestle table on which lists of stallholders had been placed beside hand-sanitizer pumps. Already a few had arrived and were laying out metal poles to be erected. Trolleys of produce were being carted with a clatter to a tarmacked lane through the centre of the park, along an avenue of trees skirting a lake.

"Sorry, boss, just coming through," said a man carrying a parasol on his shoulder, as I dilly-dallied inspecting two fearsome sculptures of dogs at the entrance to the lane.

These vicious-looking hounds are known as the Dogs of Alcibiades, based on a Greek design dating back to the fifth century BC, and have been gracing the park since 1912 after being donated by Lady Regnart. So said a public information sign, of which Victoria Park is in no short supply. A sign next to the canal had already informed me that the entrance to the park here was named after Bishop Bonner, who once owned much of the land upon which Victoria Park was established after being commissioned by Queen Victoria in 1840 and opened in 1845. This bishop had also gone under the title of "lord of the manor" of Stepney and the sign by the canal says he had been known as "Bloody Bonner" due to his enthusiastic persecution of heretics under Mary I. His old home, Bonner's Palace, was destroyed in 1845 to allow room for the new green open space.

Victoria Park was, I learn, a "breakthrough" park that was soon followed by two important acts of Parliament – the 1847 Town Improvement Clauses Act and the 1848 Public Health Act – providing local authorities with powers to set aside land for public parks for the enjoyment of the "middle or humbler classes".

It came about largely thanks to the efforts of two reforming Members of Parliament, Joseph Hume and George Frederick Young, who had convinced Queen Victoria to give royal assent after gathering a petition of 30,000 signatures. At the time, as they pointed out in a report, disease was rife and living conditions in slum dwellings dreadful among East Enders, many of whom worked in the Thames docks "swelling the resources of the empire", as the MPs persuasively put it.

Back then, the land at Bow was almost forgotten territory with a few old mouldering cottages, dismal clay pits dug for brickmaking and a reputation for being a hideout for those avoiding transportation to Australia: the area was jokingly referred to by some as Botany Bay (where Captain Phillip had arrived with his ships full of convicts before settling on Sydney Cove by what was to become the Royal Botanic Garden all those years ago). The MPs had declared in their submission to the Queen that "a park in the East End of London would probably diminish the annual deaths by several thousands". They had also astutely mentioned that this would benefit "all classes of the community... for the epidemics, whether influenza or typhus, cholera, smallpox, scarlatina [scarlet fever] or measles, which arise in the East End of the town, do not stay there, they travel to the West End and prove fatal in the wide streets and squares". Aside from an arboretum opened in Derby in 1840 – only free for the hoi polloi to enter two days a week, so not really fully "public" – no other such specifically allocated urban greenery designed as "park" (as opposed to common land) existed in Britain at the time.

Her Majesty duly gave the royal nod and the park – 218 acres in all and the first park in London to provide green space for such purposes (Richmond Park and the other royal parks, such as Green Park and St James's Park, had always simply just been there) – was duly named after her, although some now prefer to call it the People's Park and others, affectionately, Vicky Park. This is a park with many names.

A loop around is about 4 miles. Going anticlockwise from Bonner's Gate you soon come to a lake with an island upon which sits, somewhat unexpectedly, a Chinese summer-house pagoda complete with golden dragons and curly topped roofs. This was originally a display at a Chinese exhibition held at Hyde Park in 1842 but was bought by Victoria Park to add a bit of pizzazz to its newly installed lake. The landscape architect

James Pennethorne, an understudy of the famous royal architect John Nash, had been called upon to design the park and had evidently thought: *Why not?* The result was that some East End slum-dwelling children back then believed that a Chinese family lived on the island (then without a bridge).

Which is a lovely story. Although not quite so lovely on my visit, while looking across the water to a fountain and a cafe on the far shore, was my company: a big fat curious rat. The rat had been investigating an overflowing bin by the pagoda and had decided to join me, perhaps seeking a handout. None was forthcoming, yet the rat sat nearby and he/she and I regarded the view of the ducks and the Canada geese for a while before the creature scurried away. Bins with rubbish slopping out were all about the park that Sunday morning, although the workers in fluorescent jackets soon cleared up.

Evidence of lockdown festivities (and other lockdown traits of human behaviour).

After the pagoda – a replacement of the original, which had been badly damaged in the Second World War – the path around the park follows another stretch of canal between tall plane trees. Then it traverses the lake, where two abstract sculptures rise from the water (commissioned by the Romanian Cultural Institute and Tower Hamlets Council), passes the circular Pavilion Café and a community board advertising yoga, mindfulness classes and social events organized by "Queer Newham", and crosses a road into a section of fields. Council tower blocks rise on the right beyond the cosy-looking *Rose & Gin*, *Spirit of Freedom* and *B's Nest* canal barges, while joggers follow the pedestrianized road by the path. Traffic was long ago banned in the park as there had been awful traffic jams.

This is a pleasant walk on a quiet Sunday morning, heading in the direction of the Olympic Stadium built for the 2012 Games and where West Ham United play, about a mile away across the A12.

Floodlights were on for some reason and thoughts of Mo Farah, Jessica Ennis-Hill and others' exploits during that heady summer sprang to mind as the park curved around beyond a building, appropriately, home to a local running club: the Victoria Park Harriers and Tower Hamlets Athletics Club. The park attracts many joggers, some exceedingly quick runners and the occasional boxer in training, shadow punching between feints: the East End may be increasingly gentrified, but it is still tough round the edges.

Next door to the athletics club is a disused lodge for patrolmen built in the early days of the park "to safe keep the regulations of the park in so distant and lawless a neighbourhood as Hackney Wick", says a useful little sign. Close by are two old stone alcoves that were originally on a long-lost version of London Bridge dating from the eighteenth century, according to another useful little sign. Meanwhile, not far onward is the site of a Second World War prisoner-of-war camp (now a field) as well as bowling greens and tennis courts where Fred Perry once practised before winning the Wimbledon Championship. In 1895, there were 32 cricket pitches in the park, 37 tennis courts, athletics tracks, a bathing lake (which still exists although bathing is now banned) and "four gymnasia", says yet another useful little sign.

Many of these useful little signs are by the gates, which are worth detours for their titbits. Victoria Park, you cannot help thinking halfway round, could be one of the world's best parks for useful little signs.

Around this section of the north of the park, you begin to consider its People's Park tag. For a start there is the People's Park Tavern with its motto "A Pub for the People, Inspired by the People", closed due to the ongoing lockdown with its picnic benches on the artificial grass empty when I passed.

Then you come to a section of the park renowned for its political gatherings, with speakers as diverse as the nineteenth-century writer, socialist activist, printmaker and textile designer William Morris, the playwright George Bernard Shaw, the suffragette Sylvia Pankhurst (whose May Day demonstration in 1913 saw violent police opposition) and – not mentioned on any of the useful little signs I spotted – the leader of the British Union of Fascists, Oswald Mosley, who held rallies attended by his blackshirt supporters in 1936.

Much earlier, in 1848, Chartist campaigners had held regular gatherings in the park, calling for more representative government, much to the ill ease of those at the top. A meeting in June of that year had turned violent and been broken up by authorities bearing cudgels. The park's tradition of anti-establishment thinking was forged from those days onward. An area close to Royal Gate, directly north of Bonner Gate, was soon earmarked for speakers, just as at Speakers' Corner in Hyde Park. Locals dubbed the many debates held there as "forum or agin-em" (for them or against them). It is possible that Queen Victoria may not have been entirely amused by how matters were panning out in her new namesake park. There is no statue of her, interestingly, within the park's grounds.

Beyond this "forum or agin-em" corner you come to an extraordinarily OTT Gothic water fountain funded by a Victorian philanthropist, Baroness Burdett-Coutts (of the Coutts banking family), to the tune of what would be £500,000 in today's money. Unveiled in 1862, this was an early, particularly flamboyant example of virtue signalling, complete with marble cherubs, that was appreciated for its fresh supplies of clean water even if the requirement for quite such artistry was rather lost to those used to scooping water from the park's dirty lakes.

Beyond this mad decorative fountain (no longer seemingly working), the path trailed around back to the Sunday market.

By 9.30 a.m., this had become a veritable hive of activity. Afghan and Nigerian street food stalls had set up, Thai, Malaysian, Bolivian, Indian, Greek, Lebanese and Japanese stalls, too; no cockles, whelks or jellied eels of East End fame (that I saw). Businesses had yet to open and it was all highly organized. Street-food stalls filled one section, separated to keep customers in queues from overlapping, while grocery stalls in a similar configuration completed another, overflowing with artisan breads, organic cheeses, wild mushrooms, Sicilian pastries, hot sauces, Spanish churros and game pies.

Stallholders exchanged banter and checked out rivals' produce; voices, like their wares, from across the globe. This may have been the middle of a lockdown, but a world party was about to begin: all corners covered, just about. The show must go on! Delicious smells wafted across Bishop Bonner's old fields. Ethnic music played on stereos. Signs were being pinned up for two-for-one sausage rolls. Compared with the stags, the swans, the great spotted woodpeckers and the vast expanses of bracken and oaks of Richmond Park, just 15 miles away across the capital, this was another world. Another park.

My 4 miles were up.

By the lake, home to the world's oldest model boat club (though no boats were about on my visit), milky light fell in streaks on the placid water and the fountain splashed and fizzled in the direction of the pagoda and its fat curious rat.

Sitting on a bench near a pair of London Ambulance workers with Australian accents, I sipped a Pavilion Café coffee served by an American. The ambulance workers wore green overalls and looked as though they had finished a night shift. They were discussing their futures: "When I go back to Sydney" – making me think of the lovely Royal Botanic Garden way back in New South Wales. Dog walkers, families and post-run joggers filled other benches. All were taken. A queue snaked out of the cafe, where a man on the door dished out sanitizer and checked everyone wore face masks.

Welcome to park life 2020-style.

No wonder there had been such an uproar when Tower Hamlets Council had had the temerity to attempt to close Vicky Park when the pandemic began. Even early on a Sunday morning in the height of a lockdown it was alive with bustle and business.

Being used, being loved.

Just as parks should be, wherever they may be.

AFTERWORD

Cometh the worldwide lockdown, cometh the park. Just about all of us have grown more familiar with our local green spaces of late. Just about all of us city dwellers have learned to appreciate our neighbourhood parks just a little bit more.

To be fair, we have not exactly had much choice.

As far as Richmond Park goes, I now know it like the back of my hand. While writing this lockdown book about urban parks, I must have circled its perimeter 50 times or more, witnessing the months clicking by and the park's popularity ebb and flow according to latest R-rate figures, vaccination breakthroughs, overseas quarantines and – ever-so-keenly-monitored and constantly shifting – "travel corridors" of officially sanctioned countries where travel has been periodically, temporarily, allowed. Never have the British people been quite so au fait with the latest Foreign, Commonwealth and Development Office advice.

All the while, I have seen antlers grow, bellies fatten, babies born, stags roar, stags charge at one another, stags calm down and winter set in. Men and women in Lycra have pedalled by on increasingly expensive bikes. Joggers have grown in number, then fallen away as exercise regimes dropped off. Bins have overflowed with bottles and cans at weekends whenever it has been warm enough for a party; par for the course in Richmond and Victoria Parks alike, though I have never spotted a Richmond rat.

As frustrating as it may have been not to move about freely, there has been a pleasure of sorts in going local.

Once the realization dawned that travel further afield was no longer able to happen, all the usual holiday pressure was off. No worries about airfares creeping up if you leave it too long. No sweating about coordinating time off and asking bosses for leave. No angst about whether the hotel/villa/apartment is really as good as in its cleverly angled online pictures.

Just a quiet summer pottering about: fixing up the garden, doing a bit of DIY, going for walks in the park.

It has also been a time to let your mind wander; to escape in box sets (never have the British people been quite so opinionated about the latest long-running television series) and books. Including travel books. Travel in the mind has had, for a while, to take the place of travel in reality (as I had found and soon embraced when "setting off" around the world in urban parks from my study). Armchair travel, a quaint notion to most not so long ago when actual travel was so freely and cheaply available, has become a means of both stimulation and release.

Just a few months earlier this had simply not been the case. Why sit in your living room and dream of faraway places when you could book a break in a few clicks if your bank balance allowed? Not that bank balances needed much in reserve. Not with return tickets to Spain and Italy for £40. Marseilles, Biarritz, Florence, Rome? Why not just go?

Except suddenly we couldn't.

Remembering and discovering more about so many parks has, for me, been both a way of "escape" when actual escape has been impossible as well as a series of wonderful revelations. So many secret corners from Sydney to San Francisco, Pyongyang to Port-au-Prince, Khartoum to Kathmandu, Manila to Minsk, Athens to Anuradhapura (no problems with alliteration on a round-the-world journey). So many encounters. So many stories. So many histories (including so many shocking colonial histories). So many "park heroes" whose past interventions saved the day – from John Lewis at Sheen Gate and his troubles with the tricksy Princess Amelia back in 1755, onward.* So many pockets of green and calm.

---

* John Lewis' gravestone can be found on the south side of St Mary Magdalene Church in Richmond. There is also a fine portrait of him by T. Stewart, a pupil of Joshua Reynolds, that hangs in the Riverside Room in the Old Town Hall, Richmond, looking appropriately no-nonsense with a walking stick, appropriately once again, clasped in his right hand.

So yes, urban parks bring enormous pleasure – not just going to them (Google's mysterious mobility checker found visits to UK parks have leaped by a quarter since the pandemic began), but recalling them, too.

And not wishing to bang the park drum too much, although this is probably way, way too late now: *If only there were more*. The sheer scale of cities such as Beijing, Manila, Lima, Bogotá and Kathmandu (especially), not to mention New York City or London, has made this a matter of priority. The world's cities need parks… and the people who live in them want them very much, too.

The great twentieth-century travel writer Bruce Chatwin, that unofficial patron saint of Motion, often wrote about human restlessness. He believed that human beings have a migratory drive to walk long distances and that this "drive" is connected to our central nervous systems: that we *need* to travel. When we cannot, he said, we get restless and in these "warped" circumstances we have a tendency to find "outlets in violence, greed, status-seeking or a mania for the new". To travel, Chatwin believed (convincingly), is part of the human condition.

By logic, when we cannot move far away, we need to move close by.

Which is where urban parks come in, especially recently.

So, here's to parks! Here's to how they make life better in so many places on our big, bad, crowded planet.

ACKNOWLEDGEMENTS

Many thanks to all those who assisted on these travels; far too many to mention. Recalling so many adventures was, frankly, a treat during the various lockdowns. Other than walks in Richmond Park or along the Thames, armchair (desk chair) travel was the only travel available and remembering the kindness of people met on the journeys often brought a warm glow on darkest lockdown days. Special thanks during this period are due to the park-keepers of Richmond Park who gallantly cleared the mess of summer gatherings. I also owe "lockdown thanks" to the staff of Riva News, my local newsagent, and those at Sainsbury's Local on White Hart Lane. When the pandemic was at its most frightening at the beginning, they kept going (keeping the rest of us going); just as health and care workers did up and down the country.

As ever I owe a debt of gratitude to my parents Robert and Christine Chesshyre for listening to my book-related stories, my brother Edward Chesshyre and to Ben Clatworthy for their read-throughs, my sister Kate for her excellent advice this year, my aunt Meg Chesshyre, Danny Kelly, Jamie Fox and Zsuzsa Simko. Kasia Piotrowska was a wonderful companion around Richmond Park so many times and of course at other times. Special thanks also to Mark Palmer, travel editor of the *Daily Mail*, Hattie Sime, deputy travel editor at the *Daily Mail* and Hugo Brown of the *Daily Mail*'s lively *Escape* travel section. Thanks also to Sarah Hartley, travel editor of the *Mail on Sunday*, Michael Mosbacher, Bob Low and Christopher Montgomery of *The Critic*, as well as to Helena Caletta and the staff of Open Book in Richmond and to Stanfords maps in Covent Garden for being so all-round great.

Claire Plimmer, editorial director at Summersdale, made this book possible, as ever; her belief in the idea provided the push it required. Thanks also to Debbie Chapman for her review read, Hannah Adams for her first-rate edit, Emily Kearns for her sharp-eyed copy-edit, Natalya Kahn for her attentive proofreading, Hamish Braid for the neat graphics and Jasmin Burkitt for getting word out and about so well.

The talented artist Andrew Halliday kindly provided the photograph of Central Park in New York City (andrewhallidayfineart.co.uk).

BIBLIOGRAPHY

Al Gathafi, Muammar *The Green Book* (2009, World Center for the Study and Research of the Green Book)

Bartram, John, with John Karter *Park Life: The Memoirs of a Royal Parks Gamekeeper* (2017, Metro Books)

Bhasin, Raaja *Shimla on Foot: Ten Walks* (2007, Rupa)

Calvino, Italo *Invisible Cities* (1997, Vintage; first published in Great Britain by Secker & Warburg in 1974)

Collingridge, Vanessa *The Story of Australia* (2008, Andre Deutsch)

de Botton, Alain *The Art of Travel* (2002, Hamish Hamilton)

de Maistre, Xavier *A Journey Around My Room* (2017, Alma Classics; first published in 1794)

Elborough, Travis *A Walk in the Park: The Life and Times of a People's Institution* (2017, Vintage; first published by Jonathan Cape in 2016)

Ferlinghetti, Lawrence *Ferlinghetti's Greatest Poems* (2017, W. W. Norton & Company)

Fleming, Fergus *Cassell's Tales of Endurance* (2004, Weidenfeld & Nicholson)

Fletcher Jones, Pamela *Richmond Park: Portrait of a Royal Playground* (1972, Phillimore)

Greene, Graham *Our Man in Havana* (2001, Vintage; first published by William Heinemann in 1958)

Greene, Graham *The Comedians* (1971, Penguin Books; first published by The Bodley Head in 1966)

Greene, Graham *The Quiet American* (1966, Bantam; first published by The Viking Press in 1956)

Greene, Graham *The Third Man and The Fallen Idol* (2005, Vintage; first published in Great Britain by William Heinemann in 1950)

Hollis, Leo *Cities are Good for You: The Genius of the Metropolis* (2013, Bloomsbury)

Hyde, Edward *The History of the Rebellion* (2009, Oxford University Press; first published in 1704)

Kelly, Michael *Reminiscences* (1826, Henry Colburn)

Maclean, Rory *Berlin: Image of a City* (2014, Weidenfeld & Nicolson)

Mandela, Nelson *Long Walk to Freedom* (1995, Abacus; first published by Little Brown & Co in 1994)

Manley, Deborah *The Walker's Anthology* (2013, Trailblazer Publications)

McDowall, David *Richmond Park: The Walker's Historical Guide* (1996, David McDowall)

Melville, Herman *Moby-Dick* (2016, Macmillan Collector's Library; first published in 1851)

Obama, Barack *Dreams from My Father* (2008, Canongate; first published by Crown Publishers in 1995)

Raban, Jonathan *Soft City* (1998, The Harvill Press; first published by Hamish Hamilton in 1974)

Rankin, Ian *The Falls* (2001, Orion Books)

Roberts, Andrew *Churchill* (2019, Penguin Books; first published by Allen Lane in 2018)

Sanghera, Sathnam *Empireland: How Imperialism Has Shaped Modern Britain* (2021, Viking)

Temple, Grenville *Excursions in the Mediterranean* (1835, Saunders and Otley)

Vargas Llosa, Mario *Aunt Julia and the Scriptwriter*, translated by Helen R. Lane (2002, Faber and Faber; first published in Great Britain in 1983)

Willoughby, Robert *North Korea* (2007, Bradt)

Winchester, Simon *Outposts* (1985, Hodder and Stoughton)

Zychowicz, Izabella *The Royal Łazienki* (2018, The Royal Łazienki Museum)